爱，浪漫和婚姻的 99 个重点

中英双语版

[美] 江柏德（John M. Probandt）◎著
王　梅◎译

Aline forever is my Love for You. Thank you.

"Yes I Do" For Ever Love & happiness
your wife aline

INFORMATION ABOUT *THE 99 POINTS* SERIES

This is another volume in a series of mini books titled *The 99 Points*. This series covers a wide range of subjects, from business to love. These publications explore many varied and interesting subjects. They contain practical information doled out in bite-size, stand-alone pieces. Each book is packed with useful information on the subject covered. A list of books in the series can be seen at http:// the 99points.com. These books are designed to be read in less than an hour but to provide a lifetime's worth of knowledge. We use a larger font to make every book easy on the eyes and assure that the reader is never intimidated. In addition, unlike a typical book, ours are not designed as a cover-to-cover read. The points do not build upon one another in the typical manner of an essential, logical transition. Instead, the reader can open to any page, and the particular point will have meaning without having to read the rest of the book or the preceding points.

Societies are constantly evolving, and people are not reading books as often as they did in the past. The demands on our time, as well as all of the readily available informational resources through the internet and social media are major factors influencing this trend. However, learning is still a key element for success, and facilitating the learning process is the guiding principle behind *The 99 Points* series of books. All books in the series are designed to be read in one hour or less, and each book provides essential advice in ninety-nine short segments on the designated subject so that the information can be absorbed effectively and utilized immediately.

关于 *The 99 Points* 系列丛书

本书是 *The 99 Points* 系列丛书中的一本。该丛书涉及多个领域，涵盖从商业到爱情等方面，探究形形色色且异常有趣的主题。这些书短小精悍、独立成章，并适宜出版，每本都包含其相关主题的实用信息，旨在让读者在一小时内读完，并能受益终身。我们使用易读字体，方便观看，并确保读者不会望而生畏。此外，与一般书籍不同，本书不需要从头到尾通读，每一条目都自成宇宙，各条目之间没有必然联系，读者可以随意打开任何一页阅读。

社会在不断发展，人们不像以前那样喜爱读书，这主要归因于阅读太过费时，通过互联网和社交媒体就能得到即时可用的信息资源。然而，学习仍然是取得成功的关键因素，促进学习过程正是 *The 99 Points* 系列丛书的初衷。该系列中每本书都设计成可在一小时或更短时间内读完，且每本书都在特定的主题上提供了 99 条简短的建议，便于信息得以有效吸收和利用。

ABOUT THIS BOOK

The goal of the ninety-nine stand-alone points is to enhance the romance in your marriage. The book was inspired by my lovely wife. I am the luckiest man in the world to have her. I wanted to offer some personal knowledge and experience about our successful marriage that will help other couples create the magic that she and I share. Unlike the others that I have written, this book is straight from my heart. It is a guide to love, caring, and passion. If even one of these 99 points touches you and improves your marriage, it will be a success.

My wife is different from any other woman I have met. She has so many endearing and unique qualities. She is simple in many ways, but also complicated. She has more common sense than a hundred other people combined. She is elegant, beautiful, sophisticated, and alluring, but that beauty pales when compared to all her other qualities. She is intelligent, but also worldly wise in a more profound way, and her soul is magical. When we hug, cuddle, or hold hands, our souls become one. She is pure, honest, loyal, and always sweet and kind. She is the nicest person I have ever known.

As you can tell, I adore, love, and cherish her. I will never leave her, and she will never leave me. No matter what future problems we might face, God and love will keep us together to survive even the worst storm. We are the "Good Luck Couple" and God has blessed us in this way. Ours is a relationship that was created by fate. We are blessed, and together we count our blessings daily.

关于本书

书中 99 条独立建议旨在加强婚姻中的浪漫气息。本书的灵感来自我的爱妻。拥有她，使我一跃成为世界上最幸运的男人。我想在此提供一些幸福婚姻的私密知识和个人经验，让其他情侣和夫妻也能分享我们拥有的魔力。与我撰写的其他书籍不同，本书内容均为我的肺腑之言。本书是爱、浪漫和婚姻的指南。如果这 99 条中但凡有一条能触动到你、能改善你的婚姻，那我就算是功德圆满了。

我太太和我见过的其他女人完全不同，她有很多可爱和独特的品质。她在很多方面都很简单，但同时又很复杂。她比一百个人加起来还精明，她优雅、美丽、成熟、迷人，但与她的其他品质相比，这些美便会黯然失色。她很聪明，也懂得人情世故，她的灵魂很是神奇。当我们拥抱、相依或牵手时，我俩的灵魂就会合而为一。她纯洁、正直、忠诚，且总是善解人意。在我的认知里，她是最美好的人。

如你所知，我崇拜她、爱恋她、珍惜她。我永远不会离开她，她亦如是。无论我们未来会面临什么艰难险阻，上帝和爱情都会让我们团结在一起，无惧风霜雪雨。我们是“幸运伴侣”，上帝以这种方式祝福了我们，我俩命中注定要在一起，我们是有福之人，每天都会一起惜福感恩。

THE TRUE STORY

On a particularly beautiful day in Dubai, I walked into a convenience store called Zoom, the Dubai equivalent of 7-11. Little did I know at the time, but walking into that Zoom store would change my life for the better and forever. While in the Zoom store, I had the great fortune of meeting a lovely lady. The truth is, I almost did not meet her, but fate stepped in and there was magic in the air.

When I entered the store, at 10:30 in the morning, I was the only customer. I walked to the fruit department and grabbed a banana and an apple. This zoom store had a configuration that included a queue line and two cashiers.

When I went to pay, the cashier informed me that this store was different from the others. Unlike most Zoom stores, where fruits and vegetables are weighed by the cashier, in this one they had to be weighed in the fruit department. There were no other customers in the store, so that was no big deal. I told the cashier that I understood and that I would be glad to return to the fruit department to weigh my items. He then let me know that he was the one who had to weigh the items and that I should wait at the cashier stand for him to complete that task.

As he walked away, a group of people suddenly came in the store. Similar to a 7/11, at Zoom people generally make small purchases, so shopping and checking out doesn't take long. On this occasion, however, In a flash there were nine people in the queue to buy their items, but only one cashier because the other one was in the fruit department weighing my items, and he was delayed in returning because people were asking him questions back in the fruit department.

Suddenly I noticed an incredibly beautiful woman standing at the end of the line. I said to myself that I would love to meet her, but I quickly concluded that, due to the configuration of the queue, it would be impossible. I then thought that merely seeing such a

真实故事

在迪拜，一个特别美丽的日子里，我走进了一家名为Zoom的便利店，相当于7-11的那种小店。当时我全然不知，走进那家便利店将会永久改变我的生活。在Zoom店里，我有幸遇到一位可爱的女士。其实我差点错过她，但命运之神及时降临，世界充满了魔力。

当我在上午十点半走进那家店时，我是店里唯一的顾客。我走到水果区，拿了一根香蕉和一个苹果。这家店的收银区有一条队列和两个收银员。

当我去付款时，收银员告诉我这家店与其他店不同。一般在Zoom店里，水果和蔬菜都是在收银台由收银员称重，而这家店必须在水果区称重。店里没有其他顾客，我觉得无所谓，告诉收银员能理解，愿意回到水果区去称重，然而收银员说应由他去称重，我只需要在收银台等他回来。

当收银员走去称重时，一群顾客突然走进店里。与7-11类似，在Zoom店里，顾客通常只买小件商品，所以购物和结账不会花很长时间。然而这一次，转眼间有九个人在排队结账，但只有一个收银员，因为另一个在水果区给我的东西称重，他耽搁了，因为水果区有人在问他问题。

突然，我注意到一位非常漂亮的女士站在队伍的最后。我有心结识她，但很快得出结论，按照这个排队方式，估计不太可能。我当时就想，仅仅能看到这么漂亮的女子，我这一天也算鸿运当头了。

时间飞逝，给我称重的收银员还没回来，这时命运之神降临了，前面的八个人居然都结账走人了，就像变魔术一样，那位漂亮女士站在我身边另一

beautiful woman had started my day off on the right foot.

Time passed, as the cashier who was weighing my banana and apple was increasingly delayed. Then fate stepped in as the eight people in front of the woman completed their purchases. Like magic, she was standing next to me beside the other cashier stand. There is a word used by locals in Dubai termed "Inshallah." This word means God willing. Well, God was willing, as what happened next could only be from the grace of God.

I looked at her, and she looked at me. I smiled at her, and she smiled at me. I then said "Hello," and she replied, "I do not speak English." Having lived overseas for many years, I was aware that sometimes when people say they do not speak English, it is possible they do. Often inexperienced English speakers are shy because their command of the language is not perfect.

At that point, I asked her a question that came out of nowhere, "Would you like to go on a date with me?" To my surprise, she said "Yes." I am from America, and she is from Syria. In spite of what normally would be significant challenges, such as our different religions, language barriers, and cultures, we both felt an extraordinarily powerful, exciting, mutual attraction, and we have been in harmony with each other since that day. During the eighteen months between when we first met to when we were married, we grew closer, and our love grew stronger every day.

The story gets even better. Most people are familiar with Zoom, the popular conference calling service with the same brand name as the store in which we met. That service played a key role in our extraordinary story of love, romance, and marriage.

In Dubai, there are significant challenges for foreign couples seeking to get married. Aware of this problem, I began searching for a solution, which eventually turned out to be an online service named "Loyal Weddings," located in Provo, Utah, in the United States. The service was able provide us a wedding license issued by government authorities in the U.S., and on January 18 of 2023, we were married on a Zoom call. I am blessed and thankful that we are together. She is the nicest, most beautiful, and kindest person I have ever known. It seems an incredible coincidence, but it's true, we met at the Zoom store and were married on a Zoom call. Hence, ours is a "Zoom-to-Zoom" story of love, romance, and marriage. Our union as husband and wife is beyond imaginable, and best of all it is a true story.

More recent good news is that our romantic story will be revealed on the big screen as we are planning a feature film that will do just that: tell the story. It is our hope that the

个收银台旁边。迪拜本地有一个词叫“Inshallah”，意思是上帝的旨意，好吧，是上帝的意愿，因为接下来发生的一切只能是上帝的恩典。

我看着她，她也看着我，我对她微笑，她也对我微笑。然后我说“哈喽”，她回答说：“我不会说英语。”在海外生活多年后，我发现当有人说自己不会说英语时，其实很可能会说。缺乏英语交流经验的人往往很害羞，主要因为他们的英语不是很流利。

就在那一刻，我突然凭空问她一句：“咱俩约会可以吗？”令我吃惊的是，她说：“可以。”我来自美国，她来自叙利亚。尽管我们之间信仰不同、语言不同、文化不同，可以说困难重重，但我们都感受到非常强大、令人兴奋的吸引力，从那天起我们一直和睦相处，从初遇到结婚这 18 个月里，我们越来越亲密，我们的爱一天比一天浓烈。

故事至此变得愈发精彩。大家都熟悉 Zoom，一款常用的电话会议软件，和我俩初遇的那家便利店同名。这款软件也在我们非凡的爱情、浪漫和婚姻故事中发挥了关键作用。

在迪拜，外国夫妇想要结婚真是难于登天。意识到这个问题后，我开始四处想办法，最终找到一家位于美国犹他州普罗沃市名为“忠诚婚礼”（Loyal Weddings）的在线服务公司，该公司能为我们提供美国政府颁发的结婚证书。于是，2023 年 1 月 18 日，我们通过 Zoom 会议软件在线结婚。我很幸运，也很感恩，我们能从此相伴。她是我所认识的最聪明、最美丽、最善良的人。这简直是不可思议的巧合，但绝对真实，我们是在 Zoom 便利店相识的，又通过 Zoom 软件在线结婚，因而这是关于爱情、浪漫和婚姻的“从 Zoom 到 Zoom”的神奇故事。我们的结合令人难以想象，最绝的是这是个真实的故事。

最新的好消息是，我们正筹拍一部电影，我们的爱情故事将被搬上大银幕。希望这部基于我们个人生活经历的故事片能够改变很多人的生活，让世

feature film, which is based on our personal life experience, will change many lives, as it gives people everywhere hope that just maybe they can have a similar experience as we have had.

The feature film will be a story of fate, love, commitment, and communication (even though we speak different languages). Our love story of meeting by a chance encounter in the Zoom market which led to the Zoom call wedding is the definition of a story book romance.

This book does not describe the adventure of our personal romance, love, and marriage, however. Instead, it is composed of 99 tips that will be the prescription, the "Rx," needed for a happy, loving, romantic, and lasting "forever marriage" for anyone. We are confident that these points will make you smile, fill you with hope, and touch your life in a wonderful way like the Zoom-to-Zoom adventure has impacted ours.

Zoom-to-Zoom is our story, and I hope it inspires others to believe that there is indeed magic in the air. Thank you for reading this book.

界各地的人们点燃希望之火，让大家也能拥有和我们一样的美好经历。

这部影片是关于命运、爱情、承诺和沟通的故事（尽管我们说不同的语言）。我们的爱情故事从 Zoom 便利店的偶然相遇开始，再到 Zoom 软件的线上婚礼，这些都如小说中的浪漫情节。

本书并非细述关于我们浪漫、爱情和婚姻的冒险经历，而是由 99 条建议组成，这些建议就像药方一样，是拥有幸福、甜蜜、浪漫和持久婚姻的“处方药”。相信本书的观点会让你展开笑颜、充满希望，并以奇妙的方式触动你的生活，就像我们从 Zoom 到 Zoom 神奇经历的感受一样。

从 Zoom 到 Zoom 的奇缘是我们的真实故事，希望能激励大家相信现实中确实拥有魔力。感谢阅读本书。

Contents

1. Forget the Past, Live in the Present and Realize Long Term Happiness ······ 002
2. Encouragement ······ 004
3. Little Things Mean so Much ······ 006
4. Remove Negative People from Your Life ······ 010
5. Always Start any Talk With a Postive ······ 012
6. Have Fun Together ······ 014
7. Plan Intimacy (Don't Just Wait for the Moment, It may Never Come) ······ 016
8. Take a Class Together ······ 018
9. Switch Things up Once in a While. It's Very Romantic ······ 018
10. Learn to Like the Music your Spouse Likes ······ 020
11. Hold Hands Often ······ 024
12. An Open Inviation ······ 026
13. Freedom Is an Optical Illusion ······ 028
14. The Grass is Always Greenest when it is Watered and Receives Sunshine ······ 030
15. Love is More than Good Looks ······ 034
16. Thoughts Create Actions ······ 036
17. Silly, Outragous, and Fun ······ 038
18. Becoming Friends is Important ······ 040
19. Learn from the Internet and Make any Day or Night a Great Memory ······ 042
20. Tell Your Spouse they are Lovely ······ 044
21. The Magic of Touch ······ 048
22. To Win is Always to Lose ······ 050
23. Compliments Often ······ 052
24. Always Show Respect ······ 054

目录

1. 用心经营 …… 003
2. 互相鼓励 …… 005
3. 小事不小 …… 007
4. 远离小人 …… 011
5. 沟通技巧 …… 013
6. 共享欢乐 …… 015
7. 亲密行程 …… 017
8. 一起学习 …… 019
9. 偶尔浪漫 …… 019
10. 分享音乐 …… 021
11. 时常牵手 …… 025
12. 公开邀请 …… 027
13. 诠释自由 …… 029
14. 悉心呵护 …… 031
15. 无关外表 …… 035
16. 阳光心态 …… 037
17. 一起搞笑 …… 039
18. 成为朋友 …… 041
19. 在线学习 …… 043
20. 赞美伴侣 …… 045
21. 身体接触 …… 049
22. 不争对错 …… 051
23. 相互赞誉 …… 053

25. Just Forget Yelling ······ 056
26. A Photo is a Reminder of the Love Your Share ······ 060
27. Check In During the Day ······ 064
28. Be Immature Together ······ 066
29. Dress Nicely, be Attractive, and Care About Your Appearance ······ 068
30. You are not Your Spouse's Parent. You are Partners ······ 072
31. Trust ······ 074
32. We are all Victims, so Just let it Go ······ 078
33. Accept Your Spouse's Quirks ······ 080
34. Don't Ever Try to Change Your Spouse. Accept Who they are, Both the Good and the Bad ······ 082
35. Good Luck and Fate are Real, so Count Your Blessings ······ 084
36. Find Time to be alone Every Day ······ 086
37. Never Treat Your Spouse Like a Maid ······ 088
38. Dream Big Dreams Together ······ 090
39. In Sickness and In Health is a Must ······ 092
40. "Mindset" : If You Ever Wished You had a Magic Wand, Read This Point ······ 094
41. Lunch Dates Are Cool to Break up the Day ······ 098
42. When Your Spouse is Doing Some Mundane Chore, Step in Without Being Asked, and Help ······ 100
43. Take On Projects Immediately. Delaying is Never Your Friend ······ 102
44. Packaging is Every Bit as Important as Whats Inside ······ 104
45. Surprises will Keep the Romance Alive ······ 108
46. Nighttime is Never the Right Time ······ 112
47. Never Lose Your Cool ······ 116
48. Chocolate and Flowers Go a Long Way ······ 118
49. Long Walks. Meditation, or a Trip to the Gym are Great Ways to Overcome Confusion and Find Peace ······ 122
50. Being Kind is Always Important ······ 124
51. Compromise is a Must ······ 126
52. Empowerment ······ 128
53. Empathy ······ 130
54. Don't Always be the Boss ······ 132
55. Understand that People Change ······ 134
56. Never be a Know-it-all with Your Spouse ······ 136

24. 尊重伴侣……055
25. 切忌喊叫……057
26. 一起拍照……061
27. 随时联系……065
28. 保持童心……067
29. 注重形象……069
30. 避免说教……073
31. 相互信任……075
32. 学会放下……079
33. 适应怪癖……081
34. 学会包容……083
35. 惜福感恩……085
36. 独处时间……087
37. 并非佣人……089
38. 一起梦想……091
39. 同甘共苦……093
40. 拥有魔杖……095
41. 共进午餐……099
42. 主动帮忙……101
43. 拖延害人……103
44. 包装自己……105
45. 制造惊喜……109
46. 最佳时间……113
47. 保持冷静……117
48. 经典礼物……119
49. 放松大脑……123
50. 善待他人……125
51. 学会妥协……127
52. 赋予力量……129
53. 学会共情……131

57. Don't Forget to Smile ······ 138
58. Do not Strangle Your Relationship by Putting Your Spouse on a Budget ······ 140
59. Consider Having a Pet ······ 142
60. If You Want a Romantic Marriage, Stay in Shape ······ 144
61. If You want to Show You Care, Buy Health Insurance ······ 146
62. At Times, You Must Get out of Balance to be in Balance ······ 148
63. Don't Flirt Your Way into Trouble ······ 150
64. Learn to Take the Blame and Apologize ······ 154
65. Writing Notes Can Alleviate Stress ······ 156
66. Stop only Looking at Your Phone ······ 158
67. Build Traditions and Keep them Alive ······ 160
68. Never Question if You Made a Good Decision Once You are Married ······ 162
69. Tough Talks are Best when Well Thought Out ······ 164
70. Are Horoscopes Accurate Predictors of Future Marriage Happiness? ······ 166
71. Wine, Dine, and Have a Happy Marriage ······ 168
72. Routines are the Opposite of Boring—They will Add Spice to Your Love Life ······ 170
73. Spoken Words Mean Little—Actions Mean Everything ······ 172
74. Fomo - the Fear of Missing Out ······ 174
75. Understand Your Partner's Spiritual Needs ······ 176
76. Start Small On New Ventures ······ 178
77. At Times it is Important to Give a Firm no, but not Often ······ 180
78. Help Me Understand ······ 182
79. Learn Body Language (How to Read and how to Use it) ······ 184
80. Keep a Power Note of 25 Reasons Why You Love Your Spouse ······ 186
81. When It Comes to Making Love, Always Think of Your Spouse's Needs First ······ 190
82. Be Loyal and Avoid All Temptation ······ 192
83. Understand the Goals of the One You Love and Help them Achieve them ······ 194
84. Every Day is Valentine's Day ······ 196
85. Staycations Work, So Mix it up ······ 198
86. Take Time to Recharge From a Hard Week, Month or Year. Slow Down and Enjoy Your Love Nest with Your Phones Turned Off ······ 200

54. 别装老板 …… 133
55. 人都会变 …… 135
56. 学无止境 …… 137
57. 时常微笑 …… 139
58. 共同预算 …… 141
59. 养只宠物 …… 143
60. 保持体形 …… 145
61. 健康保险 …… 147
62. 保持平衡 …… 149
63. 避免调情 …… 151
64. 学会道歉 …… 155
65. 写备忘录 …… 157
66. 少玩手机 …… 159
67. 形成传统 …… 161
68. 不要质疑 …… 163
69. 艰难对话 …… 165
70. 星座占卜 …… 167
71. 美酒佳肴 …… 169
72. 日常习惯 …… 171
73. 实际行动 …… 173
74. 活在当下 …… 175
75. 精神需求 …… 177
76. 谨慎投入 …… 179
77. 偶尔拒绝 …… 181
78. 深入理解 …… 183
79. 肢体语言 …… 185
80. 写出理由 …… 187
81. 伴侣优先 …… 191
82. 避免诱惑 …… 193
83. 实现梦想 …… 195

87. Gentlemen, do You Want more Romance and Sex in Your Marriage? Simply Clean the Bathroom ······ 202
88. Work on always Being a Better Person. It Shows You Care ······ 204
89. Know What will Calm Both You and Your Spouse Down the Fastest, and Learn a Technique to Make that Happen ······ 206
90. Ask Your Spouse if there are Things that You do that are Annoying, then Modify Your Behavior ······ 208
91. Publicly Praise Your Spouse. Make them not only Look Good, but Amazing! ······ 210
92. Never Tell Outsiders Your Private Matters. Instead Tell Your Spouse. Open Communication is a Must ······ 212
93. Say Thank You Every Single Day, both in Prayer and to Your Spouse. Show Gratitude ······ 214
94. Game Night ······ 216
95. Explore Your Neighborhood ······ 218
96. Do Something that Frightens You ······ 220
97. Double Date ······ 222
98. Mood Swings ······ 224
99. Mind Reading Never Works ······ 226

84. 天天过节 …… 197
85. 周边度假 …… 199
86. 二人世界 …… 201
87. 清洁浴室 …… 203
88. 提升自我 …… 205
89. 快速冷静 …… 207
90. 做出改变 …… 209
91. 当众赞扬 …… 211
92. 保护隐私 …… 213
93. 感恩之心 …… 215
94. 游戏之夜 …… 217
95. 周围环境 …… 219
96. 克服恐惧 …… 221
97. 四人约会 …… 223
98. 情绪波动 …… 225
99. 避免猜测 …… 227

1. FORGET THE PAST, LIVE IN THE PRESENT AND REALIZE LONG TERM HAPPINESS

With marriage, your most important goal is happiness. A happy marriage is the combination of a natural and a conscious effort. You must keep things in balance. To be in balance is to assure an endearing, enduring, and happy marriage. Passion, love, and a burning desire are a good start, but you must also possess a genuine attitude of appreciation. Be thankful every day that you are married to this wonderful person. All of this must be tempered with patience and perseverance. A happy marriage requires an ongoing conscious effort by both people. With these and other elements in place you can have a marriage that turns into a forever lasting love story. Never compare your spouse to other people, instead be positive and focus on their great qualities and why you are so lucky to have this wonderful person in your life.

Evolution is a good word when we talk about marriage, as time changes things, you must move with the times. A strong marriage requires working for years to maintain a healthy foundation of good marital skills which you can learn and then implement to fit any situation. Remember, time creates change, so a marriage is based on the principles of being dynamic, not static.

In business, to finally achieve prosperity takes effort and time. Marriage is similar, except with marriage, you have a head start. The day people marry, they are in love. By the mere fact of getting married in the first place, they are already a success, unlike in business, where you often start with nothing.

I believe that much of love and marriage is due to fate. However, fate alone is not enough to create and maintain a happy relationship, which also requires that each do their part from the wedding day onward. The simple fact is that a good marriage is hard work over long periods of time.

With marriage, what you do in the present will also impact the long-term relationship. A great analogy is that of comparing being married to praying. God can help you and

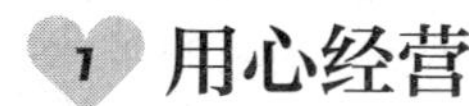

1 用心经营

在婚姻中，最重要的目标是幸福，幸福的婚姻需要通过经意和不经意的努力相结合而实现。只有保持平衡，才能拥有温暖、持久和幸福的婚姻。激情、爱恋和欲念只是美好的开始，之后则必须拥有真诚感恩的心态。能和这么好的人成婚，每天都要心存感激，所有这一切都必须用耐心和毅力加以调和。幸福的婚姻需要双方不断用心经营，外加其他因素，才能成为永恒的爱情故事。永远不要将爱人与他人比较，要积极关注伴侣的优秀品质，要感恩自己能如此幸运地拥有这么美好的人。

当我们谈论婚姻时，改进很重要，随着时间的变化，我们必须与时俱进。牢固的婚姻需要经过多年的用心经营，才能保持良好婚内技巧的健康基础，你可以学习并运用这些技巧来适应任何情况。要知道，时间能产生变化，所以婚姻是建立在动态而非静态的原则之上的。

做生意时，需要长久的努力才能最终实现盈利，婚姻亦是如此。只是婚姻会有一个良好的开端，两人结婚之时便已经相互爱恋，所以仅仅是结婚这件事本身，就已经算是成功了，不像做生意，常常白手起家。

我相信很多爱情和婚姻都是缘分使然。然而，单靠缘分不足以建立和维系幸福的婚姻，双方需要从婚礼那天起就各司其职。简而言之，美满的婚姻需要长期用心经营。

在婚姻中，你现在的所作所为也会影响到将来的长远关系。有一个恰当的比喻，就是把结婚比作祈祷。上帝可以帮助你回应祷告，但要实现这些祷告则需要行动。良好的婚姻不是自然发生的，需要有意采取措施来确保婚姻

answer your prayers, but for those prayers to be realized requires action. A healthy marriage does not happen by autopilot alone. You must take conscious steps to assure that the marriage is healthy. You are sailing a ship that depends not only on mutual love, but also daily expressions of caring, empathetic listening, emotional support, and even good health, all with a cause-and-effect relationship at the core.

In life as well as business, keeping perspective is always important. You must be able to control expectations and not imagine too much too soon or you will likely renounce a plausible idea and torpedo any subsequent dreams of success. All too often people don't appreciate how much work and foundation are required before success becomes "overnight." Do not give up too soon! Marriage is the same. You must control your expectations so that they coincide with the mindset of your spouse. You must take each day step-by-step and not imagine too much at once.

An analogy to enjoying a happy marriage is to consider a Chinese Bamboo tree. Normally, these trees take four years to sprout. Then six weeks later, they grow to a height of ninety feet! Envision planting the seed then watering and fertilizing it for four years and not seeing any results. Then, suddenly, like the tree, your idea becomes a towering success. Marriage is the same. It depends on a strong foundation, like the Chinese Bamboo tree. Every little thing you do will increase the foundations of trust, loyalty, communication, love, commitment, caring, being empathetic, and more. Over many years, the marriage can become an ever stronger, more loving bond and last forever as it grows every day. A better life for both husband and wife will be the end result.

2. ENCOURAGEMENT

You can never underestimate the value of encouragement. We all have dreams for our lives, but we do not always have the self-esteem, resources, or wherewithal to achieve them on our own. Maybe we become distracted from realizing our dreams by the many intricacies and demands of our daily lives. However, a significant other can turn those obstacles around.

健康。你们正在远航的这艘婚姻之船，不仅依赖于彼此之爱，还依赖于日常的关怀表达、感同身受、情感支持，甚至健康的体魄，所有这些都以因果关系为核心。

无论是在生活中还是在工作中，拥有远见非常重要。一定要控制期望，贪多嚼不烂，欲速则不达。人们往往会忽略在一夜成功之前需要付出的努力和积累。不要轻言放弃！婚姻也是一样。必须控制自己的期望，要与伴侣的心态一致，要一步一步过好每一天，不能一口吃个胖子。

可以把享受幸福的婚姻比作竹子。通常情况下，竹子需要 4 年才能发芽，而仅仅六个星期后便能长到 90 英尺高！想象一下，你播种之后，连续 4 年浇水和施肥，却看不到任何成果，然后突然间，它就能变成参天大树。婚姻就像竹子一样，依赖于坚实的根基。你所做的每一件小事都会加强信任、忠诚、沟通、关爱、承诺、体贴、同情等基础，多年之后，婚姻就会变得更加牢固、更加美满，并且随着每天成长而持续到永远，最终的成果就是夫妻双方的感情能够天长地久。

2 互相鼓励

千万不要低估鼓励的意义。我们都拥有自己的人生梦想，但总是没有足够的自信、资源或钱财去实现，又或许在实现梦想的过程中，会受各种日常生活琐事和需求的影响，然而你的伴侣能够帮助你排除这些障碍。

I have a dear friend who had anger problems his whole life. No matter what he did, he could not overcome them, and they just kept getting worse as he got older. One day, he met a lovely lady at a conference. They connected immediately, and before long they were living together. She had been at a job she hated for years, where she had been underpaid and unable to get a promotion, or even garner the nerves to quit and move on. They were both stuck with problems they had not been able to fix on their own, but little did they know, as their love grew and their respect for each blossomed, things would change.

After about a year in their relationship, I started to notice my friend no longer displayed the telltale signs of his anger issues. In fact, it seemed they had all but gone away. His significant other had received a raise, a promotion, and an entirely new job, which she loved. So, what happened? The answer, encouragement.

She encourages him to be a better man. Consequently, he worked on himself and made a conscious effort to overcome the anger issues he had suffered his whole life, managing to conquer this lifelong problem in less than a year. He also encouraged her to demand a better position and a higher salary. She was terrified to do so, but through his love and encouragement, she was able to achieve what she had previously believed to be impossible. Later, when she was dissatisfied with her job, he was able to encourage her to move on and find a career she truly loved.

My friend and his now wife were able to better themselves both personally and professionally through encouraging one another. You can never underestimate the value of your words to the person that you love, or theirs to you. They say people cannot change, and often that is true, but with encouragement and love, all things are possible.

3. LITTLE THINGS MEAN SO MUCH

In life, we often do not realize how important the little things are that we do. Actions often seem to be meaningless. The truth is that even when it appears nothing is happening, in actuality you can be taking quantum leaps forward. An interesting analogy

我有一个好友，脾气不太好，尝试了很多方法都无济于事，而且随着年龄的增长，越来越严重。某天，他在开会时遇到了一位可爱的女士，两人一见如故，不久就生活在一起了。该女士多年来一直在做一份不喜欢的工作，薪水过低，无法升职，她也没有勇气另谋高就。两人都被自身无法解决的问题困住了，但他们不知道，随着两人彼此相爱和彼此尊重，事情在潜移默化间发生了变化。

在两人共同生活了大约一年之后，我发现老友的脾气有好转的迹象，实际上他不再乱发脾气了，他的爱人也得到了加薪、晋升，后来甚至换了一份全新且喜欢的工作。那么到底发生了什么？答案就是鼓励。

女主人鼓励先生成为更好的人，因此他狠下功夫，用心克服积习难改的坏脾气，在不到一年的时间里就攻克了这个困扰他多年的难题。先生也鼓励女主人去争取更好的职位和更高的薪水。女主人一直不敢冒险，但在先生的关爱和鼓励下，终于实现了以前认为根本不可能的事。之后她在对自己的工作依旧不甚满意时，先生又鼓励她重新求职，直到她找到自己真正喜欢的职业。

我的朋友和他妻子通过互相鼓励，在自身和职业方面都取得了进步。千万不能低估鼓励对于所爱之人的意义，反之亦然。人们常说人是无法改变的，也许说得没错，但有了鼓励和关爱，一切皆有可能。

3 小事不小

在生活中，我们常常意识不到小事有多重要。一些事情往往看起来毫无意义，甚至表面上看起来什么都没有发生，但实际上你可能已经取得了巨大的飞跃。假如你一直在跑步机上锻炼，看起来好像没什么效果，而事实恰恰

is the treadmill. If you exercise on the treadmill, it appears that you are going nowhere. The opposite is true, as regularly exercising on the treadmill will improve your physical health and mental wellbeing. It will allow your mind time to relax. When you exercise your body, it automatically increases the production of endorphins, your brain's feel-good neurotransmitters. As endorphins are released, stress is released. Even when it seems you are running in place, often you are making great advances.

In a marriage, the little things you do may seem like they are meaningless (regularly telling your spouse that you love them, saying thank you often, even small chores such as cleaning the bathroom) but all of these add up to a strong, more loving, and happy marriage. Effort and consciousness always move things forward. Often the difference is so small that it's not initially noticed. Yet in reality, overtime, these little things keep the momentum within your marriage alive, and your romance sizzling.

Romantic movies always lean on the big romantic gesture to demonstrate how much people love one another. These types of feature films are fun to watch. The problem is that in real life, they are not realistic. Besides, even grandiose gestures get old if done too often. If you want to keep your spouse happy, I have found that it is the small things we do for one another every day that really matter. We all have our little stresses in life. To have someone that will relieve some of them can make a big difference and immediately enhance a person's mood.

If my wife and I are relaxing and watching television, and she mentions that she is thirsty, I am happy to get up and get her something to drink. You may think that such a small gesture would go unnoticed, however it never does. Similarly, if I say I am hungry, she is more than happy to cook for me. When she is hungry, I will do the same, although many times I order the food instead of cooking, as I am not nearly as good of a chef as she is.

Small gestures do not have to take the form of physical gifts. It could be a nice word here and there that turns you or your significant other's day around. In a relationship, the big things are great, but in the long-term, it really is the small things that make all of the difference.

My wife and I both make a conscious effort to do the things that make life more pleasant in small ways every day. As a result, both of our lives have become better. Whenever I go to the store, I think about her and try to get things she would like. If she happens to be at the store, she does the same. These tiny gestures are a great way to let your spouse know how much you appreciate them.

相反，定期在跑步机上锻炼可以改善身心健康，能让大脑有时间放松。当你锻炼身体时，体内会自行增加内啡肽的产生，内啡肽是大脑中让人感觉良好的神经递质。随着内啡肽的释放，压力也随之释放。即使看起来你在原地踏步，但实际上却取得了很大进步。

在婚姻中，你做的一些小事情（如经常告诉对方你的爱意，经常说谢谢，甚至是清洁浴室这样的小杂务）可能看起来毫无意义，但所有这些小事加起来能让婚姻更牢固、更有爱、更幸福。用心努力总能推动事情向前发展，这种变化通常很小，一开始并不容易察觉，然而随着时间的推移，这些小事情会让婚姻保持浪漫、活力四射。

爱情电影总是依靠特别浪漫的情节来展示恋人间是多么相爱的。这些类型的故事看看就好，在现实生活中根本不可能存在。此外，即使是最浪漫的举动，如果做得太过频繁，也会显得老套。如果真想让恋人快乐，我觉得每天为彼此做些小事才真正有效。我们在生活中都有些小压力，如果有人能排解一二，就会产生很大的不同，能立竿见影地改善另一个人的情绪。

假果我和太太正闲在一起看电视，正好她口渴了，我会很高兴地给她拿点饮料。你可能认为这样的小事没人在意，但事实并非如此。同样，如果我饿了，她会非常乐意为我下厨；当她饿的时候，我也会这样做，虽然更多时候我是点外卖而不是做饭，因为我的厨艺远不如她。

小惊喜不一定是礼物，也可以是动听的话语，时不时说上两句，能改善两人的情绪。在一段感情中，大事固然重要，但从长远来看，小事更关键。

我和太太每天都会用心做一些小事，让生活变得更加愉悦，结果是我们的生活确实变得更好了。每当我去商店的时候都会想着她，买一些她喜欢的东西。如果她碰巧在商店，她也会这样做。这些微小的举动是让对方知道你心存感激的好方法。

4. REMOVE NEGATIVE PEOPLE FROM YOUR LIFE

One important thing I have learned in my life is that you should not hate anyone. That is just the wrong, self-defeating mindset. Everyone is doing what they think is best and trying to survive. However, that does not mean you need to associate with those whose behavior you don't like. There are always going to be people in your life who are jealous of your relationship, your job, your home, or your accomplishments. Such individuals can cause no end of pain and strife between you and your spouse if you let them. Their harmful attitude can wreak havoc when permitted to go unchecked. As a result, I have found it best to cut such people entirely out of my life.

My wife is my best friend, and the love of my life. I do not want to bring people around her who will say negative things that could hurt her feelings, her ambitions, or our relationship. These people often come as wolves in sheep's clothing. They appear kind and nurturing on the surface, but underneath they are small-minded and want to see you fail. There are a number of reasons people are like this, none of which are relevant. When you encounter this type of person, the best course of action is to steer away from them, no matter the reason for their behavior. Do not be rude or insult them, just find a reason to be busy when they want to see you.

I once had a friend who I brought around my wife. He was very kind and they appeared to hit it off. I was very happy they both got along as we could all enjoy activities together. After a while, I noticed my wife acting a little standoffish towards me. When I inquired why, I discovered my "friend" had been making up stories about me when I was not around. I assured her that they were untrue and cut that friend out of our lives. Before I knew it, things were back to normal. Had I kept this person involved in our life or tried to confront him, the problem would have been exacerbated. Often the best course of action to assure there are no more disruptions to your happy home is a complete removal of negative individuals from your life.

4 远离小人

我在生活中学到的重要事情是，不应该仇恨任何人，仇恨的心态很不好，损人不利己。为了生存，每个人都会做利于自己的事情。当然，你也没必要和那些不喜欢的人交往。生活中总会有人嫉妒你的感情、工作、家庭或成就，如果放任不管，这样的人会给你和伴侣造成无休止的痛苦和麻烦。如果听之任之，这些负能量会造成严重破坏，因此，最好把这种人从生活中完全剔除。

我太太是我最好的朋友，也是我一生挚爱。我不想因周围的人说一些负面的话，而伤害她的感受、尊严或者我俩的关系。这些人往往是披着羊皮的狼，表面看起来很和善、很有教养，但实际上心胸狭窄，巴不得看到别人失败，他们这样做出于各种原因。当你遇到这种人时，不管他们是出于什么原因，最好的办法就是远离。当他们想约你的时候，也没必要伤了和气，找个借口拒绝就是了。

我曾经带一个朋友来见我太太，他人很好，和我太太也谈得来，两人相处得不错，这让我很高兴，方便我们以后能一起出去玩。之后，我发现太太对我有些许冷淡，当我询问原因时，发现这位朋友趁我不在的时候编排我。我向太太保证那些事都是无中生有，并和这个朋友断了联系。亡羊补牢，犹未迟也。如果让这种人不断扰乱我们的生活，或者直接与之对峙，情况只会更糟。所以，要确保幸福家庭不受干扰，最好的办法就是把负能量的小人从身边彻底清除。

5. ALWAYS START ANY TALK WITH A POSITIVE

Whether you are speaking to a business partner, a family member, a friend, or most importantly your significant other, it is important to start each talk with something positive. This is a well-known technique for delivering tough news. It lets the other person know that you value them and are not chastising them but are at worse delivering constructive criticism. If you are the manager at your job, and you have to reprimand an employee, it is strongly suggested that you begin the talk by mentioning something they did right.

"Hi employee X. Thank you for seeing me. I really appreciate how you always finish your work on time, but in the future could you pay a little more attention to the details."

This approach will soften the blow and not put the other person on the defensive, so you can imagine how important it is with your spouse. I never set out to hurt my wife's feelings, but when we need to have a serious discussion, I want her to listen to me, and not instantly become adversarial. If you launch right into your complaint, that negative reaction is inevitable. To start off the conversation with "baby, I love you" is a great opening. At that point, the touchy subject can be explored, and the outcome will most likely be much more productive.

I have seen this approach work firsthand because my wife uses it on me. She was once upset that I did not immediately put my dirty clothes in the hamper. As opposed demanding to know why I did this, she instead first complimented me on how I always keep our house so clean and tidy. She then went on to request that in the future, it would be nice if I would never leave dirty clothes on the floor by our bed. Rather than being offended, I was happy to comply. Actually, I was embarrassed because it is just lazy not to take five seconds to put dirty clothes in the hamper.

A lot of potential issues in personal relationships are about the approach. Misunderstandings happen so easily, it is best to develop a strategy to cut down on them as much as possible. I have found that always saying something nice is a great way to start. By the way, it is also a great way to end the conversation, or maybe better, a kiss.

5 沟通技巧

和生意伙伴、家庭成员、亲朋好友或者亲密伴侣交谈时，一开始要首先肯定对方，这很重要，在说严肃话题时，这是众所周知的技巧，能让对方知道你重视他们，不是在责备，而是在提供建设性的批评。如果你是经理，不得不批评一名员工，强烈建议你在谈话开始时先肯定对方。

“你好，x 员工，谢谢你来见我，你总是能按时完成工作，我真的很感激，但是以后能不能在细节上多注意一点？”

这种说法更加柔和，不会引起对方的逆反心理，因此，可以想象，这样做在情侣间有多重要。我从不想忽视我太太的感受，但当我们需要进行严肃谈话时，我希望她能倾听我的意见，而不是立刻充满敌意。如果一上来就直奔主题，负面反应便不可避免。用“宝贝，我爱你”来开始谈话是很好的开场白，然后水到渠成地就可以探讨敏感话题了，结果很可能会更有成效。

我亲身体验过这种方法，因为我太太就曾这样对待过我。有一回，她因我没立即把脏衣服放进洗衣篮里而生气，但她并没有直接质问我，而是先表扬我，说我总是把家里收拾得特别干净整洁，接着又说以后最好不要把脏衣服扔到床边的地板上。我非但没有生气，反而很乐意照办。其实我很尴尬，觉得自己简直太懒了，居然不肯花五秒钟把脏衣服放进洗衣篮里。

亲密关系中的很多潜在矛盾都与处理的方式方法有关，人与人之间很容易产生误解，所以一定要想办法尽可能减少误解。我发现，在谈话开始时说一些动听的话就很有用，顺便说一下，这也是结束谈话的好方法，或者一个吻的效果会更好。

6. HAVE FUN TOGETHER

This point should go without saying, but that doesn't mean it shouldn't be said. You and your significant other should have fun together. You can be romantic, create a family, and maybe even work together, but as the journey progresses, you should also be enjoying one another's company. My wife is my best friend. We have fun, whether we are just sitting on the couch or going on a lavish vacation. We always find ways to make each other laugh. We are so blessed that we enjoy every second together, and I am not exaggerating. She always makes me feel special, and that is a great feeling. Whether we are playing stupid games or making dumb jokes, we always manage to have a good time in all situations.

Many people seem to underestimate the importance of having fun with your spouse. I have seen this phenomenon play out in my own past relationships. Many people fall into a rut after being in a relationship with someone for extended periods of time. This is dangerous, as it is easy to take someone for granted. Sometimes you even begin to resent one another. The daily grind of life is enough to wear anyone down, and that is why it is so important you make a conscious effort to have fun with your spouse every chance you get.

It is so easy to enjoy your significant other's company with even the most minimal effort. Flash back to the days of dating and remember how much fun you used have together. I personally like to tell a joke over dinner, or break our diets with a fun treat. It doesn't have to be big, just something that makes both people smile. Sometimes we will even get into tickle fights. I know it sounds immature, but so what, I love her and so why not have fun.

Life can get tough, but remember you have married your best friend. Do not forget what brought you together and always work to enjoy each other's company. There is no excuse for not trying to make one another smile every chance you get. Life is a gift, and I enjoy it the most when I am in the company of my lovely wife.

6 共享欢乐

这一条不必多说，却不能不说。你和爱人应该共享欢乐。你们可以享受各种浪漫，也可以组建家庭，甚至一起工作，但随着人生旅程的展开，你们也应该享受彼此的陪伴。我太太是我最好的朋友，不管是待在家里还是去享受奢华假期，我们都很开心。我们总能找到办法逗对方笑。我们是如此幸运，不夸张地说，我俩享受在一起的每一秒。她总是让我觉得自己与众不同，这种感觉特爽。无论是玩无聊的游戏还是开愚蠢的玩笑，我俩总是想方设法在任何情境下都玩得开心。

很多人都低估了与伴侣共享欢乐的重要性，我回想起自己之前的恋情也是如此。很多人在与某人交往一段时间后就陷入老一套，这样很危险，因为人们很容易把与某人的关系视为理所当然，有时甚至开始怨恨对方。生活中的各种琐事已足以让任何人意志消沉，因此要用心经营两人的感情，与伴侣一起享受每一刻，这一点很重要。

即使是最微不足道的努力，也能让彼此享受陪伴。回想一下以前约会的日子，两人曾经在一起多么开心。我个人比较喜欢在晚餐时讲个笑话，或者换家有意思的餐馆改变一下饮食环境或口味，类似于这些平凡小事，只要能让两个人都高兴就好。有时，我们甚至会相互呵痒，我知道这样太过幼稚，但那又怎样，我爱她，能开心有什么不好呢？

生活可能会变得艰难，但记住你娶了最好的朋友。别忘了是什么让你们走到了一起，要努力享受彼此的陪伴，要时刻想办法让对方高兴。生命是一份礼物，当我和爱妻在一起时，最是享受。

7. PLAN INTIMACY (DON'T JUST WAIT FOR THE MOMENT, IT MAY NEVER COME)

Movies have set a standard where it appears that intimacy is something that must be planned and executed with precision. A well laid plan is not actually that romantic in real life as it becomes too mechanical. Yes, I am a planner, but in many cases it has been a random spontaneous idea that created the most lasting memories.

It is so much fun to plan a romantic evening for my sweetheart. It could involve booking a reservation at some fancy restaurant, dressing up, and then having a night on the town. We might even cap it off with some champagne and rose petals. No doubt this sounds like an exceptional time, and it does set expectations rather high, maybe too high, because as contradictory as it seems, those expectations can cut down on the intimacy if you plan these kinds of special occasions too often. If anything goes wrong, it can spoil the whole evening and the intimacy you have planned.

While we do enjoy such romantic evenings from time to time, we like to be intimate on all occasions. After all, is there a better way to start a day? I love to hold and touch my wife every chance I get. I do not often plan out our intimate outings with such detail, as I like to leave a little room for spontaneity.

I have watched many of my friends diligently plan their intimate rendezvous. I have observed that overplanning will normally create an end result that will feel manufactured and is just not real. Too much planning is not romantic. Romance must have a natural ebb and flow to feel real. Romance can be lost by too much planning. I have found that the best way to be intimate is to never miss a moment. Instead of trying to create that special situation, just go with the flow and harmony will be achieved. Don't wait for that special moment. That special moment is now. Do not miss it!

7 亲密行程

电影里已经形成了一套模式，好像亲密关系必须精心策划并精准执行。其实，刻意制定的计划在现实生活中并不那么浪漫，反而显得太过机械、呆板。没错，我是一个喜欢规划的人，但在很多情况下，一个随意的想法更能形成持久的记忆。

为心上人策划一个浪漫的夜晚真是太有意思了，包括预定高档餐厅，盛装打扮，然后在城里度过一晚，甚至可以用香槟和玫瑰花瓣作为结尾彩蛋。毫无疑问，这绝对是特殊的时刻，我们设定了很高的期望，但它也许太高了。说起来有些矛盾，如果频繁策划这类特殊场合的约会，这些过高的期望就会拉低亲密感，一旦中间出现任何差错，可能会毁掉整个夜晚以及亲密计划。

虽然偶尔也会享受这样浪漫的夜晚，但我们更喜欢在所有场合都保持亲密，毕竟这是开启新一天的最好方式。我喜欢一有机会就拥抱和爱抚我太太，我不会经常详细规划我们的亲密行程，因为我喜欢给说走就走、自然而发的约会留一点空间。

很多朋友都会不辞辛苦地计划亲密行程，但我认为过度规划容易让人感觉刻意和虚伪。规划太多并不浪漫，浪漫必须有自然的起伏转折才能让人感觉真实，太精心的计划会失去浪漫。我发现，最好的亲密方式就是不错过任何一个时刻，而不是试图创造那种特殊的时刻，其实只要顺其自然，和谐自会实现。不要等待那个特别的时刻，特别的时刻就是现在，千万不要错过！

8. TAKE A CLASS TOGETHER

My wife and I enjoy going to a show, dining at a fancy restaurant, or seeing a Broadway play as much as anyone else. While these things never get old, we also like to try new things. So why not take a few classes together? Classes are a great way to bond and get excited. What you learn will always stimulate your mind.

Learning a new skill or hobby together, unlike a Broadway play, is an everyday activity. We get to help each other master the said skill both in a class and at home by ourselves. Personally, we like to make an evening out of attending a class. Then all week long we can practice together, getting better and better. For those of you who do not want to leave the house, there are plenty of courses avail- able online. Talk about fun! Learning new things is always a win.

Our favorite classes so far have been French cooking and salsa dancing. We have even made some new friends. We always take short videos during such adventures and watch them later and laugh.

We have since taken other classes together which have been equally enjoyable. It is fun to learn new skills and hobbies with your partner that you can enjoy into the future. Find an activity you and your significant other are interested in learning, and learn it together. You can help each other grow and thus grow closer to each other.

9. SWITCH THINGS UP ONCE IN A WHILE. IT'S VERY ROMANTIC

Having a routine in life is crucial to success. It keeps you focused and on track, allowing you to reach and exceed your goals. The same is true in a relationship. Having a set date night every week can make sure that no matter how busy you or your spouse get, you will

8 一起学习

我和爱人与其他人一样喜欢看演出、在高档餐厅吃饭或者欣赏百老汇戏剧，虽然这些永远不会过时，但我们也喜欢尝试新鲜事物。所以，为什么不一起参加培训课程呢？上课是增进感情和激发兴趣的好方法，学到的知识还能促进思维。

与观看百老汇戏剧不同，一起学习新技能或新爱好是每天都能参与的日常活动。无论是在课堂上还是在家里，我们都可以互相帮助，掌握上述技能。就我个人而言，我更喜欢晚上去上课，然后整个星期我们可以一起练习，循序渐进。对于那些不想离开家的人来说，网上也有很多课程可供选择。说到乐趣，能学习新鲜事物就是最大的乐趣。

到目前为止，我们最喜欢的课程是法式烹饪和萨尔萨舞。我俩甚至还结交了一些新朋友，并在上课时拍摄了一些短视频，回家再看时会无比欢乐。

自此，我们又一起学习了其他同样令人愉快的课程。和伴侣一起学习新技能和新爱好很有意思，令人回味无穷。找一个两人都感兴趣的课程，一起学习，你们可以帮助彼此成长，从而更亲密。

9 偶尔浪漫

有规律的生活是成功的关键，能让人集中精力、按部就班地达到甚至超越自身目标。在亲密关系中也是如此，每周有一个固定的约会之夜能够确保无论两人有多忙，依然会找时间出去享受彼此的陪伴。我和爱人都很期待每

still find the time to go out and enjoy each other's company. My spouse and I look forward to our special nights all week, and eagerly plan what we are going to do. We usually end up doing the same type of thing, dinner somewhere and maybe a few drinks. Every now and again we will attend an event or some other activity that is slightly different, but those only arise so often. While this ritual is a beloved tradition in our relationship, I have found it is still important to mix things up from time to time.

I like to surprise my wife on a random night with tickets to a show she has mentioned, or set up an elaborate dinner at home she did not expect. It is these surprises that keep the spark of our relationship burning bright. You cannot underestimate the importance of a daily routine, but at the end of the day, it is still just a routine. Routines get boring after a while, no matter how much you attempt to spice them up. In order to keep your weekly routines from growing stale, you need to add something fun and unexpected to your relationship from time to time.

I once arrived home early on a random Tuesday and blindfolded my better half, only to chauffer her into a car where I would not let her speak until we reached an exhibit she had been talking about for months. When we arrived I removed the blindfold to see the look of sheer joy and excitement on her face. It warmed my heart to make her so happy, and it warmed hers knowing that I had put so much effort in on a random day just to see her smile.

It is important to have and maintain routines in your relationship and life, but every now and again, toss in something new!

10. LEARN TO LIKE THE MUSIC YOUR SPOUSE LIKES

Music has been dubbed the gateway to the soul, and it is easy to understand why. It has a way of making you feel emotions that are brand new or have long lain dormant. Certain songs can be incredibly personal and have a special meaning that lasts forever. If you are going to share your life with someone, it is important to get to know and like the same

周那些特别的夜晚，并兴致勃勃地制定计划。其实每次也都大同小异，找个地方吃顿饭，也许小酌几杯。我们偶尔也会参加一些稍微不同的活动，但也不是经常。虽然这种一成不变的方式我俩都很满意，但我发现偶尔改变一下也很重要。

我喜欢在一个随意的晚上给爱人送上小惊喜，比如她一直念叨的演出门票，或者瞒着她在家里精心准备晚餐。正是这些惊喜让我们的爱情火花闪烁耀眼。尽管不能低估每天一成不变的重要性，但它毕竟太过规律了。无论怎么想方设法给日常生活增添情趣，过一段时间后依旧会变得平淡无奇。为了不让规律的生活变得乏味，我们需要偶尔增添一些小确幸和小惊喜。

有一次，我在一个普通的星期二提早回家，蒙住爱人眼睛，让她坐进车里，不让她提问，最后带她来到她已经提了好几个月的展览现场。当我们到达时，我摘掉爱人的眼罩，看到她脸上呈现出异常喜悦和兴奋的表情。能让她这么开心我真太高兴了，当她知道我为这普通的一天花了这么多心血，就是为了让她开心时，她被深深地感动了。

在恋爱和生活中保持规律很重要，但偶尔也要浪漫一下！

10 分享音乐

都说音乐与灵魂相通，确实如此，音乐能让人感受从未拥有过的情绪或唤醒蛰伏多年的情感。有些歌曲更能触动某些人，并对其具有永恒的特殊含义。一起共同生活的伴侣，一定要了解并欣赏对方的音乐喜好，这点非常重要，反之亦然。你永远不可能和别人对同一首歌产生同样的共鸣，这没关

music as your partner, and visa versa. You will never have the same connection to a song as another person, and that's okay. You show your partner you care by just sincerely listening to it.

When your partner discovers a new song that really touches their heart, and they want to share it with you, take the time to enjoy it with them. To fully share a life, you do not have to love everything the other person cares about, as you are unique individuals, and sometimes it is those differences that allow you to learn and become a better person. However, if something means a lot to you or your partner, you each need to learn to experience it with them.

If you do not learn to enjoy the same music, it can be a major point of contention. Whenever you are on a drive, or one of you feels like listening to a song, it will instantly bug your partner and likely lead to resentment or a fight. However, if you put in the time to listen to what they like, you can learn to appreciate it. Obviously it has merit, as the person you love enjoys it. Music, like many things in life, is largely an acquired taste. By taking the time to listen to genres you may not initially like, you can learn to appreciate them, even if you still do not listen to that music when you are alone.

I want my wife to be comfortable listening to her music around me, and when I find a song I truly enjoy, I want to be able to share it with her. We come from different cultures and naturally grew up listening to different music. As a result, we have different musical tastes; however, we have both tried to appreciate each other's tastes and have thus grown closer together. This effort may seem like a small thing, but it is the small things that make a life meaningful.

My wife loves Arabic music. I had never listened to this type of music in my entire life until I met her. When I first heard it, I did not like it. To me, it was made up of strange sounds that I was unfamiliar with. Nonetheless, I kept listening and slowly I learned to tolerate the music. Then a wonderful thing happened, I started to love Arab music. Often, all it takes is to be open to something new and to try it, as was the case with me and Arab music. With time, my tastes adapted to what was once unfamiliar and it slowly grew on me. Learning to like this type of music has absolutely added a spice of love and romance to our marriage.

系，你可以通过真诚聆听来表达对伴侣的关心。

当伴侣发现一首真正能触动心灵的歌曲并愿意和你分享时，请你花点时间一起欣赏。真正生活在一起的人，没必要迎合对方喜欢的一切，因为你们都是独立个体，有时，正是这些差异让你不断学习并且更加优秀。然而，如果某件事对你或伴侣来说确实很重要，就需要学会和对方一起体验。

如果两人不能欣赏同样的音乐，这很可能会成为吵架的根源。当你们在开车或者其中一人想听歌曲时，这也许会打扰到另一位，并可能升级为愤怒或争吵。然而，如果你花时间去听对方喜欢的歌曲，慢慢也能学会欣赏，这些音乐能让你所爱之人喜欢，必定不俗。像生活中的许多事情一样，音乐在很大程度上是一种后天养成的品位，通过花些时间多听一些本身不太喜欢的音乐，你也能学会欣赏，即使独处时你仍然不会听这些。

我希望爱人在我身边能舒心自在地听音乐，当我找到一首特别喜欢的歌曲时，也希望能够与她分享。我们来自不同的文化背景，聆听不同的音乐长大，音乐品位自然不同。然而，我们都在努力尝试欣赏对方的喜好，因此，我们的感情更加亲密。这种努力可能看起来是小事，但正是这些小事使生活变得有意义。

我太太喜欢听阿拉伯音乐。在遇到她之前，我从来没听过这个类型的音乐。当我第一次听时，真心不喜欢，对我来说，它们就是由一些不熟悉的奇怪声音组成的。尽管如此，我还是继续听，慢慢学会了忍受这种音乐。然后，奇妙的事情发生了，我开始喜欢上阿拉伯音乐了。其实，我们所需要的只是对新鲜事物敞开胸怀就好了，就像我对阿拉伯音乐一样，经过一段时间，我慢慢适应了曾经的不熟悉，并渐渐喜欢上它，学会喜欢这种音乐绝对为我们的婚姻增添了浪漫情趣。

11. HOLD HANDS OFTEN

I love to hold hands or link arms with my sweetheart. I mean, I love it! It does not matter if we are taking a stroll along the beach, shopping at the mall, or sitting at home enjoying our favorite sitcom. It provides a sense of physical and emotional connection for both of us, which is important to maintaining a strong relationship.

Similar to a prescription drug the doctor gives when you are sick, I have found that holding hands will also bring good health to the relationship. I have found that even if we are not happy with one another at a particular moment, it is still important to hold hands and show affection. More than once, holding hands has been a mood changer. This act, although small, is comforting and often even empowering. In assures both of us that whatever the current disagreement is over, our love for each other overrides any disagreement. It is the catalyst that can help us move past the problem and on to more happy times.

Beyond this, or any anecdote I could provide, it is medically proven that holding hands is good for you. It boosts oxytocin which has been dubbed "the love hormone." Oxytocin helps to build the bond between you and your partner and strengthens feelings of closeness. As you can imagine, this also provides a sense of security for both people, which in turn can reduce stress.

Holding hands is an important activity for any couple. I know I feel incomplete when I am out and not holding my wife's hand. I like to keep her close, as it makes me feel loved and gives me the strength to accomplish any goal. Holding hands may seem like a small thing, but to me, it is invaluable.

11 时常牵手

我喜欢和心上人牵着手或挽着臂，我是说，我太喜欢这种感觉了！无论是在海边散步、在商场购物，还是坐在家里看最喜欢的情景喜剧，都是如此。牵手让双方随时能有身体和情感上的联系，这对维持感情的牢固很重要。

就像生病时医生开的处方药一样，我发现牵手也会让两人的关系更好。即使两人闹矛盾的时候，牵手表达爱意仍然很重要。牵手不止一次改变了我们的情绪，这一举动虽然微不足道，但却令人感到欣慰，甚至威力巨大，它表明，无论目前两人有什么分歧，我们对彼此的爱都会战胜一切。牵手是一种催化剂，可以帮助我们越过障碍，走向欢乐。

除此之外，现代医学也证明牵手有益，时常牵手有利于产生催产素，也就是所谓的“爱情荷尔蒙”。催产素有助于在伴侣之间建立联系，增强亲密感。想象一下，这也为双方提供了安全感，从而可以减轻压力。

牵手对任何情侣来说都很重要。当我因外出而不能和爱人牵手时，我会感觉自己不完整。我喜欢和她在一起，因为这能让我感到被爱，给予我完成任何目标的力量。牵手可能看起来只是一件小事，但对我来说特别宝贵。

12. AN OPEN INVITATION

I let my wife know that, with very few exceptions, she is invited anywhere I go. Many of my meetings are boring, even to me, and I do not believe she would ever want to attend them, but the point is that if she wanted to, it is okay with me. I give her an open invitation to go everywhere I go. She may not want to go, but simply because I always invite her, trust is created beyond measure.

Thirty years ago, people seldom brought their spouses with them to anything. This practice has changed, as I now go to many business meetings where the couple is present. I always invite my wife to everything I do, as we have an open invitation policy between us. I believe the change in people's thinking came about because it gradually became very prestigious to be known as a power couple. For me, this makes sense, as you are empowering your spouse by including them. It will also create more empathy because they will see just how hard you really work and the challenges that you face on a daily level.

When I was young, I used to get so emotionally involved in an opportunity that I missed the red flags my instincts were warning me about. Nowadays, my better half is often by my side in meetings, and she picks up on things I may miss, like a lack of logic in a proposal or some other tell-tale issue. The fishbowl concept can also come into play, where the rookie sees more than the experienced person, as they are looking at the opportunity or problem from a fresh new perspective. The idea of an open invitation is a winning way to approach life and business. The many benefits from following this approach bring you and your spouse closer together.

There are countless other benefits to having an open invitation policy that make it a winning approach to marriage. I have learned to respect my wife even more through this practice. She has surprised me more than once with her wisdom and insight.

12 公开邀请

我让爱人知道，除了极少数例外，无论我去哪里，她都能跟我一起去。我参加的很多会议其实都很无聊，甚至我自己都难以忍受，我认为她肯定不想参加，但关键是如果她愿意参加，我也同意。我会公开邀请她到我去的任何地方，她可能不想去，但仅仅因为我总是邀请她，信任就产生了。

三十年前，人们很少带伴侣出席任何活动，但现在风气已经完全改变了，我参加过的很多商务会议都是夫妇同时出席的。因为我和爱人之间有公开邀请的想法，所以我总是邀请她参加我出席的活动。我相信现在的风气之所以发生变化，是因为夫妇同心会更有社会威望。对我来说的确如此，因为可以通过邀请伴侣来赋予对方权利，这样也会产生更多的同情之心，因为对方会看到我有多努力工作，以及每天面临的挑战。

我年轻时在做生意上常常感情用事，从而忽视直觉带来的危险信号。如今我太太经常陪我一起开会，她会注意到我可能忽略的一些细节，比如提案缺乏逻辑或其他一些明显的问题。“鱼缸”概念说的就是这个道理，新手往往比有经验的人看到的更多，因为他们会从全新的角度看待问题。公开邀请的想法对生活和事业都大有裨益，遵循这种方法能让你和伴侣更亲密。

公开邀请还有很多益处，是通往幸福婚姻的必胜之路，通过这一做法，我变得更加尊重对方，而她的智慧和见识也不止一次惊艳到我。

13. FREEDOM IS AN OPTICAL ILLUSION

To me, happiness is never about freedom. The concept of freedom is actually a mirage. This is one of the many reasons why I married the love of my life. Having complete freedom leads to a lack of discipline, direction, and joy. Committing to something and especially to someone is the surest path to enjoying a wonderful life. Commitment gives focus to what is good. With focus and loyalty, which are byproducts of commitment, obstacles to happiness are removed, such as confusion and uncertainty. Clarity is easy to maintain when you make commitments. More importantly, with commitment, communication becomes easier and love will in turn grow infinitely and indefinitely. Life is about achieving a healthy mindset and making wise choices. Absolute freedom is a recipe to fail and be doomed to a miserable life.

Most people never understand this reality. True freedom comes from making connections and commitments to others, such as in marriage. I have many acquaintances, both male and female, who are old, single, and miserable as a result of never committing to anyone or anything. Being committed allows a person to focus on specific goals and actions, which is part of any formula to success. It is nature's formula. With too many options, success is rarely achieved. It is easy to choose a productive path when the options are narrowed down, but when there are too many, selecting the right one is impossible. The fewer options available, the higher the chances of success. So take my advice and commit fully to whatever it is you are doing (such as marriage, a diet, your job, etc.). With full and total commitment your future will be filled with unlimited success, joy and happiness. Just remember, if you really want freedom, all it takes is commitment. The concept of freedom for many is an optical illusion. It may seem odd, but commitment creates an environment that results in greater freedom, not less.

My wife and I are able to communicate with no problem even though we do so in broken English. Occasionally there are challenges, and we must use the translator on our phones, but we always get the message across. Living in China for over a decade, I learned that speaking the same language is not as important as we might think.

13 诠释自由

对我来说，幸福和自由毫不相干，所谓的自由不过是海市蜃楼，了解这一点是我能娶到一生挚爱的众多原因之一。拥有完全的自由会导致缺乏纪律、目标和快乐。专注于某事，尤其是某人，是享受美好生活最有效的途径。承诺让人专注于美好，专注和忠诚是承诺的副产品，能清除通往幸福的障碍，比如困惑和犹豫。当你做出承诺时，对方就不会困惑。更重要的是，有了承诺，沟通变得更容易，感情也会不断增长。生活就是要保持良好的心态，做出明智的选择，毫无意义的自由是失败的前奏，它注定要过悲惨的生活。

多数人都不明白这一现实，真正的自由来源于与他人建立联系和做出承诺，就像婚姻。我认识的各色男女，他们大多最后都孤独终老，因为从未对任何人或任何事做出过承诺而痛苦不堪。承诺能让人专注于具体的目标和行动，这正是成功的秘诀之一，是自然规律。选项太多，则很难取得成功，缩小选择范围，更容易选择一条富有成效之路，所以，接受我的建议，致力于眼前的事情（比如婚姻、节食、工作等），全身心地投入，你的未来将充满无限的成功、快乐和幸福。要知道，如果真的想要自由，就要做出承诺，对很多人来说，自由不过是一种错觉。虽然说起来很奇怪，但因承诺而营造出的环境能产生更多的自由。

我和爱人能够毫无障碍地交流，即使她用的是蹩脚的英文，当然，我们偶尔也会遇到困难，要用手机里的翻译软件，但我们总是能把要说的意思传达出去。我在中国生活了十多年，发现说同一种语言并没想象中那么重要。

The most important foundations of any such relationship are mutual caring, accepting of a new culture, learning to read body language, touching, listening, and showing respect. Yes translation machines can easily get you past the spoken word issues, but that is not enough. We fell in love through caring, observing, appreciating, and respecting each other. When you add up all the seemingly small gestures, like holding hands, cuddling, looking into each other's eyes, hugging, and sharing, before long a forever love is created. I am a big believer in counting my blessings, and I let her know that I am the luckiest man in the world to have her as my wife.

14. THE GRASS IS ALWAYS GREENEST WHEN IT IS WATERED AND RECEIVES SUNSHINE

It is normal to sometimes find your mind wandering. To wish for something new and exciting is human nature. We all look around trying to find that something better which will change our lives forever. Don't look now, but you may already have that something extra. To dream is a good thing as it helps us create goals and grow. The problem is, if it is taken too far, disaster may result. Your dream may be a better job, a nicer house, a luxury car, or something similar. Some people may even question if they could have made a better choice in marriage.

Dreams are healthy, but dwelling in that dream too often can make you lose your way in the journey of life to achieve success and happiness. If you are constantly dwelling on what you do not have, you will come to abhor what you do have. Relationships, especially marriage, are like plants. A plant must have the proper amount of sunshine, good soil, and be adequately watered to flourish. A plant will only grow and flower with the right attention. On the other hand, if we focus on the green grass on the other side of the hill, the result will be a slowly but surely weakening of the marriage.

It is so easy to complain and wish for something you do not have. Some people spend 24 hours each day wondering "what if," while ignoring "what is." This is an unhealthy cycle if it continues day after day. Such a person may begin by blaming other people, uncontrollable

亲密关系中最重要的基础是相互关心，接受新的文化，学会肢体语言，以及抚摸、倾听和尊重。翻译软件确实可以轻松渡过对话难关，但这还远远不够，我们通过互相关心、关注、欣赏和尊重而相爱。当你把所有看似微不足道的动作，比如牵手、依偎、相视、拥抱、分享，全部累加起来，不久就能形成永恒之爱。我是一个知福的人，我让她知道，有她做我的太太，我就是世界上最幸运的男人。

14 悉心呵护

偶尔发现自己想入非非很正常，追逐新鲜、刺激是人之本性。我们环顾左右，总想找到更好的东西来改变生活。其实不用找，你很可能已经拥有了。有梦想是好事，能帮助我们制定目标并且成长，问题是，如果梦做得过头，就会造成麻烦。你的梦想可能是一份更好的工作、一栋更美的房子、一辆豪车或类似的东西，还有些人甚至想要换个更好的伴侣。

有梦想很好，但过于沉溺于梦想会让人在通往成功和幸福的道路上迷失自我。如果一味纠结于没有的东西，就会厌恶所拥有的。人际关系，尤其是婚恋关系，就像植物一样，必须有充足的阳光、肥沃的土壤和适量的水分才能茁壮成长。植物只有在悉心呵护下才能生长和开花，如果我们总是这山望着那山高，必定会慢慢削弱婚姻关系。

人很容易抱怨并存非分之想，有些人每天二十四小时都在想“如果……会怎么样”，而忽略了“当下”。如果长此以往，将会形成恶性循环。这种人一开始可能会把自己的不快乐归咎于他人、外在原因和运气不好。虽然可能

circumstances, and old-fashioned bad luck for their unhappiness. While there may be external factors, the primary cause of failure is almost always with the person themselves.

Relationships are like plants. They are fragile and require attention and nurturing. With both relationships and plants, the moment we stop watering, block out the sunshine, or take them for granted, they begin to wither. At the beginning the decline will be slow and unnoticed. Certainly, there will be subtle signs, but most likely they will be overlooked. Maybe it is the constant cancelation of notable events with your spouse, postponing a vacation, or something similar. After a while, this behavior will result in a weakened marriage because the person is focusing on things that are shiny and new instead of cultivating what they already have. Such preoccupations may result in neither you nor your spouse caring about plans you have made. Maybe even a birthday or anniversary is forgotten, and the lack of care and attention continues to unravel going forward.

Being valued is double sided and goes both ways, of course. Over time, selfish and uncaring behavior from one partner will create what they get in return from the other. Of course, the new focus of your attention, such as a new person, will always be excited to hear from you. Think about it, you may spend enormous amounts of time and money on this person (not them on you) and treat them like they are the most important thing in the world, while ignoring your spouse. You start listening to them, caring what they say and sharing new ideas to help them achieve their goals. They have your undivided attention, and they feel valued. To put it back into metaphorical terms, the new grass is lush and green and that is because you are watering it. While your old grass (your spouse) is withering from neglect.

Let's shift attention back to romance and having a happy marriage. Once you decide to invest the same energy "watering" your existing marriage, you will be astonished with the results. If you divorce, it may take years of heartache and frustration to find a new spouse. Why not count the blessings you already possess and make the person you are with feel special every single day.

By pursuing a new relationship, not only are you attempting to create something from the unknown, but trust me, there are always other suiters, and you will have competition. If you compete against yourself by focusing on what you already have (your spouse) you will reap the rewards of bliss and joy. Watering the grass in your own backyard will create a competitive, winning attitude and a home field advantage for you. This is logic at its best. As you already know, the soil of your marriage is fertile and just needs the proper amount of

确实有外部因素，但失败的主要根源在于个人。

感情就像植物一样脆弱，需要悉心呵护，无论是情感还是植物，一旦我们停止浇水，遮住阳光，或者视其为理所当然，就会慢慢枯萎。一开始，这种变化会非常缓慢而不易察觉，当然，也会有一些微妙的迹象，但很容易被忽略，也许是不再与伴侣一起参加重要活动或推迟度假等类似的事情。一段时间以后，这种行为会导致婚姻关系变差，因为人们喜欢关注新鲜酷炫的东西，而不是呵护已经拥有的东西，这种情况会导致两人都不关心一起制定的计划，甚至会忘记生日或周年纪念日，缺少关心和爱护会导致婚姻破裂。

彼此间的重视是相互的，当然也会走向两个极端。一方长久以来自私和冷漠的行为会导致另一方做出同样的回应。当然，如果你有新的关注点，比如看上别人，新的人会很乐意同你交往，想想看，你可能在此人身上花了大量的时间和大把的金钱（而不是反过来），把新人当作世界上最重要的人，而忽略了你的伴侣。你开始听从、在意新人，想方设法助其实现目标。新人拥有你全心全意的关注，被重视，被呵护，用比喻的话来说，新草郁郁葱葱，那是因为你浇了水，而旧草（你的伴侣）因被忽视而枯萎。

让我们再重新回到浪漫和幸福婚姻的话题上来。一旦你决定投入同样的精力来“浇灌”现有的婚姻，结果会令你惊讶。如果离婚的话，可能要心痛和沮丧数年才能重新找到意中人，那为什么不珍惜已经拥有的幸福，让伴侣每天都感到特别呢？

追求一段新的感情，不仅是在前途未卜中白手起家，而且相信我，你还会因遇到其他的追求者而面临竞争。如果你专注于已经拥有的（你的伴侣），就相当于和自己竞争，会收获幸福和喜悦的回报。给自家后院的草浇水会给你带来肯定成功的心态和主场优势，这是最好的逻辑，如你所知，婚姻的土壤是肥沃的，只需要适量的阳光和水分就能让你们的感情开花结果。

如果你对待伴侣就像你还在“约会”一样，你就会特别感激对方。如果

sunshine and water to make your relationship a flowery success.

If you treat your spouse like you are still "dating," then you will suddenly appreciate them that much more. If you take the time and focus to pray and count your blessings for this person, your behavior toward them will change, and theirs toward you. Just like it took time for the relationship to nearly fail, it will now take time and consistent behavior for it to again be healthy. Be consistent in your approach, and the results will amaze you. By putting your spouse first, your attitude will change from the grass is greener on the other side to appreciation and counting your blessings for what you already have.

Be proactive in your spouse's life by asking questions. Do not assume you know what keeps them up at night, ask them instead. While people normally do not change significantly, we do all evolve. There is always something new you can learn about your spouse which will in turn create a better relationship.

The idea of perspective is a funny thing, because what we may view as weeds in our own backyard may be lush green fields to others, and vice versa. Always recognize just how lucky you are to have married the person you are with. Your approach will create a mindset of caring, loving, and happiness. It will let your spouse know they are cared about, respected, adored, and appreciated. Do not let your relationships perish from neglect. The grass is always greener where you water it the most. The best strategy is to treat your spouse like you are courting and the result will be a lasting, healthy, and happy marriage. Let your spouse know every single day that you are listening to them, that you love them, and that they are the most important person in your life. The results will be a honeymoon that lasts forever.

15. LOVE IS MORE THAN GOOD LOOKS

I love you is a wonderful way to start all conversations with your spouse. You may also want to add sentiments like I truly care about you, I respect you, I appreciate you, and Wow! How lucky I am to have you.

In all life situations, perspective is important in determining why something happened.

你花时间专注祈祷，为爱人祈福，你对爱人的态度就会改变，反之亦然。就像一段感情会经历很长时间才会凋谢一样，现在要想恢复健康也需要长时间坚持不懈的努力。坚持下去，结果会让你大吃一惊。把伴侣放在第一位，你的态度就会从“这山望着那山高”转变为欣赏和珍惜自己所拥有的一切。

要积极主动地询问你的伴侣，比如对方为什么夜不能寐，不要想当然，应该直接问。虽然人一般不会发生显著的变化，但人都在变，你总能从伴侣身上学到新的东西，这反过来又会让你们的关系更好。

每个人的观点、看法各不相同，因为在我们看来，自家后院的杂草对别人来说可能是郁郁葱葱的绿地，反之亦然。要时刻明白，能娶到这个人，自己是多么幸运。这种想法能营造出关心、爱恋和幸福的心态，让对方知道你的关注、尊重、崇拜和欣赏。不要让感情因为忽视而枯萎。水浇得多的地方，草总是最绿的。最好的办法是像求爱时一样对待伴侣，这样就能拥有长久、健康、幸福的婚姻。每时每刻都要让伴侣知道有你陪护在身边，伴侣是你生命中最重要的人，你们也因此能拥有一个永远持续的蜜月。

15 无关外表

在和伴侣开始所有谈话之前要先说“我爱你”，还可以加上这些话：“我特别关心你。”“尊重你。”“感激你。”“哇！能拥有你真是太幸运了。”

在各种生活情境中，判断事情发生的原因很重要。要分析造就每件事成

It Is always a good idea to analyze what made this or that a success. How did the situation evolve from interest in dating each other to being together forever in love and married.

My wife's beauty first got my attention in the Zoom convenience store. I thought that she was the most beautiful woman in the world. When I first saw her, I wanted to find a way to get to know her. It appeared impossible, but fate stepped in, and we are now married.

Later she won my heart, not from how she looked, but from the way she held me, cuddled with me, kissed me, and her cute, fun, no drama personality. I got to know the real person as time passed, and I fell in love like never before.

When wonderful things happen as they did with us, it is best to accept your good fortune and go with the flow. I believe in fate and do not question why we are now happily married. Sometimes it is best to accept a gift such as love without questioning why. I give thanks for her marrying me. I love her for who she is, not just for how she looks. She is still beautiful, but she is so much more. Overtime I fell in love with this wonderful woman for who she is, not for her appearance!

16. THOUGHTS CREATE ACTIONS

What you think about long enough can eventually become a reality. The more you dwell on something, the more likely it is that it will happen. If you have negative thoughts too often they may trigger actions that will produce a disaster. Eventually, the subconscious mind will obsess about these thoughts and work toward realizing them. That leads to trouble. If your spouse has an annoying habit and you think to yourself, "if they do this again, I will get angry," guess what? You will get angry.

The good news is that you can consciously focus on positive thoughts and get the same result. I do this simple strategy every day. I first say to myself whatever I want to manifest, and then I write it down. Because I repeat these actions daily, they get embedded in my

功的根源，是怎么从感兴趣的约会开始，进而发展到想要永远在一起并最终结婚的。

我太太的美貌从我们在 Zoom 便利店初遇时就引起了我的注意，我认为她是世界上最漂亮的女人。当我第一次见到她时，就想方设法地想结识她，当时看似不可能的事，终因命运之神降临而令我们终成眷属。

后来她赢得了我的心，不是因为她长得多漂亮，而是因为她抱我、搂我、吻我的方式，还有她可爱、有趣、不做作的个性。我渐渐了解了她这个真实的人，并前所未有地坠入爱河。

当美好的事情发生时，就像我俩这种情况，要顺其自然地接受好运。我相信缘分，从不质疑我们的幸福婚姻。有时候，要接受上天安排的礼物，比如爱情，不用问为什么。我感谢她嫁给我，我爱她不仅是因为她的美貌，更因为她的为人，她现在依然很漂亮，而且比以前更漂亮。随着时光流转，我爱上了这个了不起的女人，爱她这个人，而无关外表！

16 阳光心态

越是想什么就越容易来什么，越是琢磨一件事，就越有可能发生。如果你经常有消极的想法，就会引发导致灾难的行为，甚至于潜意识里会被这些想法所困扰，并促使其成为现实，这种想法会造成麻烦。如果你的伴侣有令人讨厌的习惯，而你一直对自己说：“如果对方再这样做，我会生气的。”你猜怎么着？结果你真的就会生气。

好的方面是，你可以有意识地让自己以积极乐观的方式想问题，也许就能得到同样的结果。我每天都这么做，首先对自己说出想要实现的目标，然

subconscious and slowly work their way into my reality. I begin to believe them so much that eventually my subconscious mind reacts in only positive ways, and that becomes part of my daily life.

For example, I constantly think about how lucky I am to be married to my lovely life partner. What can I do today to make her happy? Guess what? Every day I do something to make her happy. It might be the smallest of gestures, like opening the door for her, but it will make a difference. I think to myself how can I make my wife feel important? As time passes, I do things that make her feel important without trying. For example, I am writing this book that you are reading right now, and I know that will make her smile.

Trust me, this simple and easy exercise is almost effortless and assures that your relationship stays strong, instead of becoming brittle. It is a way to keep any relationship happy. It is time tested formula, and as long as you follow this recipe of consciously putting good thoughts in your head, over time you will experience positive results. Eventually your subconscious will take over your conscious mind, and you will find yourself naturally taking the very actions you previously had to consciously think about.

17. SILLY, OUTRAGEOUS, AND FUN

People love a person who is elegant, sophisticated, debonair, suave, cultured, dashing, and refined. Often you may have noticed that people who possess these characteristics are very attractive to the opposite sex and "lucky in Love." There have been thousands of Hollywood movies based on this premise. Such a person will rise above all other suiters. To be courted by a person of such character can be enough for anyone to fall in love.

However, such an attractive person might also be boring, predictable, and no fun at all. We all like to laugh and be with people who make us laugh. I like to think of myself as having these sophisticated characteristics, excepting the boring personality of course. I always dress for success and carry myself in such a way that people might immediately realize I am successful in whatever I do. I speak with sophistication, I am well read, and I

后写下来。因为我每天都在重复这些动作，它就会嵌入我的潜意识，慢慢促进梦想实现。我现在特别相信这种方法，遇事时潜意识里只会以积极阳光的方式做出反应，这已成为我日常生活的一部分。

例如，我总想自己有多幸运，能娶到这么可爱的伴侣，那今天该做点什么才能让她高兴呢？结果每天我都想办法让她开心。有可能是帮她开门这种微小的举动，但很有效。我总是想怎样才能让太太觉得她自己很重要。随着时间的流逝，我毫不费力地做了一些让她自我感觉重要的事情，比如我写了大家正在读的这本书，我知道这会让她高兴。

相信我，这种简单易行的方法最省力，能保证两人关系更加牢固，是能经受住时间考验、让感情更加幸福的最好方法，只要你遵循这一秘诀，有意营造阳光的心态，你就会慢慢体验到积极的结果。潜意识也会影响思维，你会自然而然采取以前需要深思熟虑的行动。

17 一起搞笑

人们都会喜欢优雅成熟、温和娴静、满腹经纶、沉稳体面的人。通常你会发现，拥有这些特性的人特别能吸引异性，而且“桃花运很旺”，有很多好莱坞电影都是以此为蓝本的。这种人能胜过无数情敌，如果能被具有这种性格魅力的人追求，任何人都会坠入爱河。

然而，这么有吸引力的人很可能会无趣，可以想象，肯定特别没意思。我们都喜欢笑，喜欢和能让我们欢乐的人在一起。我愿意自己具有这种成熟性格，当然除去无聊这一条。我喜欢穿着得体，给人一种成功人士的感觉，我谈吐不凡、博览群书，且善于观察，这些优势使我在工作上和生活中都能

am a great observer of small things, which in business and in life often provides me with an advantage over others.

There is another side of my personality, also, and in a relationship, the other side is more powerful than the sophisticated side. I sometimes will do silly, outrageous things that are remembered for years. They add humor to an otherwise predictable life. I do not do these things in the presence of others in order to avoid embarrassing my spouse; however, in a private environment, it is a different story. I only do them for the benefit and the laughter they create for her.

For example, once when she was taking a shower, I walked in fully dressed in a tuxedo. I proclaimed, "I am here to help make sure you are clean." She laughed and will always remember this moment. No one except the two of us shared this event, making it a special memory and a very private moment (until now). It might be fun and create a great memory to both jump in a swimming pool with all our clothes on, or to go to a cheap hamburger stand and bring a bottle of expensive champagne. Costume parties are always fun also, as we get to change our personalities for a little while. The fun pictures and the awesome memories that are created from such activities are a great way to keep your relationship or marriage alive and healthy.

18. BECOMING FRIENDS IS IMPORTANT

Being married should not mean being bored. Routines are important to be successful in life and in marriage, but it is easy to fall into routines that are tiring. There comes a time to break up routines to keep things fresh. Part of the equation of a successful marriage is realizing that you are not only in love with your spouse but that this person is also your best friend.

My spouse is the person I tell all my secrets to, and I know that she will care about and listen to what I say. I never hide anything from her, and this makes our relationship strong. She is the person who will listen when I need to be heard. She is the person who can help

优于他人。

我的个性也有另一面，在恋爱时，另一面比成熟的一面更强大。我有时会做一些愚蠢、搞笑的事情，让人难以忘怀，也能给原本平凡的生活增添一缕幽默。我不会在外人面前做这些事，以免让伴侣感到难堪，然而就我们俩的时候，就完全是另一回事了。我这样做只是为了让她高兴。

例如，有一次她正在洗澡，我穿着燕尾服郑重其事地走进浴室。我说："我来这里视察一下你是否洗干净了。"她乐坏了，表示会永远记住这一幕。除我们两人以外，没有人知道这件事，这是一段特别的记忆和非常私密的时刻（直到现在都是）。穿着衣服一起跳进泳池，或者带一瓶昂贵的香槟去街边汉堡摊，也非常搞笑，能留下美好回忆。化装舞会也不错，因为可以短暂改变自己的人设。在这些活动中拍出来的有趣照片和美好回忆有利于保持良好的婚恋关系。

18 成为朋友

婚后生活并不意味着无聊。日常习惯对于美好的生活和婚姻都很重要，但我们很容易陷入令人生厌的例行公事中。有时候，我们要打破常规、保持新鲜。在美满的婚姻中，你要意识到自己不仅要爱伴侣，这个人也是你最好的朋友。

我会对爱人倾诉所有秘密，而且我知道她会在意并认真倾听，我从不向她隐瞒任何事情，这让我们的感情更加牢固。当我需要吐露心声的时候，她

put what's troubling me into perspective and offer a solution.

Maybe the primary job of your partner is only to listen and not offer advice. I have found many times that if I just talk to someone whom I trust, the very act of speaking my mind clarifies the issues and creates a solution. This person is one with whom you can share all your wildest and craziest dreams and maybe they can help you make those dreams come true.

You marry because you love someone, and when you recognize that they are also your best friend, you will realize you have what I call a total win. In life we sometimes need a shoulder to cry on and somebody who will listen. To have a supportive spouse is a win every time.

19. LEARN FROM THE INTERNET AND MAKE ANY DAY OR NIGHT A GREAT MEMORY

We all love a great massage. I know a massage makes me feel relaxed and rested. There are many other things I love, such as a good meal. Have you ever realized that just maybe your spouse may love the same things as you? With this in mind, I have used YouTube and other platforms to learn new skills, such as how to give a world class massage.

There are so many platforms where you can learn just about anything from seasoned professionals and experts. The library of educational videos is nearly unlimited, and many are from experts in the field. For example, I learned how to give a massage from professionals who teach the spa professionals. I have gotten so good at giving a massage using this method, I could probably get a job at a spa (assuming I was able to get a license).

You can learn in depth techniques and various tips that only the pros know from such sources. I learned that a great massage is more than technique. There are different measures of touch and pressure points that set massage therapists apart. How about adding relaxing music and maybe a candle to put the experience over the top. After the massage, you might lay out fresh fruit and nourishing drinks presented in an elegant manner. Small details down to the cup used are important. One of the videos pointed out that even the type of oil

会耐心倾听，并能帮助我正确看待困难，提供解决方案。

也许你的伴侣只要倾听就好，无须提供建议。我发现，很多时候，只要能和信任的人交谈，说出自己的想法，这一行为本身就能让事态明朗，并找到解决方案。这个人是能与之分享所有痴心妄想和疯狂梦想的人，也许还能帮助你实现梦想。

结婚是因为你爱这个人，当你想到此人也能成为你最好的朋友时，就会意识到自己赢了。在生活中，我们有时需要一个可以依靠的肩膀和一个愿意倾听的人，有一个支持你的伴侣，就是最大的胜利。

19 在线学习

我们都特别享受按摩，它能让人放松和休息。我还喜欢很多东西，比如厨艺。你有没有想过，也许你的伴侣也喜欢同样的东西？想到这，我就去“油管”（YouTube）和其他平台上学习新技能，比如如何掌握一流的按摩技法。

在很多平台上，你都可以跟随经验丰富的专业人士学习各种课程，教育视频库几乎涵盖一切，其中很多都是来自该领域的专家。例如，我从SPA专业人士那里学会了如何按摩，我现在已经很擅长做这种按摩了，都能在SPA中心找工作了（如果我能拿到证书的话）。

可以从这些资源中深入学习只有专业人士才掌握的技术和各种技巧。我发现，一流的按摩不仅仅靠技术，按压位置和按压手法确实能区分出按摩师的优劣，但是如果再播放一段轻松的音乐，或者点燃一支蜡烛，那就更加完美了。按摩结束后，还可以摆上新鲜的水果和滋补饮料，要讲究摆放细节，

matters. by watching these videos, I learned that a great massage is much more than simply rubbing someone's back. A great massage has many elements to make it an experience that will be cherished.

The list of things you can do to make your spouse feel special is vast. Just use your imagination. That little extra effort and attention to detail is always how you get the win. Cooking, like massages, can be learned on the internet from the world's greatest chefs. If your spouse loves a certain dish, why not learn to make it? Just like a massage, a good meal is much more than just the food. If they like wine, do you have a good one that pairs well with what you are serving? Is the ambiance of the room romantic enough for the occasion? Did you buy candles? Room temperature also matters in setting the mood. How about the dinnerware that you are serving the food on? Have you thought about the music you might play? Attention to the small details upgrades what you have planned from special to something that will be remembered forever. Go the extra mile and pay attention to every detail.

Whatever it is that you plan, and it can be anything, learn as much as you can from videos, books, and other sources before you undertake the challenge. It does not have to be a massage or a meal, it can be anything. You can even use the internet as a private coach for dance lessons. There are so many fun things that you can learn to show your spouse that you not only love them but that you care. Often knowing someone loves you is not enough. You must also show that you care and do it over and over again.

20. TELL YOUR SPOUSE THEY ARE LOVELY

Being told you are lovely is a wonderful compliment. To me it is better than beautiful, as it means the person is not only physically attractive but that they are also charming and worth remembering.

Giving compliments creates a greater level of optimism, satisfaction, and happiness. Compliments create positive, warm energy for both people. Similar to the giving of physical gifts, both the giver and receiver will benefit from the experience. The mood change created

小到所用的杯子都很重要。其中一个视频还强调，按摩精油的类型也很讲究。通过观看这些视频，我了解到按摩不是捏捏肩膀这么简单，一流的按摩需要很多方面相互调和，才能让体验者享受其中。

能让伴侣感到特别的事情有很多，要发挥想象力，这些小小的努力和对细节的关注正是你获胜的原因。厨艺和按摩一样，也能在网上向世界顶级大师学习。如果爱人喜欢某道菜，为什么不学着做呢？就像按摩一样，一顿美餐不仅仅在于食物本身，如果爱人喜欢小酌，你是否有佐餐的好酒？房间布置得是否浪漫？是否准备了蜡烛？室温对营造气氛也很重要，盛菜的餐具也要考究，播放的音乐也要考虑，注意这些细节能让这个特别的日子成为永恒的记忆。一定要加倍努力，注意细节。

无论你计划做什么，在开始之前，尽量从视频、书籍和其他资源中学习。不一定是按摩或厨艺，可以是任何方面，甚至可以在网上学习舞蹈。有很多有趣的事情都可以学，这表明你不仅爱着伴侣，而且关心伴侣。知道别人爱你是不够的，还必须不断表现出你的关心。

20 赞美伴侣

说对方可爱是最好的赞美，对我来说，比漂亮更好，因为可爱意味着此人不仅外表有魅力，而且个性很迷人，能让人记忆深刻。

赞美能让人更乐观、更满足、更快乐，能给双方都带来积极温暖的能量，和送礼物一样，送礼者和收礼者都会从中受益。在某些情况下，适当的

by a compliment can be one that lasts for days, based on the situation. A kind, genuine, thoughtful compliment is like a form of magic, as it has the power to turn someone's day around in an instant, and can make them feel proud, happy, and appreciated.

Everyone loves to be complimented. It is an ego booster. It can make a down day turn into a happy day. Of course, the opposite is true when you say negative things about someone, as it can ruin their day. Look at the social media influencers who have millions of adoring followers. Suddenly one person finds something about them that is unattractive, and just that one comment causes the person to go into a depression. I have read that social media influencers are among the highest in suicide rates in the world because of their "haters."

You will not be with your spouse 24/7. During the times when you will be apart, someone may say something that causes them become depressed. I believe it is my job to counteract such a situation. Therefore, when my spouse returns, I always find something sincere to compliment her on. The compliment can be about her appearance or maybe an achievement of that day. Maybe you say that she has made your day a happy one simply with her electrifying presence. I sincerely believe it is my job to be my spouse's biggest cheerleader and support group, and it is such a great job. Think about it, when you say something that makes another person feel good, you will also get a feeling of joy. When I give a compliment and it makes the person smile, I also feel happy.

Compliments like "baby you look lovely today" always have a positive impact on your spouse. It is impossible to offer such compliments too of- ten. People love hearing nice things and being noticed. Genuine compliments build relationships, improve communication, motivate people, and boost self-esteem and self-importance. A genuine compliment will enhance and nurture your loving relationship. So, make sure the compliments you give are real and genuine. Do not make up things that you do not believe. Trust me, there is always something you can find about your spouse to compliment. Even if it is the same compliment every time, that works.

Never underestimate the power of a "your nails look fabulous" or "that pink dress was made for you" or "the way you treat me makes me feel great!" The compliment could be just skin deep, like your ring is so lovely, or maybe a more important attribute, personality trait, or accomplishment. For example, to say, "You have such good judgement. I wish I had that ability" is powerful. I simply say "Baby, you are so lovely today" as my fallback, and she never gets tired of hearing it.

赞美所产生的情绪变化可以持续数天。善意、真诚、体贴的赞美就像魔法一样，能瞬间改变人的情绪，让人感到骄傲、快乐和感激。

每个人都喜欢被赞美，这能够提升自我价值，也能让失落的一天变成快乐的一天。当然，当你说别人坏话时，也能破坏他人的情绪。看看那些拥有百万粉丝的网红，如果突然有人发现该网红身上有什么负面消息，仅仅是一句评论就能让此人抑郁。有报道称网红是世界上自杀率最高者之一，就因为他们拥有众多“仇恨者”。

你不可能二十四小时都陪在伴侣身边，当两人不在一起时，就会有人说一些意志消沉的话，而我的职责就是应对这种情况。因此，当太太回来时，我总是真诚地赞美她，可以夸她的外表，也可以夸她当天做的事，或者说因为她的存在，我过得很快乐。我由衷相信我就是她人生中的啦啦队长，给她拍手喝彩就是我的职责。要知道，当你表扬别人时，你也会感到快乐。当我赞美他人、让他人高兴时，我就会快乐。

“宝贝，你今天看起来很可爱”这样的赞美一定能对伴侣产生积极的影响。但你不可能总说这一句。人们喜欢动听的话并且被他人关心。真诚的赞美能建立感情、改善沟通、激励他人，并能增强自尊和提升自我。真心的赞美能增进和滋养恋爱关系，所以一定要发自内心，不能说违心的话。相信我，你肯定能在对方身上找到值得赞美的方面，就算每次都是同样的话也没关系。

永远不要低估“你的指甲真漂亮”“那条粉色裙子太配你了”“你对我真好，我太高兴了！”这些话。赞美可以是表面上的，比如“你的戒指太可爱了”，或者是个性特征、成就方面等深层次的，比如“你有很强的判断能力，真希望我也行”这种话就很有说服力，还可以用最简单的话“宝贝，你今天太可爱了”作为应急，对方永远听不腻。

21. THE MAGIC OF TOUCH

The importance of physical touch in a relationship cannot be emphasized enough. In fact, we have another entire point on just holding hands. Touch is so powerful it is equivalent to that of a magic wand. Touch gives someone a feeling of being understood, accepted, and cared about. To feel cared about, and to know that you matter to the other person is both powerful and calming. The ongoing experience of physical touch builds trust by showing that you are there for and with the other person.

Touch can be a powerful way of communicating emotions without using words. Touch offers a subtle approach in how we interact with our partner. A hug can communicate positive emotions, such as love, safety, and appreciation. When I hug my spouse, I feel amazing and experience an emotional high that is out of this world. It reminds me that I am important to her. Hugs, holding hands, sitting next to each other with our bodies touching and cuddling at night make us both feel warm, cared about, and loved.

As mentioned in point 11 about the importance of holding hands, human beings have a hormone directly associated with touch and bonding called Oxytocin, the "love hormone" or the "cuddle hormone." This hormone is created when people hold hands, or cuddle, and it is critical to human development as demonstrated when a mother first holds her newborn baby. Oxytocin is both a hormone and a neurotransmitter that facilitates communication within our brains and bodies. It inhibits stress and increases calmness.

My wife and I are always touching each other in powerful and meaningful ways. When we walk, sit in a car, train, or plane, we always hold hands. At night we cuddle all night long, and as a result, we always wake up fully rested. If we have been apart, we hug the second we see each other. Sometimes, she will give me a long deep hug that reaches my soul. I actually look forward to getting in bed for more than just sex. It is so powerful in our relationship that often just a hug can overcome any issue.

If you want a healthy marriage, touch can be a great elixir. If you have not been touching your spouse on a regular basis, learn a new habit and make it part of your

21 身体接触

身体接触在恋爱关系中的重要性怎么强调都不为过，实际上我们之前也提到过，仅仅牵手都很重要。接触就像一根魔杖，能给人被理解、被接受和被关心的感觉。让你感受到被关爱，知道你对别人很重要，这种感觉既温暖又安心。持续不断的身体接触可以建立信任，表明你一直都在身边。

身体接触是不需要语言就能交流情感的有效方法，为伴侣之间的互动提供了一种含蓄的方式。拥抱可以传达积极的情绪，比如关爱、安全和感激。当我拥抱爱人时，感觉特别棒，能体验到一种超凡脱俗的情感，让我明白自己对于她很重要。拥抱牵手、相互依偎、搂抱而眠，让我俩感到温暖、体贴、关爱。

正如在第 11 条目中提到牵手的重要性，人类有一种与身体接触直接相关的激素，叫作催产素，即“爱情荷尔蒙”或“拥抱激素”。这种激素在人们牵手或拥抱时产生，对人类的发展至关重要——当母亲第一次怀抱新生儿时就证明了这一点。催产素既是一种激素，也是一种神经递质，能促进大脑和身体之间的信息传递，可以抑制压力，让人平和。

我和爱人总是以有效且有意义的方式相互触摸。当我们走路、乘坐汽车、火车或飞机时，总是手牵着手。晚上我们整夜搂抱在一起，醒来时总是精神饱满。如果我们一时分别，会在见到对方时立即拥抱。有时，她会给我一个深深的拥抱，能直达我的灵魂。其实，我很期待上床，但不只是为了做爱。身体接触在我们的关系中非常重要，一个拥抱就能让我们克服任何难题。

想要拥有健康的婚姻，身体接触是最好的灵丹妙药。如果你不懂得应该

routine. I believe one of the reasons our relationship is so strong is because we are always touching each other. I think this happened because of the language barrier. It was a way to show affection during the times we could not understand each other through the spoken word. Before long, it became just part of who we are, and it is one of the main reasons our relationship is so strong. Touch is a gift that costs nothing and can give a relationship that loving edge for a lifetime.

22. TO WIN IS ALWAYS TO LOSE

It does not matter how well two people are matched, occasionally there will be friction that leads to disagreement. This cannot be avoided. At that point, how you handle the situation is crucial. To just rollover and give in is often a must. However, I advise sometimes that it is best to first make your point gently before completely giving in because by planting the seed, you will avoid the disagreement happening over and over again. In addition, if you want a healthy relationship, on unimportant matters, just let whatever the issue is go and say nothing.

To win an argument with your spouse is to lose. It will slowly pull the two of you apart. To embarrass your spouse is never a winning formula. No matter how much you feel that your opinion is correct, the other person also feels they are justified in their assessment and conclusion. You must take this into account and accept that the opinion of your spouse matters. I work under the assumption and mindset that her opinion matters more than mine. My strategy is simple, her opinion matters, and I must accept and listen before reacting. Because we have a language barrier, this strategy is especially important. Since developing this strategy, it has spilled over and helped me in my business life. Now, I let trivial issues go and just keep moving forward toward successful goals.

It is natural to sometimes say no, and sometimes I say, “No-no-no!” When I catch myself doing this, I slow down immediately and rethink my position. I listen before saying anything else. I often find that I was wrong. When you look at a conflict from a different

经常触摸伴侣，那就要养成这个新习惯，使之成为日常生活的一部分。我相信，我俩关系如此牢固，就是因为我们总是互相触摸，我想这是因为语言障碍造成的，在我们无法通过语言相互理解的时候，这是一种表达爱意的方式，久而久之就成为我们生活的一部分，这也是我俩关系如此牢固的主要原因之一。身体接触是不需要花费任何代价的礼物，能让一段浓烈的感情持续一生。

22 不争对错

无论两个人多么般配，偶尔也会因小摩擦而起冲突，这是无法避免的。在这种情况下，如何处理至关重要，妥协和让步肯定毋庸置疑。然而，我建议在完全认输之前最好先温和地表达自己的观点，这样先慢慢灌输，就能避免循环往复地出现同一分歧。此外，如果你想让两人感情和谐美满，在不重要的事情上就算了吧，什么都别说。

赢得与伴侣的争论其实是一种失败，会让两人关系慢慢疏远。让对方难堪绝不是好方法，无论你觉得自己的观点多么正确，对方也会觉得自己的判断和结论有理，你必须考虑到这一点，接受对方的意见很重要。我总是保持这种想法和心态，认为她的意见比我的更重要，我的策略很简单，她的意见很重要，我必须在做出回应之前接受并倾听。由于我们有语言障碍，这个策略尤为重要。自从制定了这个策略，它的效果居然延伸到生意上，对我很有帮助。现在，我对鸡毛蒜皮的小事都不在意，要继续朝着成功的目标前进。

有时说“不”是很自然的，有时我会说：“不，不，不！”当我发现这种情况时，就会立即慢下来，重新思考自己的立场，要先听后说，事后我经常发现是自己错了。当你从不同的角度看待冲突时，往往会得出新的结论。

angle, often you will come to a new conclusion.

It can be very satisfying to let your partner know that you are right and they are wrong. But trust me, this is an approach to disaster, and you must change your mindset. It really does not matter who is right. Being in-sync with perfect harmony should be your goal. Being right all the time will hurt the person you love. From big things to small, if you feel you have to be right, you must break the pattern and change your mindset. Often a person's deep need to be right prevents them from having relationships that are as supportive and meaningful as they should be.

It's hard to break this pattern, and like most things that are hard to do, it starts with small steps. You must learn to learn how to react in ways that are not defensive. Learning to let moments pass without reacting to them will build a strong and lasting relationship.

You will be pleasantly surprised by how much these incremental changes in your attitude will improve your relationship. Little things always mean a lot. Eventually, situations that once were sure to turn into fights pass by without conflict. This should be your goal. Since we were young, we were always taught to win the game, but in relationships, losing often creates the win. Like everyone else I love being right, but I have learned that to win is often to lose. To first listen instead of reacting is my strategy, and it has proved to be very successful. To stop defending my position and to respect, honor, and love my spouse as my first priority is the true win. If that means often accepting something I may initially disagree with, I am okay with this outcome.

23. COMPLIMENTS OFTEN

They say diamonds are a girl's best friend, and while they are definitely a part of my wife's social circle, I have come to believe that compliments go further. Diamonds are fun to show off and make you feel beautiful and admired, but compliments show you love your spouse and make you like yourself, which is more important. I greatly care for my wife's self-esteem, but the haters of the world have a strange way of making her feel like she is not

让对方知道你是对的、对方是错的，也许能满足你自己的虚荣心，但相信我，这种方法非常可怕，你必须改变心态，不争对错。谁对谁错真的无关紧要。两人和谐美满才应该是目标。什么都是你对，会伤害你爱的人。无论大事小事，不能觉得自己都是对的，你必须打破这种模式，改变心态。人通常会根深蒂固地认为自己永远正确，这样就无法拥有本该相互支持的美好感情。

要打破这种模式很难，就像很多难事一样，要先从一小步开始。你必须先学会如何以温和的方式做出回应，学会顺其自然，冷静下来先不回应，才能建立牢固而持久的感情。

你会惊喜地发现，这些态度上的改变能改善两人关系。小事往往很重要，最终那些注定会演变成争吵的冲突会平静地过去，这才应该是你的目标。我们从小就被教导要赢得比赛，但在感情中，先输才会赢。和所有人一样，我也喜欢自己什么都对，但我明白争执对错本身就输了。我的策略是先倾听而不是先回应，事实证明这种策略非常成功。不要再为自己辩解，把尊重和敬爱伴侣作为首要任务，才是真正的胜利。如果这意味着我要接受最初不太认可的事，那也无所谓。

23 相互赞誉

都说钻石是女孩最好的朋友，没错，钻石绝对是我太太社交圈的一部分，但我越来越相信，赞誉更胜一筹。炫目的钻石使人很有成就感，认为自己很漂亮、令人艳羡，而赞誉表明你爱对方，也能让你喜欢自己，这才是更重要的。我非常在意我太太的自尊，但是世界上那些记恨她的人总有奇怪的

pretty enough, smart enough, etc. These criticisms are of course untrue, and I let her know how beautiful she is every day. Whenever she says or does something clever or kind, which is often, I let her know that I understand and appreciate whatever it is. If you are going to have a successful marriage, it is crucial to compliment each other as often as possible. You are already thinking it, so you may as well say it.

If compliments rather than diamonds are a girl's best friend, they are a man's everything. There is an old joke that if you compliment a man's shirt, not only will he never throw it away, he will wear it every day going forward. In general, men are starved for compliments. They get them so rarely, that when they do, it is like giving a starving man a meal. They mean even more when coming from their significant other. I know that when my wife compliments me, I feel like I can take over the world. I do better in business, and I am happier all day long.

Couples should be comfortable complimenting each other, and they should do so often. The world can be a harsh place. The media creates unrealistic expectations of people that naturally hurt their self-esteem and self-image. If this goes unchecked, it can cause legitimate psychological issues. However, if the person you love goes out of their way to let you know that you are not only enough, but smart, beautiful, and kind, it can change the critical narrative.

24. ALWAYS SHOW RESPECT

It should go without saying that you should always show respect, not only to your friends and family, but anyone you meet in life. It is basic manners and anyone with class abides by it. Strangely, there is one exception. Whether it is because you have such a close and intimate relationship, or because you spend so much time together, we sometimes forget to treat our spouse with respect, and instead expect things from them.

My wife is by far the most important person in my life, and as such she deserves more respect than anyone else. I have caught myself in the past beginning to expect things from

方式让她觉得自己不够漂亮、不够聪明等。这些说法当然都不对，我每天都要让她知道自己有多漂亮。每当她说出或做出一些聪明或善良的事情时，她确实经常如此，我都会让她知道我的理解和感激。如果你想拥有美满的婚姻，时常相互赞誉至关重要。你已经在想了，赶紧说出来吧。

如果说钻石是女孩最好的朋友，那么赞誉就是男人的一切。有一个老式笑话：如果你称赞一个男人的衬衫，他就永远都不会扔掉，而且还会每天穿着。一般来说，男人都渴望得到赞扬，他们却很少能有这种机会。如果一旦得到，他们就会像饿极了的人看到美食一样，若这些赞誉来自另一半，则更是意义重大。就我而言，当太太称赞我时，我就会感觉全世界都属于我，生意会更兴隆，整天都特别开心。

伴侣之间要乐于相互赞誉，而且应该经常如此。世界本就残酷，媒体又总是制造不切实际的期望，这自然会伤害人们的自尊和自我形象，如果置之不理，还会导致严重的心理问题。然而，如果你爱的人特意让你知道，你不仅够格，而且聪明、美丽、善良，就能改变负面影响。

24 尊重伴侣

毋庸置疑，应该时刻尊重他人，不仅对朋友和家人，对生活中遇到的任何人都理应如此，这是基本礼仪，任何有教养的人都会遵守。但奇怪的是，确实有一个例外，不管是因为两人关系太过亲密，还是因为在一起的时间太长，人们有时会忘记尊重自己的伴侣，反而要求得到对方的尊重。

到目前为止，我太太是我生命中最重要的人，因此她，比任何人都值得

her, and then not showing the proper amount of gratitude when she complies. Luckily, my mindset catches me like a safety net and subconsciously pulls me back onto the right path. In retrospect, I feel horrible about these instances even though they rarely happen. In each case, I slow down and do some deep thinking to figure out why they occurred. Usually, I behave in this reprehensible way when I get overly busy, stressed, or overwhelmed. Which, if you think about it, makes sense. That does not excuse the behavior, and being disrespectful to the one person who could ease your tension does little to help solve your basic problem. It also does not make practical sense. When I was rude to my wife, she would naturally get upset, and it would start a whole new set of problems for me.

I have learned to always be respectful to my wife, even when I am personally in a bad mood. My normal behavior is to consistently treat her with respect and let her know how I feel. It took much deep thought and meditation to figure out this simple life lesson. I call it the "respect, don't expect" formula. When you begin to feel like you may snap, pay extra close attention to how you treat your spouse and do the opposite. They do not deserve to be the recipient of your bad day, and further, it will not make it better.

It is funny, my wife has caught on to this, so on those bad days, she will say, "So you have had some negative challenges today?" Meaning, I was treating her so well that she knew I was overcompensating for my bad day at work. We both laugh. Even this will elevate my mood. Go out of your way to let your significant other know that they are respected, admired and appreciated.

25. JUST FORGET YELLING

Yelling is great if you are at a sporting event and cheering for your team, or maybe even booing the opposition. It is even useful when you are in a loud bar or restaurant and need to communicate. Further, how are you going to talk to someone on the other side of a wide river if not by yelling? These examples, however, are not the type of yelling I am talking

尊重。曾经有段时间，我发现自己开始对她有所要求，而当她顺从我时，我却没有因此而心生感激。幸运的是，我的思维像安全网一样发现了情况，下意识地把我拉回了正确的轨道。尽管这种情况很少发生，但我回想起来还是觉得可怕。每经一事，我都会静下心来，进行深入思考，找出原因。通常来说，当我特别忙碌、压力过大或不堪重负时，就会以这种错误的方式行事。如果你仔细想想，这也确实可以理解，但这并不能成为错误行为的借口，而且不尊重那个替你缓解压力的人并不能解决根本问题，也没有任何实际意义。当我对太太无礼时，她自然会生气，这会给我带来一系列新的问题。

我认识到，应该永远尊重太太，即使在心情不好的时候也一样，要始终尊重她，并让她知道我的感受。我通过深思熟虑才明白这一简单的人生道理，我称之为“要尊重，勿要求”公式。当你感觉自己要崩溃时，要格外注意对待伴侣的态度，然后反其道而行之，对方不应该成为你糟糕心情的承受者，而且这样不会解决任何问题。

有意思的是，我太太已经发觉这种情况了，所以在我糟心的时候，她会说:“你今天遇到麻烦了吧？”意思是，我对她很好，她知道我是在补偿工作中的糟糕心情。我们都笑了，即使这样也能改善我的情绪。要尽你所能让对方知道被尊重、被欣赏和被感激。

25 切忌喊叫

如果看体育比赛时为自己的队伍加油，或者向对手喝倒彩，大声喊叫没有问题。在嘈杂的酒吧或餐厅交谈时，也需要大声喊叫。要想跟河对岸的人说话，也只能大声喊叫。当然，这些例子并不是我所说的那种大声喊叫，我

about. I am talking about yelling out of anger. It is never a good idea to yell or even to raise your voice at anyone. This behavior shows a lack of self-restraint, and it makes you look weak. Yelling or raising your voice at your spouse is the worst of all.

Relationships can turn into a boiling pot when a disagreement arises. When you have an argument with most people, you inevitably leave and go home, and naturally cool off. When you live with the person, you do not get the luxury of having time to cool off. Instead you are stuck with them, and in that time, many couples like to snipe at one another. This can turn a little disagreement into a massive argument, and eventually someone may lose their cool.

The key to avoid this trap is to develop a strategy. Mine is to find an excuse to breathe and put things in perspective. Just going to the bathroom can give you enough time to analyze what is the problem and be ready with a rational, cool approach to resolving it. This is a much better way to handle the situation than allowing it to escalate to yelling.

My beautiful wife and I of course try to avoid this whole scenario as much as possible, but things happen. What is important is to never reach the point where you lose your cool and begin to shout. Once you raise your voice, the argument is over and you have lost. It does not matter whether you were right or wrong. I had to learn this the hard way when I was in my twenties, and it has cost me many relationships. When I look back now, I feel foolish. Why would I ever yell or raise my voice at anyone? Nothing positive has every resulted from that behavior.

I have learned that if I begin to feel like my wife and I are in a pressure cooker, and our frustration with each other is rising, I will find a way to pause and refresh, or as they say in the computer industry, hit the reset button. “Baby, lets slow down so I can better understand the situation.” Such situations are gratitude builders because after an episode where a challenge has been created and a solution is found, both people will feel better about each other. A short pause can begin to depressurize the situation and allow everything to return to normal. I love my wife and never want to make her feel otherwise.

指的是发脾气。对任何人大声喊叫甚至提高嗓门说话都很不好，这种行为表明你缺乏自制力，而且会让人觉得你软弱无能，对伴侣大声喊叫或提高嗓门则是最糟糕的。

当出现分歧时，两人的关系就会变成沸腾的锅。当你和别人发生争执时，可以躲开对方然后回家，自然而然会冷静下来；而当你和同住人争执时，没有时间供你冷静，你俩会僵持在一起，这时多数夫妻就会互相攻击，然后把一个小分歧变成大争论，最后就会有人失去冷静。

避免这种困境的关键是要制定一个策略，我一般会找个借口冷静一下，以便分析原因，只要去趟洗手间就能有足够的时间来分析问题所在，然后找到理性、冷静的方法来解决问题。用这种方式处理问题效果会更好，千万不要升级到大喊大叫。

我和我的漂亮太太当然会尽量避免这种事情发生，但确实还是会发生，重要的是千万不要因此失去冷静而冲对方大声喊叫。一旦你提高嗓门，争论是结束了，你却输了，对错其实都不重要。在我二十多岁的时候，经历过惨痛教训后我才明白了这个道理，而当时却让我痛失了几段感情。现在回想起来，我觉得自己很愚蠢，为什么要对别人大声喊叫或提高嗓门呢？这种行为没有任何实际意义。

我现在明白，一旦发觉和太太发生了冲突，就像待在高压锅里时，我们对彼此的失望情绪就会上升，我会像计算机术语所说的那样，要想办法暂停和刷新，或者按下重置按钮。“宝贝，让我们慢慢来，看看到底怎么回事。”这样做能让对方心存感激，因为在发生冲突并找到解决方法之后，双方的感情会更好。短暂的停顿可以减轻压力，让一切恢复正常。我爱太太，从不想让她有其他感觉。

26. A PHOTO IS A REMINDER OF THE LOVE YOUR SHARE

My goal is to make as many memories with my wife as possible by taking pictures. We have a "feel good" library at hand to remind us of our love for each other. I cannot possibly hope to recall all our times together with detail, but when I look at a photo, like magic, I remember.

Even seconds after a photo is taken, a warm feeling of happiness is felt by both people. The biggest reason I like to take photos with my wife is to keep my spirits up throughout the week. Whenever things are not going my way, or I begin to feel a little depressed, I pull out my phone and I scroll through all of the good times we have had together. Looking at the smile on her face reminds me of how blessed I am, and what a great life I have.

Beyond this, it is simply fun to take photos and commemorate and memorialize our life together. I have always liked to take photos in every situation. I think they are a useful tool in business and a fun keepsake. This is doubly true with my wife as she is a photo queen. I can go through my camera roll and relive our whole relationship at any time.

Not only do I like to take pictures of my wife and me for myself, but I like to show them off to close friends. She makes me happy, and I want to share the joy with the people we are close to.

She and I take pictures in all situations. Whether we are out on the town, seeing the sights, or simply having a glass of wine on our balcony, we like to take photos together. I personally do not use social media, but if I did, she would be the only subject I posted to it. It is a good idea to take as many photos of you and your significant other as you can. It only takes a second, and you will cherish them for a lifetime.

More than just taking the pictures, I believe it is also important to display them. I like to keep a photo of my beautiful wife in as many places as possible because I like to look at them frequently. They remind me of how blessed I am. Her photo brings me up when I am down and raises me even higher when I am already up, reminding me that she is the most

26 一起拍照

我的目标是通过多拍照片，留下和爱人的美好回忆。我们有一个“感觉良好”的私人收藏，能不断提醒我们之间的美好感情。我不可能单靠记忆回想起所有美好时光的细节，但当我看着照片时，就像拥有了魔法一样，全都能回想起来。

即使是刚刚拍完照片，也能让两人立刻拥有幸福温暖的感觉。我喜欢和太太一起拍照，最大原因是能让我整个星期都精神饱满。每当事不如愿，或者情绪不佳时，我就拿出手机，翻看那些我们一起度过美好时光的照片，看着她脸上的笑容，我便会想到自己多么幸福，生活多么美好。

除此之外，拍照能纪念我们在一起的生活点滴，这很有意思。在任何时候，我都喜欢拍照，而且在生意场上一起照相也会有所助益，还能作为有趣的回忆。对于我太太来说更是如此，因为她是拍照女王。我可以随时翻看相册，重温我们的美好时光。

我不仅喜欢为我俩拍照，还喜欢向亲密的朋友炫耀。她让我快乐，我愿意和亲近的人分享快乐。

我俩随时随地都会拍照，不管是在城里玩，还是去看风景，或者只是在阳台上小酌一杯，都喜欢一起拍照。我一般不会在社交媒体上发照片，但如果我分享，她将是我发布的唯一主题。要尽量多为两人拍照，只需要一秒，你却会珍惜一生。

除了拍照，我认为把照片摆放出来也很重要。我喜欢在各个角落摆放太太的美照，因为我愿意随时能看到，提醒自己是多么幸运。她的照片在

important person in my life. It is a beautiful thing. Certainly Facebook, Instagram, TikTok, Snapchat and other platforms have proved beyond a shadow of a doubt that almost all people love looking at photos of themselves.

Some people may think it is over the top to have pictures of your significant other hung all over the place, and maybe it is, but I don't care. I also think it is good for you and your relationship. Why wouldn't you want to think about the love of your life? It is a constant reminder of the bond you share. I also want my wife to see just how much I love her, and a picture of the two of us together on the wall does just that.

I suggest that everyone have several pictures of their husband or wife in their house, on their phone, and in their office. It can strengthen your bond and keep that person always on your mind, reminding you of the love you share. During tough times, it can act as a mood enhancer, reminding you of the good things that are in your life. I like to hang photos of the two of us having fun together, relaxing, and of course, holding each other. These photos remind me of fond memories we have shared, and act as a catalyst for my imagination to plan new and exciting adventures.

In my opinion, hanging photos of your spouse all over is a MUST when it comes to keeping romance in your marriage!

Taking photos together is like taking vitamins, a healthy thing to do. A carefully chosen couples photo will reinforce the good elements of the relationship and memorialize positive emotions of your love for each other. Viewing pictures together increases the couple's attachment, infatuation, and marital satisfaction.

You always care about how you look in a picture and the same is true with your spouse. People always looks at themselves first before deciding if they like the photo. When your spouse sees a picture in which they look good, it creates instantaneous bonding. Happiness is remembered and closeness is created. Photos increase attachment, infatuation, and marital satisfaction. Just looking at pictures of the two of you has the power to make the love of your life feel more in love and satisfied with the marriage.

A related fun strategy is to put your spouse's photo as their contact in your phone. Then each time the phone rings, you will see a photo of your wonderful spouse. Think about how many calls you get each day, and you will realize how powerful this strategy can be. Any photo of the two of you that is displayed will show the positive aspects of your marriage, and more importantly, that you care.

我情绪低落的时候能让我振作起来，在我高兴的时候让我更加春风得意，提醒自己她是我生命中最重要的人，这是多么美好的事情。当然，“脸书”（Facebook）、照片墙（Instagram）、抖音（TikTok）、色拉布（Snapchat）和其他平台已经毫无疑问地证明，几乎所有人都喜欢看自己的照片。

有些人可能会认为到处挂满伴侣的照片太过分了，也许是这样，但我不在乎，我认为这样做有益于两人的感情。时常想着一生挚爱有什么错？照片能不断提醒两人的感情，我还想让太太知道我有多爱她，墙上挂着我们俩在一起的照片就是为了证明这一点。

我建议每个人都在家里、手机里和办公室里，多放几张自己丈夫或妻子的照片，这样能增强感情，让伴侣一直存在于你的脑海中，时刻提醒两人之间的爱。在困难时，能作为情绪增强剂，提醒你生活中的美好事物。我喜欢挂上我们俩在一起玩耍、放松的照片，当然还有互相拥抱的照片。这些照片让我回想起两人共同度过的美好时光，并能激发兴趣，以便规划新鲜有趣的旅程。

在我看来，如果你想拥有浪漫的婚姻，就必须挂满伴侣的照片！

一起拍照就像服用维生素一样有益身心。一张精心挑选的情侣照能强化两人感情中的美好元素，并纪念彼此相爱的正面情绪。一起看照片能增加夫妻之间的依恋、迷恋和婚姻满意度。

人总是关心自己在照片中的样子，伴侣也是如此。在决定是否喜欢这张照片之前，人们总是先看看自己。当伴侣看到自己很上相的照片时，会立刻连接情感纽带，铭记永恒幸福，使感情更加亲密。照片能增加依恋、迷恋和婚姻满意度。只要看看两人的照片，就能让两人更加相爱，让婚姻更美满。

一个有意思的方法是把伴侣的照片在手机通讯录里设为来电显示，然后每次电话一响，你就能看到爱人的照片。想想每天能接多少个电话，你就会明白这个方法有多棒。两人一起的任何照片都能表明婚姻的良好状态，更重要的是，说明你在意她。

There are no downsides to this strategy, but you should make certain your spouse likes the way they look in the photo before displaying it. Photos should illustrate the wonderful traits and behaviors of your lover and never their flaws. This approach will improve the mood of both you and your spouse, which in turn has the potential to improve your marriage.

Three last thoughts. First, consider the practice of Wu Xing, the ancient Chinese way of balancing your home. It is comprised of five elements: earth, metal, water, wood, and fire. These elements are interrelated and work together to create a complete ecosystem. An example of Feng Shui is putting photos on the east wall of any room. It is believed that this will garner more positive energy. Photos on the east wall will have the biggest impact on creating a positive vibe in your relationship.

Second, with that in mind, do not be shy about taking photos. Any model will tell you it takes approximately 200 photos to get one that is outstanding. This means you should take lots of pictures to get that good one.

Third, there is nothing wrong with editing to make the photo look that much better. There are many great apps that can help you with the editing part of the process.

27. CHECK IN DURING THE DAY

My wife has observed that we are a much happier couple than anyone she knows. She asks why do you think this has happened? I answered with the obvious. I told her that we prioritize each other as number one over all others. We listen to each other and we take action when required with no delays. Being empathetic is a good word to describe how much we love each other. Throughout each day we communicate. Maybe that communication is as simple as an emoji, but it keeps us close. It shows we are constantly thinking about each other.

Of course, there are many other reasons, but constant communication is one of the key factors in our happy marriage. We are continually reminding each other of our wonderful love. We are always on each other's minds.

这个方法没有任何毛病，但在晒照片之前，应该确定对方喜欢自己在照片中的样子。照片应该展示伴侣的优秀品质和文雅举止，而不是缺点。这种方法可以改善两人的情绪，从而改善婚姻状况。

最后三个想法：首先，考虑一下五行平衡的问题，这是中国古代平衡万物的方法，由五种元素组成：金、木、水、火、土。这些元素在相互关联、共同作用之下，生成一个完整的生态系统，讲究五行的一个实例是把照片贴在任何房间的东墙上，据说这样能吸纳更多的正能量，东墙上的照片会对两人的感情产生积极的影响。

第二，说到这里，千万不要羞于拍照。模特们都知道，大约需要拍 200 张照片才能得到一张出色的成片，这说明你应该拍很多照片才能拍到一张好照片。

第三，通过编辑让照片看起来更漂亮并没有错，有很多很棒的应用程序可以帮助编辑修图。

27 随时联系

我太太发现，我俩是她认识的人中最幸福的一对。她问为什么？我的回答显而易见，我说，因为我们把彼此放在第一位，我们互相倾听，在需要的时候直接行动，绝不拖延。共情这个词能很好地描述了我们有多爱对方。我们每天都联系，也许只是一个简单的表情符号，但它能让我们保持亲密，说明我们一直都想着对方。

当然，还有很多其他原因，不断交流是我们婚姻能够幸福的关键因素之一。我们不断提醒对方我们之间的美好爱情，时刻牵挂着彼此。

在和朋友们闲聊时，我惊讶于大多数人一整天都不联系另一半。我每天

In casual conversation with my friends, I was shocked to learn that most of them do not check in with their significant other throughout the day. I have always done so and naturally assumed that everyone did. When I questioned them as to why, they responded with statements like, "I will see her when I get home," or "Why should I? I know what she is doing!" One even went so far as to call such a habit "annoying." While I am not one to judge other people, and I truly believe to each their own, I also think checking in with your spouse throughout the day is an absolute MUST. It does not mean you must have a long, drawn-out conversation; a short message is enough.

My wife and I check in with one another at least several times a day. This may take the form of calls, texts, or sometimes funny picture messages. Usually we do not have anything important to inquire about or report, we simply enjoy talking to one another. She likes to give me updates on how her day is going and what she has been doing, and I like to listen. On the flipside, I like to do the same, but I also simply enjoy chatting with her. It provides a good midday morale boost to keep me going and focused on my business deals. She is also very smart and has good ideas that often help me with those deals. Of course, I try to do the same for her. Plus, I like to hear her voice.

I have found that talking throughout the day helps to strengthen our relationship. Far from being annoying, it is uplifting. Sometimes she will call, and I will be busy, so I inform her of that, and we will connect when I am free, or vice versa. If you do not currently check in with your significant other throughout the day, I would suggest giving it a try. It will make your days go faster also, as breaks are always needed. Talking to my wife is more than a break for me, it is an energy booster!

28. BE IMMATURE TOGETHER

Sometimes it is fun to be a kid again! It doesn't matter how old I get, I still feel like I am in my early 20's, and although I have responsibilities that prevent me from acting irresponsibly or taking unnecessary risks, that doesn't mean I don't like to act a little

都联系，自然认为其他人也一样。当我问他们原因时，回答是：“回家后就见到了。”或者：“有这个必要吗？我知道那位干什么呢！”有人甚至称这种习惯“令人讨厌”。虽然我不能评判他人，每个人都有自己的做法，但我依然认为和伴侣每天联系**十分必要**。这并不是说你必须聊很多，一条短信息就足够了。

我和太太每天至少要联系好几回，有可能打电话、发短信或有时发张有意思的图片。我们一般没有什么重要的事情要询问或报备，只是喜欢闲聊。她愿意说说这一天过得怎么样、她在做什么，而我也愿意听；反过来，我也喜欢这样做，但我更愿意听她说，这样能鼓舞我的士气，以便继续工作、专注业务。她很聪明，有很好的想法，经常帮助我做生意。当然，我也会为她做同样的事，而且我喜欢听到她的声音。

我发现，随时联系有助于加强两人感情，这样不会惹人厌烦，反而令人振奋。有时她打来电话，赶上我正忙，我会告诉她，等我有空的时候再打过去，反之亦然。如果你现在一整天都不和另一半联系，我建议你不妨一试，这样能让白天过得更快，人总是需要休息的。对我来说，和太太聊天不仅仅是休息，更是能量助推器！

28 保持童心

有时候，把自己当作小孩很有意思！不管多大年纪，我仍然觉得自己才二十岁出头，虽然说我有责任阻止自己做出不理智的行为或冒不必要的风险，但我也可以偶尔表现得不太成熟，而且我太太是能和我一起疯狂的最佳人选。

immature from time to time, and there is no one I would rather run amok with than my wife.

It may sound strange to some people, but my wife and I love to go to theme parks, like Disneyland and Universal Studios. They may be built for a younger audience, but we have a great time running around taking photos with the characters, going on the rides, and eating all of the unhealthy treats we can stomach. Sometimes, it is fun to simply let loose and act like kids. I find it nostalgic, and after such an outing, I always return home with a big smile on my face and feeling closer to my wife.

Our favorite thing to do is to play carnival games. I have been very good at shooting baskets since I was a kid, and even though I am not a kid anymore, I can still shoot very well. For some reason this skill has stayed with me. They say once you learn to ride a bike it stays with your forever. With me that saying holds true with shooting basketballs. Whenever we go to the boardwalk or anywhere with these games, I always like to win a big stuffed toy for her to take home. It makes her day when she gets to choose what character she wants. Usually, it is big stuffed bear or dog. The only problem is that our home began to fill up with these stuffed animals! The solution was simple, however; we now always randomly give away the stuffed animal to a stranger. The joy of seeing an unknown person smile is heartwarming.

Every couple will have their own preferences when it comes to those "going back to being a kid" moments. Yours could be playing video games all night, dressing up in silly outfits, or speaking to each other in funny accents. Never let the kid inside of you die, or let the excitement in your relationship fade away. You should look at your relationship like a child looks at the world. Full of wonder and hope.

29. DRESS NICELY, BE ATTRACTIVE, AND CARE ABOUT YOUR APPEARANCE

We all know that it is proper to dress up if you are going to spend a night at the opera, or if you are headed to an important business meeting. You will usually even put on a nice outfit if you are going to see a family member or friend you haven't spent time with

听起来可能有些奇怪，我和太太喜欢去主题公园，像迪士尼乐园和环球影城这些适合年轻人的地方，但我俩能在里边尽情玩乐、与角色合影、乘坐游乐设施、吃尽所有不健康食品。有时候，简单放松、童心未泯就很有趣。我觉得就像回到童年时光，回家后依然笑容灿烂，而且感觉和太太更亲近了。

我们最喜欢玩嘉年华游戏，我从小就擅长投篮，虽然现在长大了，但这项技能一直没丢。人们常说，一旦学会了骑自行车，就永远都能骑。对我来说，投篮就是如此。每当我们去木板道或任何地方玩这些游戏时，我都能赢个大毛绒玩具让她带回家，当她可以选择自己想要的玩具时会特别开心，一般会选大的毛绒熊或毛绒狗。唯一的问题是，我们家已经堆满了这些毛绒玩具！然而，解决办法很简单，我们会把玩具随便送给路人，能看到陌生人开心我们也会很暖心。

每对夫妇在“回到童年”这一时刻都会有自己的偏好，有可能整晚打电玩、穿可笑的服装，或者用奇怪的口音和对方说话。永远不要失去童心，也不要让感情趋于平淡。应该像孩子看待世界一样看待你们的关系，要充满好奇和希望。

29 注重形象

我们都知道，如果晚上外出看戏，或是参加重要的商务会议，就应该精心打扮一下，即使是去看望很久没在一起的家人或朋友，也应该穿一套漂亮衣服。然而，由于我们经常和伴侣在一起，很容易忘记为对方而打扮，其实

in a while. However, we see our significant other so often, it is so easy to forget that it is important and fun to dress up around them as well. Dressing up for a person is always a nice way to show them respect.

Naturally, most of us want to lounge in something comfortable after a hard day at work. Since you are comfortable, you do not bother changing your clothes when you head out to dinner or the movies. This soon becomes a habit, and the next thing you know, you haven't dressed up for your husband or wife for months. You may think they don't notice or care, and they may not. The good news, however, is that they will notice when you go out of your way to dress up for them. Talk about an immediate mood enhancer! You showed your spouse respect with the way you dress, and it creates an aura of sunshine. This changing of wardrobe will make your spouse realize that they are just as important to you as the billionaire you just had lunch with.

I am not advocating dressing up in a suit or nice dress every day after work. You need to able to kick your feet up in your comfortable pajamas and relax. That doesn't mean it isn't important to throw on a nice pair of slacks and a dress shirt from time to time when you and your spouse go out to dinner or the movies. However, dressing up is just the tip of the iceberg.

There is more to looking good for you partner than just your wardrobe. When you are in a relationship, you also have to focus on your physical appearance. That means maintaining good hygiene, eating right, and exercising. I do cardio for at least 30 minutes a day, no matter how busy I get, and I try to watch what I eat.

If you care about the person you are with, which I do more than anything, you want to look your best for them. That means making those sacrifices to hold off father time and maintain your health and appearance to the best of your ability. It is common for married people to give up on their appearance once they say their vows. Then, they wonder why their partner is no longer attracted to them. It doesn't take a rocket scientist to figure this out, but most people are in the dark and have no idea the impact of maintaining your appearance and health is to impress your spouse and create more romance in your marriage. Too many people just let themselves go after marriage. This is incredibly disrespectful to your significant other and to yourself. You should always strive to look the best you can for the person you love.

这很重要，也很有意思。为某人精心打扮是表达尊重的好方法。

在辛苦工作了一天之后，我们自然都想懒洋洋地躺着休息。因为贪图舒服，所以出去吃饭或看电影的时候也不想换衣服，不久就会形成习惯，接下来你能想到，会连续数月都不为伴侣打扮，可能你会认为对方不在意或不关心，也确实有这种可能性。然而，当你特意为伴侣打扮时，对方会注意到，这绝对是实时的情绪强化剂！精心打扮说明你尊重伴侣，能营造出温暖阳光的氛围。为伴侣打扮会让对方意识到自己在你心目中如同刚才一起吃午餐的亿万富翁一样重要。

我并不提倡每天下班后都穿着西装或漂亮裙子，我们确实需要穿上能舒展四肢的睡衣放松一下。但并不是说当你和伴侣出去吃饭或看电影时，偶尔穿上漂亮长裤配正装衬衫就不重要了。穿衣打扮其实只是冰山一角。

要想为了伴侣而精心打扮，光靠穿衣戴帽是不够的，恋爱时还要关注体态，要保持良好的卫生、正确的饮食并时常运动健身。不管多忙，我每天至少做 30 分钟的有氧运动，而且我在饮食上也格外注意。

如果你像我一样特别在意另一半，就会希望在伴侣面前展现出最好的自己。这意味着要做出一些牺牲来拖住时间老人，竭尽全力保持最佳体态。对于已婚人士来说，婚后往往不再注重形象，却又不理解为何在伴侣面前失去了魅力，个中原因并不需要火箭专家来解释，但多数人都不明白，保持自身外形外貌能给伴侣留下深刻印象，并在婚姻中营造更多浪漫。在婚后放任自我是对你自己和另一半极不尊重的行为。为了你爱的人，永远都要注重形象。

30. YOU ARE NOT YOUR SPOUSE'S PARENT. YOU ARE PARTNERS

You and your spouse come from different families, and you may come from different countries, cultures, or religions. There may even be an age gap. No matter how you cut it, you both have different backgrounds. That means you will probably disagree about how to do certain things. There is nothing wrong with that. In fact, it is how we grow as people. It is a beautiful thing to be exposed to another way of thinking, if you can keep an open mind. The problem is, there will sometimes be friction. When this occurs, particularly if it is due to an ingrained ideology or thought process, it is common not to understand why the other person doesn't see things the same way you do. The next step in this progressive mindset is to teach them your way, which you believe to be the right way. The problem in these situations is that usually there is no right or wrong way. Only different ways.

This story may sound silly, but I will share it anyway. I was born in Texas, and in Texas, we put mustard on our hamburgers. One day, my beautiful wife was making dinner, and she brought me a burger without mustard. I gently explained to her that I enjoyed burgers better when they have mustard and pickles. This response was silly, of course, because if I wanted mustard, why should I trouble her? I could just get up and get it myself. If I were to do it again, besides not troubling her to get the mustard for me, I might tell her how I like my burger with mustard and ask if she would like to try it. That way she learns something new about me and maybe finds a new favorite condiment.

When you cannot understand another person's way of thinking, you're very likely to try to teach them your way, but what you believe to be the correct way is not the only way. Since it is so obvious to you, you may talk down to your partner, as if you were their parent or teacher, and they are a delinquent child. This is rude and demeaning. Always treat your spouse with respect, as the love of your life.

30 避免说教

你和伴侣来自不同家庭，国家、文化或宗教都不同，甚至可能存在年龄差距。不管你怎么想办法弥合，两人终究来自不同的背景，这意味着你们会对如何处理某些事情持不同意见。这并没有错，事实上，这正是我们成长的方式。如果拥有开明的心态，能接触到另一种思维方式是好事，问题是有时会产生分歧。当这种情况发生时，特别是出于根深蒂固的想法或思维习惯时，你就会不理解，为什么对方看事情的方式和自己不一样。这种激进的心态会促使你要去教对方怎么做，你认为这是正确的方式。在这些情况下，通常没有对错，只是方式不同而已。

下面这个故事可能听起来很傻，但我还是要分享一下。我出生在得克萨斯州，在得州我们都是在汉堡上抹黄芥末。有一天，我的漂亮太太为我做晚饭，给了我一个没有芥末的汉堡。我温和地表示更喜欢有黄芥末和腌黄瓜的汉堡。这样说当然很蠢，如果我真想要芥末，何必要麻烦她，自己起来拿就好了。如果再给我一次机会，除了不对她说教之外，我还会告诉她我特别喜欢芥末汉堡，并问她是否愿意尝尝，这样她就能对我更加了解，也许还能喜欢上这种调料。

当你不能理解另一个人的思维方式时，就会试图对别人说教，但你认为正确的方式并不是唯一的方式。由于对你来说这是显而易见的，你就会用高人一等的口气和伴侣说话，好像自己是父母或老师，而对方是犯错的孩子。这样做非常无礼且有辱人格。要永远尊重伴侣，要视其为生命中的挚爱。

31. TRUST

Trust is such a small word, but it has such a powerful meaning and impact on any marriage. Trust is the core of a love being strong, lasting, and growing. To trust your spouse is empowering to the relationship. Trust creates faith and the belief that nothing can derail a marriage. I have this type of trust with my wife. I have faith in her, and she has faith in me.

Trust is spiritual. You must believe to trust. I pray often to make sure that the trust of my lovely wife will never wane. I am bold in my prayers and ask that she always trust me and that I will always do the same. I know the importance of trust, and I prioritize it. I am very thankful, and I pray every day giving thanks for my good fortune of having this wonderful woman as my wife. Each day and every hour, I consciously count my blessings to be married to her, which automatically makes my trust in her stronger and enduring.

As we all know, communication is one of the key elements in a happy marriage. Combined with great communication and sharing, trust will grow, and the words we use can be a key factor in building and keeping trust. Over the years, I have found that whenever someone tells me I am important, I feel good. With this in mind, it's a good practice to tell your spouse every day these simple words: "You are important to me."

Carefully chosen words can be an important element in building your mutual trust to higher and higher levels. Saying "I was wrong" is a good example of words that build trust. Strong people admit when they are wrong. Weak people ignore their mistakes or defend them, which weakens trust. "Tell me about it" is also an icebreaker and means that you care and will listen. This invitation builds trust because it shows your genuine engagement. Another good example might be to say, "Help me understand." This means you will listen to what they tell you.

Being empathic with your spouse and seeing their point of view is a powerful trust builder. To listen without interrupting shows again that you care. Something as simple as not looking at your phone when you are talking to your spouse will always be appreciated. Never plan your reply when your spouse is talking; instead, just intently listen with care. I

31 相互信任

信任虽然只是一个很小的词汇，对婚姻却具有重大意义和影响。信任是确保爱情坚固、持久和常青的核心。信任伴侣就是对两人的感情赋予力量。信任造就信念，让人相信没有什么能破坏婚姻关系。我对我太太就有这种信任。我相信她，她也相信我。

信任是精神上的，你必须相信才能信任。我经常祈祷，祝愿太太能永远信任我。我大胆祷告，祈求我们俩能永远相互信任。我清楚信任的重要性，所以把信任放在首位。我很感恩，每天都祈祷并感谢自己的好福气，有这么好的女子做我的太太，每时每刻我都特别惜福感恩，这让我对她的信任更加坚定和持久。

众所周知，沟通是幸福婚姻的关键因素之一。通过和伴侣沟通、分享，就能加强信任，我们所说的话语是建立和维持信任的关键因素。多年以来，我发现，每当有人夸我很重要时，我就会自我感觉良好，所以要记住这一点，每天和伴侣说“你对我很重要”，这些简单的话更有效。

说话时精心考虑措辞是让两人彼此更加信任的重要因素，说“我错了”更容易达成信任。强者会勇于承认自己的错误，弱者无视自己的错误或为错误辩解，这会削弱信任。“跟我说说”能打破僵局，说明你关心对方并愿意倾听，这种方法能达成信任，表明你很在意。另外，“给我讲讲”也意味着你愿意倾听对方要说的话。

同情伴侣并理解对方的观点能得到特别的信任。倾听而不打断更说明你关心对方。做一些简单的事情，比如当你和伴侣说话时不玩手机，对方会很

show respect to my wife by always looking her in the eyes when we talk. Slowing down and looking your spouse in the eyes when you talk or listen also sends a powerful message of love and builds trust.

Words of affection and respect as well as sharing time together help, but actions and living up to your promises mean the most. Be true to your word and follow through with your actions. Keeping your word and leading by example has excellent additional benefits. It sets the stage for your spouse to do the same. Treating your spouse with respect is crucial for a happy marriage, and it starts with keeping your promises. When I make a promise to my wife, I am willing and able to move mountains to make it reality. We must make our spouses feel safe. My wife knows this is my DNA with her, and she feels warm and secure as a direct result.

Trust always results from your consistent behavior. Your spouse will trust you when you are consistent with your actions. Regularly showing your spouse that you're there for them is an effective way to build, maintain, and grow trust. Learn to say thank you and give acknowledgments with sincere appreciation, even for the small things that your spouse does for you. This will play an important role in building trust and maintaining a loving relationship.

The power of being honest is critical to building lasting trust. To have no secrets and always be honest is imperative. Always be truthful. If you are caught telling a lie, no matter how small, your trustworthiness in the future will be questioned.

In summary, take this small word "trust" with the big meaning seriously. The relationship between trust and love is reality. Trust means trusting yourself, your own judgments, and trusting your spouse. Trust is the foundation for a healthy marriage. Lack of trust is the main reason relationships fall apart. Trust builds faith in each other, allowing the two of you to get through any and all challenges. Trust helps give your spouse space (freedom to do things on their own without your interference) and we all need this in our lives. If you're not suspicious about who your spouse spends time with, your actions will be calm, relaxed, and loving. My wife is my first priority. She knows this, and it gives her comfort and makes her very happy. At all times, I put her needs and interests before mine.

We talked about the importance of touch in another point. Touch helps to build and maintain trust. I advise to hug and hold hands as often as possible. I also make my wife's family important, and this is another factor that makes her have such strong trust in me.

感激。当伴侣说话时，别总想着怎么回答，只要专心倾听就好。当我俩说话时，我总是看着爱人的眼睛，以示尊重。当你说话或倾听时，不能着急，要看着对方的眼睛，传递爱的信息，并达成信任。

关爱和尊重的话语以及彼此陪伴都很重要，但行动和履行承诺则更重要，必须说到做到、言行一致。信守诺言、以身作则会有很多好处，也便于对方能够效仿。尊重伴侣对幸福婚姻至关重要，要从遵守诺言开始。当我对太太做出承诺时，我愿意并且能够排除万难去实现。必须要让伴侣放心，我太太知道，和她在一起已经刻在我的基因里，这让她感到温暖和安全。

信任源于一直以来的行为，当你言行一致时，对方就会信任你。经常向伴侣表明你一直陪护在其左右，是建立、维持和发展信任的有效方法。要学会说谢谢，即使对方为你做的是一件小事，也要用真诚的感激来表达谢意，这会在建立信任和维持爱情中发挥重要作用。

待人真诚对于建立持久的信任至关重要，要做到没有秘密、永远真诚。做人要诚实，如果一旦被发现说谎，无论谎言多么小，今后都会使你备受质疑。

总而言之，要认真对待“信任”这个小小词汇的重大含义。信任和爱情之间的关系很现实。信任意味着相信自己，相信自己的判断，相信自己的伴侣。信任是美满婚姻的基础。缺乏信任是感情破裂的主要原因。信任让彼此拥有信心，能够战胜任何困难。信任有助于给伴侣留有空间（不受干扰，有自己做事的自由），我们在生活中都需要这样的空间。如果不去怀疑伴侣，你就能平静、放松和充满爱意。我太太永远排在第一位，她知道这一点，这让她特别欣慰。在任何时候，我都把她的需要和利益排在我前面。

我们在另一条目里谈到过身体接触的重要性。接触有助于建立和维持信任。我建议要尽量多拥抱和牵手。我也很重视我太太的娘家，这也是她特别信任我的另一个原因。

Each little thing helps in building and maintaining a trusting, lasting, and loving marriage. I love my wife and I have complete faith and trust in this lovely lady I am lucky enough to have as my lifetime partner and companion.

32. WE ARE ALL VICTIMS, SO JUST LET IT GO

There is a saying, "second verse, same as the first." This basically means that whatever trauma you grew up with will be repeated in future relationships unless it is addressed. It will also be taken out on your future partner, dooming your relationship before it even starts. The good news is that you are not locked into this cycle, and it can be broken. I am not a physiatrist and will not get into all the methods by which this can be accomplished, but I can tell you this. . .the first step is acknowledging the past trauma and moving beyond it. This usually means forgiving the abusers and yourself. Unless you are able to do this, you are doomed to repeat the same destructive cycle you grew up with over and over again.

I do not dig into my wife's past, and she does not dig into mine. I am sure she has traumas from growing up, just as I know I do. It is not always easy to keep that base programming you received as a child from activating in your relationship when certain stimuli are present. However, it can be done. Whenever I begin to see myself behaving in a way my parents did that I did not like, I take a second to breathe and reevaluate the situation. You can never progress until you move on from the past. If you don't, it will haunt you and gain power as you age.

We must all understand that our current spouse is not responsible for what happened to us. We all have stories. If we want to forge a life together, we must learn to let it go, forgive, and move on. As they say, the best revenge is living well.

每一件小事都有助于建立和维持相互信任、长久关爱的婚姻。我爱我太太，我对这位可爱女士有绝对的信心和信任，我很幸运能拥有她作为我的终身伴侣。

32 学会放下

有一种说法："第二段总是在重复第一段。"意思是，如果在成长的过程中你曾受到过心理创伤，除非治愈，否则就会在未来的感情关系中重复出现，这也会影响你未来的伴侣，让你们的感情无疾而终。幸运的是，你不必一直困在这个循环里，可以将其打破。我不是心理治疗师，也不会讨论各种治疗方案，但我可以告诉你：首先要承认过去的创伤并告别过往，这就意味着要原谅施暴者和你自己；除非能做到这一点，否则你将注定不断重复成长过程中所经历的死循环。

我没有深究过我太太的过去，她也没有深究过我的。我确信她在成长过程中受到过创伤，应该和我一样。当类似情境出现时，要保证小时候遭遇的创伤不再重现真的很难，然而这是可以做到的。每当我看到自己的行为举止和当时父母所作所为一模一样时，我简直深恶痛绝，我会停下来深呼吸，重新进行思考。只有走出过去，才能进步，否则随着年龄的增长，往事会一直困扰你，并变得越来越强大。

我们都必须明白，现在的伴侣对我们的过往种种没有任何责任。我们都有往事，但想要共同生活，就必须学会放下、原谅，然后继续前行。俗话说，最好的报复就是活得更好。

33. ACCEPT YOUR SPOUSE'S QUIRKS

At the beginning of a relationship, it is usually those cute little quirks that initially attract you to your spouse or significant other. Strangely enough, as the relationship wears on, it becomes those same quirks that might drive you or her crazy! It makes no sense, but it is what it is.

When I was speaking with my friend about this subject, he told me his wife used to think the way he tapped his pencil when he was thinking was adorable. She even said so on several occasions. Flash forward to after they had been together for a few years and that quirk had begun to drive her crazy. She was not the only one reacting similarly. He told me how she used to do this cute thing where she played with her hair, twirling it around her forefinger and tugging on it. He initially found it adorable; however, after a while, he found himself snapping at her to stop touching her hair. How silly, right?

We all have unique little quirks or oddities, and in a positive light, they are great because they make us who we are. How boring would the world be if we were all the same? Sadly, sometimes these great little unique aspects of our personalities tend to annoy people, not because there is something intrinsically wrong with them, but because they are unique and noticeable. If your spouse has such a quirk that you find bothersome, the responsibility is on you to get used to it, not for them to stop doing it.

There are exceptions. If that quirk is something that could hurt your spouse, then it is a good idea to bring it up. For instance, that same friend used to enjoy throat lozenges in bed before sleeping. This is very dangerous, as he could easily choke to death on a lozenge. His wife forced him to stop doing this in bed. Initially he was not happy with her because it relaxed him before he slept, but in retrospect, he could see the wisdom of her decision. When my wife gives me advice, I always trust her opinion.

33 适应怪癖

在一段感情开始时，经常是对方那些可爱的小怪癖吸引到你。令人不解的是，随着感情的发展，同样的怪癖可能会让你或另一半抓狂！这简直毫无道理，但事实就是如此。

当我和好友谈论这一话题时，他说他爱人以前觉得他在思考时轻敲铅笔的样子很可爱，而且说过好多回。然而他俩在一起几年之后，这种怪癖开始让他太太抓狂。无独有偶，他告诉我他太太喜欢玩自己的头发，把头发绕在食指上，然后拉拽头发。起初他觉得这样很可爱，然而过了一段时间，他冲太太大喊大叫，让她不要玩头发。这样是不是很傻？

我们都有独特的小怪癖，从积极的角度来看，这样很好，因为这些怪癖让我们成为现在的自己，如果所有人都一模一样，那么世界将会多无聊！不幸的是，有时，我们个性中这些独特的小怪癖往往会惹恼别人，不是因为本质上有什么问题，而是因为过于独特而引人注目。如果你的伴侣有这样的怪癖，让你觉得很烦，你应该想办法适应，而不是让对方改变。

当然也有例外，如果那个怪癖可能会伤害到你的伴侣，那它就应该得到关注。例如，还是这位朋友，以前喜欢在睡前躺床上吃润喉糖。这样非常危险，很容易窒息而死。他太太对此强烈禁止。起初，他很生气，因为睡前吃糖能让他放松，但现在回想起来，他发现他太太的决定很明智。当我太太给我建议时，我总是相信她的看法。

34. DON'T EVER TRY TO CHANGE YOUR SPOUSE. ACCEPT WHO THEY ARE, BOTH THE GOOD AND THE BAD

I am so lucky that there is almost nothing about my wife that bothers me. Of course, there must be something, but I am not going to search for those negative traits. I guess I'm particularly lucky because I love everything about her. This is not the case with all couples, so I want to offer some sound advice.

It is basic human nature to try to change the world around you to best suit your current wants and needs, but those wants and needs don't necessarily represent what is best for you. Many times, as you age, you will look back at what you thought you wanted and needed ten years prior and find those desires to be ridiculous because you have grown as a person. It should be our constant goal to evolve and change into a new and better version of ourselves. However, that does not mean it is our place to change someone else.

I have many friends, both male and female, who married someone whose traits at the time they found desirable; then, after a few years, they started trying to change those aspects of their spouse's personality or career. A man might marry a woman who wears a specific style of clothing that he finds attractive, only to become irritated when she continues to dress that way after they are married. Hello! You knew she dressed that way before you said your vows! If it was such a problem, you should not have married her in the first place.

It is not your place to try to change your spouse. If something bothers you, I would hope that both of you have enough respect for one another to have a calm and civil conversation about the action or behavior and be able to find some middle ground. I would never try to change my wife, and she does not try to change me, but she will suggest I consider behaving differently in certain situations, and she is usually right. I almost always follow her suggestion and do it! To ask someone to change is difficult but to evolve or modify your behavior is easy. Like all challenges, little things mean a lot, and to move forwards step by step is always a win.

34 学会包容

我很幸运，我太太基本上没有什么烦人的毛病。当然，肯定有一些小缺点，但我不会去深究。可能是我特别幸运，因为我爱她的一切。然而，并不是所有的夫妇都如此，所以我想提供一些合理的建议。

试图改变周围环境以适应自身需求是人类的本性，但这些需求不一定对你有益。很多时候，随着年龄的增长，当你回想起十年前的需求时，因为成长的原因，会发现那些欲望其实很可笑。我们孜孜以求的目标应该是不断进步，变成崭新的、更好的自己。然而，这并不意味着我们有资格去改变别人。

我有很多朋友，他们各自与当时喜欢的对象结婚了，数年之后，他们开始想要改变伴侣的性格或事业。男人当初愿意娶穿衣风格很吸引他的女人，但当他们结婚后，如果女人继续这种风格，他就会生气。哎呀！在宣誓之前你就知道她是这种穿衣风格！如果这真算个问题，你从一开始就不应该娶她。

不要试图改变你的伴侣。如果确实有什么事困扰你，要在尊重对方的前提下，对该行为进行冷静和理智的沟通，最好能各退一步，学会包容。我永远不会去改变我太太，她也不会改变我，但她有时会建议我稍稍改变行为习惯，而且她通常是对的，我基本上都会按照她的建议去做！要求别人改变会很难，但是改变或改进自己的行为会相对容易。遇到困难时，小事情往往意义重大，要一步一步来，终会胜利。

35. GOOD LUCK AND FATE ARE REAL, SO COUNT YOUR BLESSINGS

It is important to count your blessings every day— not just when you wake up, but throughout the day and before you lay down your head at night. It is so easy to take what we have for granted. You look at TV or social media and are instantly overwhelmed with images of people on lavish vacations, driving expensive sports cars and living in multimillion dollar mansions. That is not reality for most people, and those who have those economic privileges have the same emotional problems as everyone else. A lot of the time, theirs are much worse be- cause of their wealthy lifestyles.

I have been divorced, but it was a blessing, because it brought me to the wonderful wife I have now. I would not have been the person I was when we met without what I learned from my previous life's teachings and experiences. Often what appeared bad at one point in time turned out to be good ultimately because I learned from the experience. Now, I wake up every day to the love of my life. She inspires me to do and be the best I can, and that is a blessing I do not take for granted. We live in a nice home, have food on our table, clothes on our backs, and love in our hearts. What more could you want? Everything else is just window dressing. I am the richest man in the world simply by having her as my wife.

If you count your blessings, you will be able to appreciate the beautiful life you have. Envy spawns hatred and resentment. Once you begin to envy your neighbor, not only will you hate them, you will begin to hate yourself, your spouse, your beautiful family and your life. Show gratitude for everything that you have, and do not worry about the things you don't. If you really want them, you can work for them and they will come. Count your blessings every day and show gratitude for everything you have.

35 惜福感恩

每天都要惜福感恩，在早上醒来、整个白天和临睡之前都要感恩。人们很容易把自己所拥有的一切视为理所当然。你看电视或网络上，全是人们享受奢华假期、驾驶昂贵跑车、居住高档豪宅的画面，对大多数人来说，这些并不现实，那些拥有经济特权的人与普通人一样，也有各种情感问题，很多时候，由于他们富裕的生活方式，情况只会更糟。

我曾经离过婚，但这也是福气，我因此等到了现在这个完美的太太。如果没有从前经历中的经验教训，我就不会是我俩相遇时的我。有时，在某个人生阶段不太好的事，之后也会变成好事，因为我会从中吸取教训。现在，我每天都在挚爱面前醒来，她激励我去做最好的自己，这是我的福气，绝不是理所当然。我们生活美满，桌上有食，身上有衣，心中有爱。人生如此，夫复何求？其他一切都是浮云。我之所以成为世界上最富有的人，只因我娶她为妻。

如果能惜福感恩，就能享受你所拥有的美好生活。嫉妒会产生仇恨和怨愤。一旦开始嫉妒邻居，你不仅会恨他们，也会开始恨自己、恨你的伴侣、恨你的美好家庭和生活。要感激你所拥有的一切，不要为自己没有的东西焦虑。如果你真的想要那些，可以通过自身努力而争取。每天都要惜福感恩，感激你所拥有的一切。

36. FIND TIME TO BE ALONE EVERY DAY

As much as I love my wife, and as important as it is for me to spend time with her, it is still nice to get some time to myself. I know that if she were forced to be around me 24/7, I would drive her crazy! She has told me so. That is not because she dislikes me, or even dislikes my company. It is because we all need time to ourselves in order to retain and develop our individual identities. Being apart for short periods of time gives us the opportunity to be alone with our thoughts, recharge, prioritize, put things in perspective and recalibrate. Even Superman needed his fortress of solitude.

When you are around the same person for an extended period of time, it doesn't matter who they are, or how much you love them, most likely they will eventually begin to get on your nerves. It is simple oversaturation. The little things that bug you will build up over time if you never take a break, the same way a dripping faucet will eventually cause a glass to overflow. That is why it is so important for couples to spend a little time apart each day. Vacations with family or business trips are also healthy for a relationship.

The proverb "absence makes the heart grow fonder" describes the feeling of greater affection between friends and lovers who are kept apart. This is not true in a healthy marriage. In my experience, extended absence from your spouse never makes the heart grow fonder, so I advise you to keep your times apart limited and brief. The good news is that a little time apart now and then can give each of you some valuable space. and sometimes we all need this.

I know that when I have to go away on a business trip, I return home afterward loving my wife more than when I left. It does not take a business trip to have this experience. Even after a few hours apart, I get the same feeling. Brief times away give me a chance to experience life without her, which only makes me really appreciate all of the joy she brings me when we are together. Of course, we stay in contact on the rare times either of us travels alone. In fact, we talk several times a day, but that is not a substitute for being together, and we acutely feel each other's absence when we are apart.

36 独处时间

尽管我很爱我太太，和她在一起对我来说很重要，但我还是愿意能有一些属于自己的时间。我知道，如果让她 24 小时都陪着我，她会发疯！她也这样说过。这不是因为她不喜欢我，甚至不喜欢我的陪伴，而是因为我们都需要有自己的空间。短暂的分离让我们有机会独自思考、恢复精力、统筹安排、审时度势。即使是超人，也需要自己的孤独堡垒。

当你长时间和某人在一起时，不管此人是谁，或者你有多爱此人，这个人最终都会让你心烦意乱，这就是过犹不及。如果你不及时解决，这些烦人的小问题会随着时间而积累，就像水龙头滴水最终也会溢出水杯一样。因此，夫妻每天分开一段时间非常重要。与家人一起度假或因公出差也对恋情有益。

俗话说，久别情更深，这是指离别能让朋友和恋人间的感情更深，这在美满婚姻中是不正确的。根据我的经验，长时间离别不会让两人的心变得更亲密，所以，我建议恋人分开的时间要尽量缩短。好的方面是，偶尔分开一段时间可以让各自拥有一些宝贵的空间，有时候我们都需要空间。

我发现，当我确实需要出差时，回家后会比离开时更爱我太太。其实不需要出差就能获得这种体验，即使分开几个小时，我也能有同样的感觉。短暂的分别让我有机会体验没有她的生活，这会使我更加感激我们在一起时她带给我的所有快乐。当然，我们很少单独旅行，即便有也会保持联系，实际上，我们每天都会联系好几回，但这并不能代替真正在一起；分开的时候，我们都会因对方不在而感到若有所失。

Taking time to be alone with yourself will not only strengthen your relationship, but it is also good for your mental health. Do not think something is wrong with you or your spouse because you need a little break from time to time; everyone does, but not everyone is wise enough to take advantage of it.

37. NEVER TREAT YOUR SPOUSE LIKE A MAID

I have observed a few of my friends treating their spouse like a maid. Normally it is not out of malice or some misplaced misogyny. Most of the time, it is simple sloth "laziness." My dishes are dirty, and I am tired, so I didn't do them, hoping the other person will clean them for me. What a bad attitude. Maybe the person does not view his spouse as a maid, but unintentionally that's the reality. Treating her/him with no respect by being lazy is just uncool. If this is you, then wake up, step up and be a part of the solution. In this case that means help your spouse clean the dishes.

Both my wife and I have certain duties around the house. Actually, we have a maid, but on those days when that person does not come, we both step up and clean. For instance, I vacuum and she cleans the surfaces. We split things up to keep our home tidy between the housekeeper's visits and for simplicity's sake. We are not firm in our roles, but I have found that having a general agreement will help things to run smoothly. That isn't to say that I will not clean the surfaces, or she will not vacuum sometimes.

Treating your spouse like a maid isn't about what you ask, it is how you do it. When you demand or expect something from someone, you are treating them like your maid or your servant. When you nicely request a favor, you are doing just that, requesting a favor. They are by no means obligated to comply, but it is nice when they do. Personally, I always try to do whatever my wife asks. There are potential exceptions to this response, but I have not found one yet.

There is nothing wrong with one person in a relationship doing most of the housework.

留点时间独处不仅能增强感情，而且对心理健康有好处。不要因为偶尔需要独处，就认为你或伴侣有什么问题，每个人都需要独处，但不是每个人都有足够的智慧来利用这一点。

37 并非佣人

我发现，有些朋友会把自己的伴侣当作佣人。他们这样做倒不是出于恶意或憎恨对方，多数情况都是因为懒惰。盘子脏了，但我很累，所以没刷，希望有人能帮我刷，这种想法很恶劣，也许此人并没想把伴侣当佣人，而是无意中使之变为现实。因为自己懒而不尊重对方是很无礼的行为，如果你就是这样，那就清醒一下，主动去解决问题。其实，这种时候，你可以主动帮对方刷盘子。

我和太太做家务各有分工。其实我们请了小时工，但小时工不在时，我俩都会主动打扫卫生。例如，我负责吸尘，她负责擦拭。为了方便起见，我俩分工做家务，让家里保持整洁舒适。我俩的分工并不固定，但我发现，明确分工合作的总体方针会使活干起来更顺利，这并不是说我不能擦拭，或者她不能吸尘。

是否像佣人一样对待伴侣不在于要求对方做事，而在于处理方式。当你要求或指望某人做某事时，你就把对方当作佣人了，但当你善意请求别人帮忙时，没错，这就是帮忙，对方绝对没有义务帮你，当然能帮最好。就我个人而言，我总是尽量按照太太的要求去做，基本没有例外，至少我还没发现。

In many cases, that is how things work best, but the other party should be thankful for it and appreciate the effort, rather than expecting it. You are treating someone like a maid once you begin to expect things from them. Everything you or your spouse do for one another should always be appreciated.

38. DREAM BIG DREAMS TOGETHER

Dream big. Have sky high aspirations. One of my favorite things to do is lie in bed next to my wife and plan our future together. We dream about where we will be and what we will do. We talk about places we want to visit, activities we want to do, cars we'd like to drive, and homes we'd like to own. We even discuss businesses we would like to start or run. Some of this is just fantasizing for the sake of fantasizing, and some of it will become a reality. As a couple, you need to have goals to strive toward. Without goals, a relationship will grow stagnant. As they say, if you are not going forward, you are going backwards.

Your goals may be to start a family, or they could be something as simple as organizing a vacation together. As long as you have dreams that you share, you will remain on the same path. It gives you something to hope for together and something to look forward to. Beyond that, it gives you something to work your way towards, and helps to strengthen your bond.

Working together towards a common goal is one of the best ways to build trust, love and comradery between you and your significant other. It puts you on the same page and gives you a goal to strive towards. It is easy to get lost in the shuffle of life when you do not have a goal to orient yourself towards. Rather than working with your spouse, you end up spinning your wheels in opposite directions. This can lead to tension and strife. Isn't it more fun to dream big together and then work to see those dreams come to life? A note of caution, dreaming big is okay, but don't ignore the necessity of earning enough to help you realize those dreams.

两人中的一方承担大部分家务并没有什么问题，对于多数家庭来说，这是最好的运作方式，但另一方应该对此感恩并感激伴侣的努力，而不是总惦记让别人干活。一旦你开始指望别人做事，就是在把对方当作佣人。你或你的伴侣为彼此所做的一切都应该得到感激。

38 一起梦想

人要有大梦想，要有壮志凌云的抱负。我最喜欢做的事情之一就是和太太躺在床上，一起畅想我们的未来。我们梦想着将来会去哪儿、会做什么。我们探讨想参观的地方、想参加的活动、想驾驶的豪车、想拥有的房子。我们甚至会讨论想要经营的买卖。有些梦想只是为了幻想而幻想，而有些将成为现实。作为夫妻，要有共同的奋斗目标，没有目标，感情就会停滞不前，正如人们常说的，逆水行舟，不进则退。

你们的目标可能是生个小孩，也可能是一起度假这种简单的事。只要两人有共同的梦想，就会有共同的努力方向，能让你们拥有共同的希望和期待，也能拥有前进的动力，并能增强两人的感情。

一起朝着共同的目标努力是在伴侣之间建立信任、关爱及和谐的最好方法之一，能让两人同舟共济、勇往直前。如果没有目标，就很容易迷失在生活的混乱中，不能和伴侣共同努力，最终走向相反的道路，还会导致两人关系紧张、发生冲突。一起怀揣远大的梦想，然后努力实现这些梦想，不是更有趣吗？提醒一下，有远大的梦想很好，但需要赚足够多的钱才能帮助你实现这些梦想。

39. IN SICKNESS AND IN HEALTH IS A MUST

It is easy to love someone when they are at their best—healthy and happy, gallivanting around and having a great time. They are attractive, charming, energetic, and loving. It is not so easy to love that same person when they are at their worst. Sick, feeble, weak, and scared. If you are in a relationship, you signed up for both of these people. God willing, you will have more of the former than the latter, but you can never be sure.

I love my wife as she is, and I am thankful for her health, but God forbid, if something serious happened to her and she could no longer physically take care of herself, I would remain by her side and do everything I could to make her happy. No matter what, it would not affect how much I love her.

Life can be hard, and it is full of surprises. It is a beautiful gift, but it is not without its challenges. Good health is not guaranteed, and aging is a simple fact of life. There is a reason the priest will ask in your vows if you will stay together in sickness and health. It is because that vow is the backbone of a marriage. You cannot only be around for the good times, you must also stay for the bad.

It is a beautiful concept. I am committed to my wife no matter what may happen, and she is committed to me. It gives me a sense of security knowing that whatever occurs, I will always have her. In my toughest moments, it keeps me strong. I hope my wife and I are always healthy, but I know that no matter what may come, we will at least always have each other.

39 同甘共苦

当一个人健康、快乐、自在、开心的时候，正是引人注目、风情万种、精力充沛、爱意正浓之际，我们很容易爱上此人。当这个人最糟糕的时候，患病、衰微、虚弱、焦虑之际，就很难让人去爱了。如果你正在恋爱，这两种可能性你都要承担。上帝保佑，你能拥有前者，但世事难料。

我爱我太太，感谢她很健康，但上帝保佑，万一她发生什么严重状况，以致不能自理，我也会陪在她身边，尽我所能让她快乐。不管怎样，都不会影响我对她的爱。

人生路苦，但也充满了惊喜。人生是一份精美的礼物，但也会有挑战。身体健康是无法保证的，衰老是自然规律。在婚礼上宣誓时，牧师问你们是否无论疾病还是健康都会同甘共苦，就是这个道理。誓言是婚姻的支柱，两个人要有福同享、有难同当。

这个理念很棒，无论发生什么事，我都会忠于我太太，她也会忠于我。我知道，无论发生什么，她都会陪我同甘共苦，让我倍感心安，在艰难困苦的时刻，能让我坚强。我希望我和爱人永远健康，但我知道无论发生什么，我们至少永远拥有彼此。

40. "MINDSET": IF YOU EVER WISHED YOU HAD A MAGIC WAND, READ THIS POINT

Mindset is your magic wand for having a wonderful and lasting marriage. Have you noticed that when you get totally engaged with something or someone, it is impossible to be derailed. Failure after failure means nothing because you are only focused on achieving the current task and you have the right mindset. All you are thinking about is the eventual success. With a proper mindset, you can achieve anything, and that includes having a happy and lasting marriage.

With my mindset I do not see failure as a possibility. I may get frustrated, but giving up is not in my vision. I remember once trying to fix a mechanical problem in my home. It took me maybe a hundred times to get it done, but in the end, I succeeded. I experienced failure after failure, then like magic, I completed the task.

Having challenges in our lives is not a problem if you have the proper mindset. Everyone encounters problems. The "problem" is how we view ourselves in these circumstances. We often limit ourselves by what we believe or imagine is achievable. Our mindset is the source of power to solve problems, and you can choose your mindset. Mindsets define our perceptions and impact not only thoughts, feelings, and behavior, but they can also affect physiological changes.

People who adopt positive expectations have longer and healthier relationships. I realized long ago that if my mindset allows me to see what is wrong, then I will certainly find and fix it. The problem with relationships is that circumstances can easily be read in the wrong way. For example, a salesman may call, the wife answers, and the husband hears a male voice on the phone. I have observed with friends that when a call comes in, they are always asking their spouse about who it was. They are not asking that question for any other reason than that their jealous mindset is looking for something suspicious.

If you are a person with the constant mindset of looking for something wrong, you will always find it. In the example above of the salesman calling, the result would be disastrous

40 拥有魔杖

心态是能够拥有美满持久婚姻的魔杖。你是否发现，当你全身心投入在某事或某人身上时，不可能偏离目标。一次又一次的失败都无所谓，因为你一心只想完成当前的任务，这是正确的心态，你心中所想都是最终的成功。拥有良好的心态，什么都可以实现，包括拥有一个幸福和持久的婚姻。

以我的心态，失败是不可能的。我可能会沮丧，但放弃二字不会出现在我的字典里。记得有一次我试图修理家中一个坏了的机器，我试了大约一百次才修好，期间经历了无数次失败，然后像施了魔法一样，我终于完成了任务。

如果你有正确的心态，生活中的各种挑战便不是问题。每个人都会遇到困难，"问题"在于我们如何看待自己。我们经常被自己相信或认为能做成的事所限制。心态是解决问题的力量源泉，我们可以选择拥有哪种心态，心态决定了我们的认知，不仅会影响思维、感觉和态度，还会引起生理变化。

拥有乐观期望的人会拥有更长久、更健康的感情。很久以前我就意识到，如果通过内心能够看到问题所在，那么我一定会找到原因并解决问题。感情问题在于，人们很容易以错误的方式解读实际情况。例如，推销员来电，妻子接起电话，丈夫会听到电话里是男性的声音。我从朋友那儿观察到，当电话打进来时，他们总是问自己的伴侣是谁打来的。他们这么问是因为嫉妒的心态在作祟，疑心而已。

如果你的内心总是在找寻错误，你就总能发现错误。在上面推销员来电的例子中，如果丈夫持怀疑的心态，结果会不堪设想。疑心和想象能让丈夫

should the husband have a suspicious mindset. His suspicions and imagination might cause him to make false accusations. The husband may accuse his spouse of infidelity when she is completely innocent. If this happens too many times, there will be a breaking point. Some would call this a self-fulfilling prophecy, created by a jealous mindset. If the husband in this case had a mindset of always trusting his spouse, such a situation could not happen.

My wife and I both have a simple, open mindset: one of trust, commitment, caring, empathy, love, and calmness at all times. We have talked about this and consciously made sure that we were in sync on the subject.

This issue brings us back to the importance of open communication, talking and developing congruent philosophies. In our case, even if we did not talk specifically about trust as a critical element of our mindset, it would not have been a problem because we are both trusting people by nature. However, we realize that many couples simply do not trust each other, which is a path to disaster. For this reason, a meeting of the minds must be created, and that only happens when both people agree to change their mindset.

One day, when I sat down and examined all my past successes and how I achieved them, I realized that each and every case came down to my mindset. Every time I had a winning mindset, I won. A winning mindset means I do not even consider failure as an option. If anyone looks back at their past failures, they will realize a big part of it was the mindset they had at the time. A simple comparison of how you felt about things at a particular point in time may prove useful. My bet is that you will notice a correlation between the times you failed and those in which you succeeded were due to the mindset you had at that time.

I suggest starting each day being excited and ready for a climb up the highest mountain. First and foremost, tell your spouse you love them. A big hug and a kiss go a long way in action to support these words and will increase your chances of having a good day. when I wake, I say "Darling, I am so lucky to have you as my wife, and I love you forever, so let's have a wonderful day." When we go to bed, we pray together, then tell each other how lucky we are to be married. During the day, if we are in separate places, we send multiple messages of love and appreciation (often stickers that we make from photos with an app). The result is that even on those days full of challenges where problem after problem is experienced, we both still have a great day.

Your relationship mindset has a powerful effect on your life. It's not just about positive thinking, it is as about truly believing. Being flexible with the focus on the prize is key.

作出错误的结论，可能会在妻子完全无辜的情况下指责她不忠。如果这种情况发生太多次，矛盾就会爆发。有人说这是由嫉妒心理造成的自证预言。如果丈夫能拥有始终信任妻子的心态，那么这种情况就不会发生。

我和太太都有简单、坦率的心态：信任、忠诚、体贴、同情、关爱和冷静的心态。我们已经讨论过这个问题，并刻意保持两人同步。

这个问题又回到了坦诚沟通、对话和发展一致性哲学的重要性上。就我俩而言，即使不会特意将信任作为心态的关键因素，也不会有问题，因为我们都天生信任他人。然而我发现很多夫妻根本不信任彼此，这是通往灾难的道路，因此双方必须达成共识，这需要双方都愿意改变自己的心态。

有一天，当我坐下来回顾过往所有的成就以及成功的原因时，我发现，每一次成功都源于我的心态。每当我有必胜的心态时，我就能赢。成功的心态意味着不允许失败。如果有人回顾他们过去的失败，会发现很大一部分原因是源于当时的心态。简单比较一下你在某一特定时间点对事物的感受可能会对你有所帮助，我敢打赌，你会发现失败和成功与你当时的心态密切相关。

想快乐地开始每一天，要有登高望远的心态。首先要向伴侣表达爱意，如大大的拥抱和甜蜜的吻，配合动听的话语会更有效，能让人心情愉悦。当我醒来时会说："亲爱的，我很幸运有你做我的太太，我会永远爱你，让我们开始美好的一天。"在入睡前，我们一起祈祷，然后告诉对方能在一起多么幸运。白天，如果我们没在一起，会互发充满爱意和感激的消息（用应用程序制作的照片贴画），这样的结果是，即使在那些充满挑战、经历各种困难的日子里，我们仍然能携手度过。

对待伴侣的心态能够大大地影响你的生活，不仅要有乐观的思想，还要有完全的信任，关键是要懂得变通，把注意力集中在目标上。我始终基于一个原则，就是不管这一天过得多糟糕，也不会影响我对爱人的态度。不管现

My mindset is already focused on the basic rule that even if I have the worst day, it won't impact the way I treat my wife. Regardless of the realities of the day, I will show her love, understanding, calmness, and positivity. If she is having a bad day, I encourage her to tell me about it. I then encourage her by reminding her that things will get better, and that our love is stronger than any external problem.

I know I am very lucky to have a wonderful wife, so no matter how bad the day may seem, in the end I win. Frustration is temporary, but my wife and I are forever. All that really matters to me is the love that I have for her and how I treat her. My mindset is focused on making her happy, and I will not allow external issues to ever blur my vision. I know something is bound to go wrong every day, and when it does, no matter how bad it is, I will calmly deal with it immediately. This way of thinking is also my mindset. To harness the power of your mindset is to become superhuman.

The great thing about being human is that we all have the ability to make choices. We can choose to be pessimistic about the day or we can decide to make it a positive one. It all comes down to the mindset.

I choose to have a great day, every day. I always show my wife that I love her by my actions. I am always listening, and I am a person who takes action. I love her more and more each day. A marriage that is loving, empathic, joyous, caring, and forever is the focus of my mindset. Mindset is your magic wand to achieve success in all you do, and especially to create a wonderful, loving, compassionate, intimate, warm, devoted, and forever marriage.

41. LUNCH DATES ARE COOL TO BREAK UP THE DAY

I love to go out with my wife anytime—morning, noon, and night—but there is something extra special about our lunch dates. Not only does knowing we have one planned give me confidence in my morning meetings, it gives me something to look forward to. I know that no matter how good or bad the meetings go, I will have lunch with the love of

实如何，在她面前我都保持关爱、理解、冷静和乐观的情绪。如果她哪天过得不好，我会让她说出来，然后鼓励她，告诉她事情终会好起来，我们的爱足以战胜任何困难。

我知道自己很幸运能有这样一个好太太，所以不管这一天过得有多糟糕，我依然是人生赢家。挫折是暂时的，而我和爱人会永远在一起。对我来说，真正重要的是我对她的爱和我对她的态度。我的心态就是想办法让她快乐，不让外部因素遮挡视线。我知道每天都会有一些不好的事情发生，但不管事情有多糟糕，我都会立即冷静处理，这种思维方式就是我的心态，善于利用心态就能使自己成为超人。

人类的优势在于拥有选择的能力。我们可以选择悲观地面对生活，也可以选择乐观地面对生活，这都源于心态。

我会选择过好每一天，我总是用行动向太太证明我爱她。我愿意倾听，更喜欢采取行动，我越来越爱她。这个充满爱意、情感、欢乐、关怀并能持久的婚姻是我心之所向。心态是一根魔杖，能助你取得成功，尤其是能创造一个充满美好、关爱、同情、亲密、温暖、忠诚并持久的婚姻。

41 共进午餐

我喜欢和我太太在任何时候出去玩，早上、中午和晚上都行，但是我们的午餐约会很不同。想到能共进午餐不仅让我在早会上更有信心，还让我有所期待。我知道，无论会议进行得如何，我都将与挚爱共进午餐，这很特别。午饭后，当我不得不回去参加各种会议时，会觉得自己精神饱满，能胜

my life. This is special. Then, after lunch, when I have to return to this or that meeting, I feel fully recharged and ready to accomplish all my goals for the rest of the day. I have noticed that I tend to be more successful on the days we meet for a midday meal. The funny thing is, it does not matter where we meet. I could pop in at our house for a quick bite, we could go to a fancy waterfront restaurant, or I could meet her for fast-food. As long as we get to spend some quality time together, the result is always the same.

The psychology behind this is simple. When we have something to look forward to, it boosts our mood and attitude leading up to the event. As long as you do not get so excited that you lose focus, this can put you in a better mood, which will in turn shine through in everything else you do. That means you will be more personable during this period and thus more successful at work. However, do not get confused. I am not advocating planning lunch dates with your partner because it will help you professionally, that is simply a fringe benefit.

Having the occasional lunch date with you husband or wife will bring you closer together. It gives you an opportunity to talk about each other's day thus far, exchange business ideas, and catch up. My wife will regularly provide insights on meetings that I did not see. This in turn will help me when I return to work. To gain a new perspective is always helpful. Beyond everything else, it is simply nice to see her and share a few moments together.

42. WHEN YOUR SPOUSE IS DOING SOME MUNDANE CHORE, STEP IN WITHOUT BEING ASKED, AND HELP

Everyone appreciates a little unrequested assistance. We all have those chores to do that are relatively simple but take forever. It could be sorting photos, organizing your workspace, or simple errands. No matter what the case, these chores usually get put off until they begin to feel unmanageable. So, wouldn't it be nice if, when you saw your spouse beginning such a project, you jumped in to help without even being asked?

Sharing tasks is a great way to grow closer together and have some fun. It may not

任当天余下的所有工作。我发现，在我们共进午餐的日子里，我会更容易成功。有意思的是，我们相约在哪里并不重要，有可能回家吃点东西，也有可能去一家高档的海滨餐厅，或者去吃快餐，只要我们能在一起共度美好时光，其结果都一样。

这当中蕴含的心理学原理很简单，当人们有所期待时，就会拥有更好的情绪和态度。只要你不因太过兴奋而失去重点，就能拥有更好的心情，也能在其他事情中发挥作用。你在这段时间里会更有风度，在工作上也会更成功。但是不要因此产生困惑，我并不是因为这对你的职业生涯有所帮助而提倡你和伴侣共进午餐，这只是一个附带的好处而已。

偶尔和伴侣共进午餐能拉近两人的关系，能让两人有机会聊聊这一天过得怎么样，交换业务想法，并交流各自状况。我太太总能洞察出一些被我忽略的会议细节，因而会对我的工作有所帮助，能从新的视角看问题总是有益的。除此之外，仅仅能见到她就让我很高兴，我们可以一起共享美好时光。

42 主动帮忙

每个人都喜欢不请自来的帮助。家里总有一些琐事要做，这些事情相对简单，却要花很长时间，比如整理照片、收拾工作间或者其他简单琐事。不管是什么活儿，这些家务琐事不到万不得已都没人去做，所以当你看到伴侣做这些家务时，应该主动帮忙，这不是很好吗？

一起做家务是增进彼此关系和享受乐趣的好方法。收拾工作间或整理一万张照片确实没什么意思，但如果你和合适的人一起做这些事，会不一

seem like organizing an office or sorting through 10,000 photos could be fun, but you would be surprised if you are doing it side by side with the right person. Besides, the old saying "misery love company" applies when you are doing unpleasant or boring tasks together. There are so many opportunities to laugh and make jokes when going through old knickknacks or pictures.

"Can you believe I ever dressed like that?" "Look at that hairdo; what were you thinking?" Any chore can be made fun when it is done as a couple. It can turn something which you were dreading into a priceless memory. My wife and I have created some of our favorite memories while completing some arduous task or chore, and we wouldn't trade those times for anything.

You may be saying to yourself that there is no way you can make certain tasks fun, and while I disagree, I am not right about everything. That does not change the recommendation that if your spouse is undertaking such a mission, you should offer to help. You are a team, and you are meant to tackle life together. That doesn't mean just the fun or big things, it can be the little annoying things as well. I guarantee they will appreciate your assistance and you will grow closer together for your trouble.

43. TAKE ON PROJECTS IMMEDIATELY. DELAYING IS NEVER YOUR FRIEND

I have found that in business as well as in personal relationships, delay will equal death. If you and your wife have an ambition to go to a certain restaurant or take a vacation, there is no better time than the present. I have learned the hard way that once you get an inclination to do something, it is best to do it right away, or there is a good chance it will never happen. We are all so busy in our lives that there is rarely a good time to take a break and get away. This type of thinking leads to vacations or fun outings being put off indefinitely. These are prime opportunities for you and your spouse to grow closer together, but too often instead, people allow life's circumstances to force those plans to the wayside.

样。当你们一起做烦人或无聊的琐事时，正如俗话所说的“有难同当”。你们在收拾过去物品或照片时，还能互相打趣，一起度过欢乐时光。

“你能相信我曾经打扮成那样吗？”“看那发型，你当时怎么想的？”夫妻一起做家务会很有意思，能把烦人琐事变成珍贵回忆。我和太太一起做家务会有许多美好回忆，是千金不换的幸福时光。

你可能会说，有些琐事不可能变得有意思，虽然我不同意，但我说的也不见得全对，可是我不会改变这个建议：在伴侣忙家务时，你应该主动帮忙。你们是一家人，注定要一起面对生活，不仅仅要面对有意思或重要的事情，还会面对烦人琐事。我保证对方会感激你的帮助，你们也会因为这些小事而更加亲密。

43 拖延害人

我发现，不管是在工作中还是生活中，拖延特别害人。如果你和爱人想去某家餐馆或外出度假，现在就是最佳时刻。一旦要做某事，最好马上去做，否则最后很有可能不了了之，这一点我有过惨痛的教训。大家都很忙，很少有时间休息，这种想法会导致度假或郊游被无限期推迟，而这正是能和伴侣增进感情的绝佳机会。人们往往被外部环境影响而将计划搁置。拖延会让两人感情疏远，不要等到合适的时机才去享受生活，现在就去！

这种事我听过很多次：某人计划去做健康体检，却一直拖着没去，最终

When they get put off, they tend to have the opposite effect and push people apart. Do not wait for the right moment to live your life to the fullest; do it now!

How many times have I heard of a person who planned to get a health physical and kept putting it off, dying from something that was completely avoidable had they done the checkup. When addressing problems or issues, whether with your spouse, work, health, or anything else you can think of, do them without delay.

There are several reasons to never delay. The first is simple. If you do not address an issue immediately it will slip your mind and never get accomplished. The second is a bit more serious. If you put off a problem, it is likely to compound, meaning it may have been manageable when you first noticed it, but by the time you decide it needs to be addressed, it may have grown so big that it cannot be resolved. These problems also cause subconscious stress that will make you more volatile with your partner and can thus negatively affect your relationship.

In relationships, it is best to address every issue, both good and bad, as it arises. It will help you and your partner to live a happier and more stress-free life together.

44. PACKAGING IS EVERY BIT AS IMPORTANT AS WHATS INSIDE

Product packaging is the single largest factor impacting consumers when it comes to making a purchase. A great product with poor packaging will rarely sell. Consider the perfume industry, as they excel at this concept. The packaging of perfume boxes is amazing, and after they are opened, the bottle will wow you. This is all before you even try the perfume.

Packaging lets the consumer learn information about the product. You can learn from the packaging what the product can do and how to use the product. It can make the company look compelling, powerful, and strong. The packaging will build your brand, as it communicates company values. Good packaging markets what's inside and gives the consumer confidence about the quality of the product they are buying.

In this book we are talking about marriage and romance, not products, but if you think

死于本来完全可以避免的疾病，如果当初去体检就不会这样了。当遇到问题时，无论是伴侣、工作、健康，还是任何能想到的方面，千万不要拖延，马上去做。

有两条不能拖延的理由。第一条很简单：如果不立即处理这个问题，就会忘掉，最终永远不会解决。第二条更严重：如果一直拖延，这个问题很可能会变得复杂。也许刚开始只是一个可控的小问题，但最终决定必须解决的时候，事情已经变得庞大复杂，以至于无法解决。这些问题还会对潜意识造成压力，让你和伴侣感情不稳定，从而产生负面影响。

在亲密关系中，要果断解决每一个问题，无论好坏，不能拖延，这样才能和伴侣一起拥有更快乐、更减压的生活。

44 包装自己

产品包装是影响消费者是否购买商品的最大因素。商品再好，如果包装差劲也很难卖出去。香水行业就特别擅于包装。香水盒就已经令人惊叹了，里面的香水瓶更令人叫绝，香水还没被使用就先让人信服了。

包装有助于消费者了解产品信息，人们可以从包装上了解产品功能和使用方法，也能了解经营公司的实力。包装有助于树立品牌形象，传递经营者的价值观。漂亮的包装能带动产品，让消费者对所购商品的质量充满信心。

尽管本书讨论的是婚恋关系，而不是商品，但如果你仔细想想，为什么不按伴侣喜欢的风格包装一下自己呢？衣着得体的人总能吸引我的眼球（无论男女）。如果有人喷了好闻的香水，也会引起我的注意，否则通常会忽视；

about it, why not package yourself in a way that is attractive to your spouse. A well-dressed person always catches my eye (male or female). If someone is wearing a nice scent, I may take notice of that person I might not have noticed otherwise. Well-manicured nails always get my attention also. Attractive hairstyles can give a person a commanding social and professional advantage along with stylish clothes, shoes and accessories that draw positive praise and attention. All of these noticeable factors can make a person stand out, giving them that extra boost in confidence and hence the winning edge socially and professionally. The way your dress can be alluring to others, and it will impact their opinion of you.

Everything I have written so far is common sense. People who are dating know these things. The problem is that after marriage, all too often people relax about their appearance and stop trying to impress. This is a huge mistake. No one wants to have a boring life with a person who never tries to keep up their appearance. Everyone wants to be with a person they are attracted to, and that includes after you are married.

Once you are married, I think it is more important than ever to look fantastic all the time. Going the extra mile to be alluring to your spouse is fun, especially if you make it a game. Unlike when you were in the dating game, this is a game that you will win every time. To me, winning is fun. I am not saying to spend hours each day on your looks, but an extra twenty minutes can make a world of difference in your appearance and ultimately in how attractive you are to your spouse. Flowers are great, so why not be that fresh flower. Look fabulous, smell alluring, and make your spouse proud to be married.

Even when we are doing nothing, my wife will spend a few minutes taking the time to do little things that are attractive to me, and she knows how much I appreciate the effort. On most occasions, we aren't even planning to see anyone else. "Dressing for success" is often for our eyes only. She is so attractive, sometimes she will try on an outfit even when we are not going anywhere just to see if I like it. Maybe it's only tennis dress or gym clothes, but the gesture of trying something on just for me is engaging and reminds me of how lucky I am that she is my wife. When we go to nice places, she will do the same with formal wear. She is naturally beautiful. She could dress in old clothes and still be lovely, but she chooses to look the best she can for me every day, and I appreciate it.

I try to do the same for her by always trying to go beyond what is normal in the way I dress. For example, in the morning when I take a shower, I always put on cologne. I pick nice clothes to wear when we are just sitting around. She does notice and often compliments me. Of

精心修剪的指甲也能吸引人；漂亮的发型在社交和职业方面都相当有优势；时尚的衣服、鞋子和配饰，也能得到赞美和关注。所有这些引人注目的因素都能让一个人脱颖而出、信心倍增，从而使人在社交和职业方面取得成功。你的穿着能吸引别人，也会影响别人对你的看法。

本书到目前为止所写的都是基本常识，正在约会的人都知道，问题在于人们婚后往往不再去在意自己的外表，不再想引人注目。这就大错特错了，没人愿意和不注意外表的人一起过无聊的日子，每个人都想和自己喜欢的人在一起，结婚后也不例外。

我认为婚后更应该时刻注意形象。想尽办法去吸引伴侣会很有意思，尤其是把这件事当成游戏，和约会时不同，这个游戏你肯定能赢。对我来说，能赢太好了。我并不是说每天要花几个小时来修饰自己的外表，但多花 20 分钟就能发生翻天覆地的变化，肯定能吸引到你的伴侣。鲜花多美好啊，所以为什么不成为那朵鲜花呢？看起来漂亮，闻起来香甜，也让伴侣为与你结婚而自豪。

即使我们赋闲在家，我太太也会花几分钟为能吸引我而打扮一下，她知道我会因此而感激。很多时候只有我们俩，没有别人。“人靠衣装”，我俩打扮纯粹为自己看着高兴。她很有魅力，有时即使哪儿都不去，她也会试穿一套衣服，只是为了看我是否喜欢。也许只是网球服或其他运动服，但她为我试穿衣服真是感人，让我想到娶她为妻是多么幸运。在正式场合，她也会穿正装。她天生丽质，即便穿旧衣服，也依然迷人。她每天都会在我面前展现最好的一面，我为此很感激。

我也试着为她做同样的事，也会注重穿着打扮。例如，我早上洗澡后会喷古龙水，而两人闲坐时也会挑漂亮衣服穿。她发现了会经常表扬我，当然，我也会表扬她，我们因此而彼此欣赏，这样做很有效。

即使在卧室，我们也会穿那种有意思的衣服。我喜欢看太太穿时尚内

course, I do the same. This practice builds appreciation for each other, and that's powerful.

Even when we are in the bedroom, we dress in a way that makes it fun to undress. Nice lingerie is something I love to see when my wife comes to me. Her sexy bedroom way of dressing shows me that she cares, and I am the only person who will ever see her this way. I am so appreciative that my wife goes the extra mile to look good in all situations. For a man, there may be fewer clothing options, but I do my best to look good for her all the time also. Taking the extra time to always look and smell good will always add a new spark to your relationship. That spark will be the catalyst that ignites the fire of love and romance.

To take the time to "package" yourself in a way that makes you more attractive is a winning recipe. There is another benefit. When you are outside your home, why not dress in a way that makes your spouse look good. People love to talk and gossip. Why not make them say, she or he is so lucky to be married to that person.

On the business side, you never know who you might run into. I can give you many examples where I have accidentally run into people who are important business partners. On such occasions, maybe it would not have mattered if I had been dressed like a bum, but better safe than sorry. Better to dress to impress and always win. Your wardrobe and appearance do impact the way people think and act toward you. Earning money is also important in maintaining romance in your relationship with your spouse because it gives you freedom to do all the things together we have been exploring.

The little extra effort it takes to look nice will light a candle that will burn forever. Your intimacy will always remain ignited, and your life will be better.

45. SURPRISES WILL KEEP THE ROMANCE ALIVE

Surprises break my golden rule of no secrets in a relationship. A good surprise must be a secret in order to garner the desired impact. If a person knows what is in the wrapped present, it would not be as much fun. Many rules should never be broken, but this is the

衣，这种性感的着衣方式说明她在乎我，我是唯一能看到她这样的人。我很感激太太总是保持良好的仪态。对于男人来说，衣服可选性不多，但我也会尽最大努力让自己在她面前看起来更好。花点时间让自己神清气爽，能为两人感情增添新的火花，而火花正是点燃爱情之火的催化剂。

花些时间“包装”一下自己，让自己更有吸引力，是成功的秘诀。还有一个好处：当你外出的时候，要穿得和自己的伴侣相配，人们喜欢闲聊八卦，要给他们机会去说，某人跟某人结婚真是太幸运了。

从工作角度来讲也要注意打扮，你永远不知道会遇到谁。我就曾偶遇过重要的商业伙伴，这时如果我穿得像个乞丐——当然，这也没什么关系，但正好穿着得体总比可能后悔强。最好穿着得体，让人印象深刻是成功的法宝，你的穿着打扮确实会影响别人对你的看法。赚钱对于维持你和伴侣之间的浪漫关系也很重要，因为有钱才能让你们自由自在地在一起做想做的事情。

要努力让自己更漂亮，就像点燃一支永远燃烧的蜡烛，你们的亲密关系也就此点燃，生活也会更加美好。

45 制造惊喜

惊喜打破了我所说的感情中没有秘密的黄金法则。要想获得预期的效果，一个特别的惊喜必须保密，如果对方知道包装好的礼物是什么，那就没意思了。很多规则永远都不能打破，但这个规则必须打破。所以，在感情这

one place where breaking the rules is imperative. So go ahead, have a few secrets in this one area of your relationship. Breaking that rule is so exciting when preparing a gift for the person you love. For me, the planning stages of the surprise gift are incredibly enjoyable. The planning is an adventure that involves being creative, and it is almost as thrilling as actually giving the gift.

Have you ever noticed the correlation between getting or giving a gift and the way it makes the receiver and the giver feel? The result is happiness for both. Add the element of surprise and you have an over-the-top joyful experience. I love giving gifts because it makes me feel great, and I just love making my wife smile. Of course, I love receiving gifts also because it makes me feel special. The feeling of giving or getting a gift is powerful. A gift creates a positive experience, especially if that gift is a surprise. Opening a gift changes a person's entire attitude on how they view the day, the week, the month, and sometimes even the whole year. A new perspective is gained that is glorious and memorable.

Who made the rule that gifts should only be given on special occasions? Who made the rule that gifts should be expensive? With me and my beloved wife, every single moment is a special occasion. We always feel blessed—because we are— and a simple surprise kiss from her powers me up with warm loving energy.

I may not give her a gift every single day, but I do so very often. I may not give her anything for a month, and then I will give her a surprise gift every day for five days in a row. I mix up these occasions so that they are really unexpected and a surprise. Yes, she does the same for me. However, even if it were one-sided, I would still do it. The look on her face and the joy she shows as she opens a gift is wonderful. My wife appreciates my efforts as much as the gift I give. Her reactions make my planning and efforts worthwhile. She never knows when a surprise gift will arrive. It may be a diamond, or something as simple as flowers. The fact is that surprise gifts absolutely add spice and fun to our marriage.

Surprises promote a pleasant feeling that lasts forever. Surprises make a person happy, and regarding our gift-giving, super-happy. With a surprise, the secretion of dopamine is released, causing both the recipient and the giver to experience a pleasant, natural high. Little things show that you care. Little things done in an unexpected moment are even more powerful romance builders. I am talking about breaking predictable patterns with continuous small gestures that show you care and love your spouse. You are not a robot, and neither is your spouse. A surprise gift now and then will make sure that your relationship

一领域要保有秘密。在为爱人准备礼物时，打破规则会令人兴奋。对我来说，策划惊喜礼物的阶段特别愉快，策划本身就是充满创意的冒险，和真正送出礼物的时候一样激动人心。

你有没有注意到，收送礼物以及收送礼的人心中感受之间的联系？结果是双方都很高兴，再加上惊喜的元素，你能感受极度快乐。我喜欢送礼物，因为这种感觉很棒，我也愿意让太太高兴。当然，我也喜欢收礼物，因为我能感到自己与众不同。收送礼物的感觉都很棒。礼物能给人积极的影响，尤其是充满惊喜的礼物。打开礼物的那一瞬间能改变某人看待一天、一周、一个月甚至一整年的态度，会用光辉而难忘的新视角去看待生活。

谁规定只有特殊场合才能送礼物？谁又规定礼物应该贵重？对我和爱妻来说，每一刻都是特别的时刻。我们总是感到幸福（因为我们确实如此），她只需一个简单的惊喜之吻，就能让我充满温暖甜蜜的能量。

我不会每天都送她礼物，但我会经常送。我可能一个月都不送她任何礼物，然后会连续五天每天给她一份惊喜礼物。我会打乱规律，所以每次都能出乎意料并令她惊喜，当然她也如此。然而，就算只是我单方面送礼物，我也心甘情愿。当她打开礼物时，脸上会呈现出惊讶和喜悦的神情，真是太棒了。我太太对礼物和心意同样感激，她这样做让我费尽心思地制造惊喜更加值得。她永远不知道何时会收到惊喜礼物，有可能是一颗钻石，或者只是普通鲜花。事实上，惊喜礼物确实给我们的婚姻增添了情趣和欢乐。

惊喜给人带来的愉悦感觉能持续很久。惊喜能让人开心，而送礼物更是让人超级开心。惊喜能促进释放多巴胺，使收礼者和送礼者都能拥有愉悦、自然的快乐情绪。小事情更能表明你关心对方，在意想不到的时刻做一些小事更能制造浪漫，我是指要不断用打破常规的小惊喜来表明你对伴侣的关心和在意。你不是机器人，你的伴侣也不是，偶尔送一份惊喜礼物能确保两人的感情不会平淡无奇。除了送礼物，即使是稍微用心，比如跑去开门而不用

will never become static and predictable. Besides gift-giving, even making a little extra effort, such as running to answer the door so your spouse does not have to get up can surprise them and draw a big smile.

I hear the words disruptive technology in tech talks all the time. Surprising your spouse will produce the same impact, "disruptive behavior" of a positive kind. When you disrupt a boring routine, it will bring spice and new life to your marriage. Surprise is a key ingredient for disruptive innovation. Disruptive innovators capitalize on the power of surprise by reaching further, connecting disconnected ideas, and embracing blank canvas thinking. Why not also apply these rules to your personal life? I can go on and on about the power of surprise to keep romance alive, but I think you are beginning to see my point.

Follow our example by surprising your spouse in creative and fun ways on a regular basis, and you will benefit from a much happier relationship. Of course, being creative only enhances the surprise. It is important to keep your creative juices flowing. The planning of surprises will produce a win in every way possible, especially in building and maintaining a loving, affectionate relationship.

46. NIGHTTIME IS NEVER THE RIGHT TIME

It may be controversial to say that nighttime is never the right time, but the facts bear this out. In my opinion, the most romantic part of the day is sunrise.

Most good things happen during the day, and that includes finding your partner for life. You earn money in the day, you wake up in the daytime, you normally go to school in the daytime. The list of daytime activities far outweighs the evening choices. At night, especially in bars and clubs, people are not usually looking for a life partner, but instead a one-night stand. I know almost zero people who met their spouse at night. Maybe I do a few, but the number is exceedingly small.

Most of my friends met their spouse during the day, at work, school, conferences, the gym, volunteering, playing sports like tennis, biking, jogging clubs, the chamber of

伴侣起身，也能让伴侣因惊喜而展露笑颜。

我经常在科技演讲中听到颠覆性技术这个词汇，给伴侣制造惊喜也能产生颠覆性的效果，这是一种积极的“颠覆行为”。打破无聊的常规，会给婚姻带来乐趣和新意。惊喜是颠覆性创新的关键因素。颠覆性的革新者通过不断探索，将不相关的想法联系起来，利用惊喜的力量创造崭新的思维。为什么不将这一规则应用到个人生活中呢？惊喜能让浪漫永存，这一话题根本说不完，但我想你已经明白我的意思了。

按我说的，定期以新奇有趣的方式给伴侣制造惊喜，能让两人收获更多幸福。当然，有创意才会增加惊喜，所以常变常新很重要。制造惊喜能在很多方面助你取得成功，特别是在建立和维持浓情蜜意的感情方面。

46 最佳时间

要说夜晚并不是最浪漫的时间，可能会引起争议，但事实证明确实如此。在我看来，一天中最浪漫的时候是日出时分。

很多好事都发生在日间，也包括寻找终身伴侣。你会在白天挣钱、白天起床、白天上学。日间的活动会比夜间多很多。在晚上，尤其是在酒吧和夜店里，人们不会到这些地方寻找终身伴侣，顶多是一夜情。在我认识的人中，几乎没有人是在晚上遇到另一半的，就算有也非常少。

我的朋友们都是在日间认识各自伴侣的，比如在公司、学校、会务、健身房、志愿服务等，或者在运动时，比如一起打网球、骑行、慢跑，也有可

commerce, church, book clubs, dog parks, the beach, museums, festivals of all types, farmers markets, or if you are lucky like me, at the local Zoom store.

In all of the above situations you start off with an advantage in daylight hours since there is a much greater chance of meeting someone with whom you have things in common. This is a huge advantage. For example, if you meet a person at an industry conference, it is likely you work in the same industry. Having and doing something in common absolutely increases the odds that an actual relationship will develop. If your goal is to get married and have a long, loving, and lasting relationship, explore opportunities to connect during the daytime. If you marry someone with whom you have things in common, it is logical that the chances of the marriage lasting are disproportionately increased.

Many people find nighttime to be exciting, but not me. Nighttime is sprinkled with small amounts of mystery and danger. Bad things happen all too often after midnight and at nightclubs. I like safety, and I like romance. I don't like music that is so loud a conversation is not possible.

I like to believe I am the most non-boring person I know. I am adventurous and fun to be around, but I choose to avoid nightclubs. I think I am also flexible and spontaneous. Spontaneity often creates the best times, the special moments that will be remembered forever. My wife and I like to make plans together, but we also like to be spontaneous and change our plans. Either way is often exciting and creates a great memory. We love going out at night to restaurants but not to late night clubs. Interestingly, we have found sometimes breakfast or lunch can be even more romantic than a crowded place at night. Nighttime activities, to me, are extremely overrated. I am a businessperson, and my days are important. I like to wake up feeling great. If we go out at night too often, the days tend not to be productive. I want the energy to give my wife and my work the attention they deserve, and I always do exactly that.

I am not saying to never go out at night. What I am saying is if you look at nighttime as your sole period of enjoyment, you should think again. I once heard a song called "Afternoon Delight," and to me and my friends the song is true. To have a little fun midday makes the rest of the day amazing. Why wait until late at night when you are tired and ready to sleep?

Why not have some fun when the moment strikes. I will carry this point a bit further. Go ahead and plan daytime adventures. Write down on a calendar the date and time for

能在商会、教堂、读书俱乐部、动物公园、海滩、博物馆、各种节庆活动、农贸市场，又或者像我一样幸运，在当地的 Zoom 便利店。

在上述情形中，白天比较有优势，因为更有机会遇到志同道合的人，这一点非常有利，例如，如果你在行业会议上遇到某人，很可能你们在同一行业工作。拥有相同的事业绝对会增加两人恋爱的几率。如果你想结婚，并拥有一段长久、甜蜜的感情，那就在白天寻找这种机会。如果你能与志同道合的人成婚，那么可以肯定的是，这会大大增加婚姻持久的机会。

很多人会觉得夜晚更加刺激，但我不觉得。夜晚会夹杂着些许神秘和危险，夜店里经常会在午夜过后发生不好的事情。我喜欢安全，也喜欢浪漫，我不喜欢音乐声量过高，吵得人无法交谈。

我觉得自己是最风趣幽默的人，我喜欢冒险，和我在一起会很有意思，但我基本不去夜店。我还认为自己很灵活且很随性，随性往往能抓住最好的时机，那些能永远铭记的特殊时刻。我和太太喜欢一起制定计划，但我们也喜欢随性而行、改变计划，无论哪种方式都能令人兴奋，并成为美好回忆。我们喜欢晚上出去吃饭，但不去夜店。有意思的是，我们发现，有时，早餐或午餐去拥挤的地方吃饭会比晚上去更浪漫。对我来说，夜间活动绝对被高估了。我是商人，白天对我很重要。我喜欢醒来时精神饱满，如果我们晚上出去太过频繁，白天的工作效率就会降低。我希望把精力留给值得我关注的爱人和工作，我一向如此。

并不是说不能在晚上出去，我想说的是，如果把夜晚看作唯一的快乐时光，那你应该再重新考虑一下。我曾经听过一首歌叫《午后乐事》，对我和朋友们来说，这首歌太真实了。午间开心一下能让余下时间特别欢乐。为什么要等到夜深人静、累得想睡觉的时候再出去玩呢？

为什么不在合适的时间出去呢？我再说明白点儿，赶紧在白天的时候好好玩吧，在日历上记下出去玩的日期和时间，这些午间约会能让你心有期

such an escapade. These middle of the day rendezvous will give you something to look forward to. If you want to reignite your romance, then the daytime is the answer. Do not forget the nights, but "daytime is absolutely the right time."

47. NEVER LOSE YOUR COOL

There are many ways to lose your cool. When you think about losing your cool, you probably picture you and your spouse yelling at one another. We have already explored a point about the toxicity of raising your voice with your spouse. While this is certainly one way you might lose your cool, this point is going to focus on the games we play inside of our own heads that can spin out of control and cause real world problems.

In a previous point about "mindset," we used a similar example. For simplicity's sake, and to show how these points can intertwine, we will run with that same narrative. You will see that there are multiple variables to every situation. For instance, if you think your wife is acting suspiciously, and you happen to find a business card from a business neither you nor your wife need or would ever visit, you may start to suspect something is amiss. When you ask her where it came from, if she claims not to know, that may create even more suspicion. Soon, jealousy will outweigh logic. With this suspicious mindset, all kinds of accusations about being dis- loyal will surface. The person (let's say the husband) has already convinced himself something is going on behind his back (the wife is making him wear a green hat). To the husband the situation is blurred by his warped mindset. Jealousy has been created, the pot has been stirred, and false accusations are in the air everywhere. The strange business card is confirmation of what he already suspected to be true. The next thing you know, a marriage is destroyed by his misguided mindset, all over something that only occurred in the husband's imagination and was never true. That scenario is all too common.

Human beings tend to let such narratives run rampant in our heads. These can lead to fights and breakups over small miscommunications. Having the wrong mindset does not make for a happy spouse, or a happy life.

盼，如果你想重燃爱情之火，那么白天出去是最好的选择。虽然夜晚也不错，但“白天绝对是最佳时间”。

47 保持冷静

有很多情况能让人失去冷静。说到失控，你可能就会想到和伴侣互相大喊大叫。我们已经探讨过在伴侣面前提高嗓门的劣势，虽然这肯定是能让你失去冷静的一种情形，但此条目会侧重讲人在自己大脑中的假想，这些想像会令人失控并导致现实问题。

在之前关于“心态”（“拥有魔杖”）的条目中，我们列举过类似的实例。为了方便起见，也为了表明这些条目之间会相互重叠，我们依旧沿用之前的说法，你会发现每种情况都是多元化的。例如，如果你认为妻子行为可疑，而你碰巧发现一张与你俩没有半点关系的公司名片，你就会开始疑心。当你问她名片怎么来的时，如果她说不知道，那就更加可疑了。很快，嫉妒就会压倒逻辑，有了这种多疑的心态，你就会有各种不忠的指责。这个人（比方说丈夫）已经确信妻子背着他做了什么事（给他戴绿帽）。对丈夫来说，出于扭曲的心态，情况会变得错综复杂。嫉妒之心一起，高压锅就被搅动了，丈夫会立即失去冷静，进而错误地指责对方。用一张奇怪的名片来证实疑心的事是真实的，接下来的事情你知道，婚姻会被错误的心态摧毁，所有的事情都只是丈夫的想象，从来没有发生过。这种情况真是太常见了。

人们经常让这种假想在脑海中泛滥，因为小小的沟通不畅而导致争吵和分手。错误的心态不会带来幸福的伴侣，也不会带来幸福的生活。

Try to always look at every situation from multiple points of view. Just because you have a suspicion and what you believe to be evidence doesn't make it so. I always give the benefit of doubt as a rule of thumb. Our emotions have a strange way of twisting the truth to our desires, or in this case, fears.

Instead of losing your cool, take a step back and breathe. Talk to your significant other about these fears. Do not ask your friends or family members, as they will almost certainly agree with you, and worse, that will permanently turn them against your spouse. After all, you are providing them with the same skewed evidence that caused you to draw the opinion in the first place. Your brain has a way of making you see what it wants you to see. Treat the situation objectively, as if you were a scientist, and never rush to conclusions. That is how you lose your cool, and possibly lose the love of your life.

The bottom line is not to let your imagination or anger get the best of you. Be conscious of your thoughts, and you can create a proper winning mindset. I advise to write down what you are thinking. Then occasionally self-evaluate to be sure that you are in sync when comparing your current thinking with the target mindset you jotted down.

48. CHOCOLATE AND FLOWERS GO A LONG WAY

Remind your significant other that they are special and give them something to brag about! It is difficult to give a deeply personal gift every day. For instance, if you gave your wife a diamond bracelet every morning, how long would it take her to get bored? She may, of course, reply never to gifts of diamond bracelets, but I believe otherwise. Flowers and candy, however, are consummate classic gifts that may be given frequently. and they keep on giving.

I try to bring my sweetheart flowers or some sort of sweet treat a few times a week. I do not bring such gifts on a schedule because I don't want to her come to expect it. I like to see the surprise on her face when I show up with a bouquet or her favorite candy or baked good. She loves to show her sister and friends the flowers I gave her, and she has fun arranging

要多角度看问题。仅仅因为疑心而自以为是的证据并不是事实，我总是把“假定无过”作为经验法则。人的情感会用奇怪的方式来扭曲事实，以满足想象，而在这一实例中则是出于恐惧。

与其失去冷静，不如退一步深呼吸，和伴侣谈谈你的恐惧心理。不要向朋友或亲人倾诉，因为他们肯定会同意你的观点，更糟糕的是，这会让他们从此和你的伴侣作对。毕竟，你提供的线索正是让你得出错误结论的扭曲证据。人的大脑总有办法让自己看到想看到的东西。要客观对待实际情况，就像科学家一样，不要急于下结论，否则会失去冷静，最终失去一生挚爱。

我们的底线是不要被想象或愤怒击败，要明确自己的想法，拥有积极适当的心态。我建议把自己的想法记录下来，然后适时进行自我评估，确保现在的想法和记录的目标心态同步。

48 经典礼物

要让伴侣感觉与众不同，就要送给伴侣一些可以炫耀的礼物！每天都送一份非常特别的礼物确实很难。例如，如果你每天早上送给爱人一个钻石手镯，要送多久她才会觉得无聊？当然，她可能会说不要钻石手镯，但我不这么认为。然而，鲜花和糖果是最完美的经典礼物，可以经常赠送，一直赠送。

我每周都会给心上人送几束鲜花或一些糖果。我的礼物不定期，因为我不想让这成为她意料之中的事。当我手捧一束鲜花，拿出她最喜欢的糖果或烘焙食品出现在她面前时，就能看到她脸上惊讶的表情。她喜欢把我送的鲜花

them around the house. Plus, these are gifts for both of us. We can both enjoy the beauty and the scent of the flowers, or share the desserts while cuddling in bed.

It does not take much to bring home a bouquet of flowers or your spouse's favorite dessert, but for some reason, this tends to slip people's minds. I would advise you to make a habit out of it. Bring home one of the two choices at least once a week. It will make your spouse happy, and in so doing, make you happy. We are all happier when the person we care about has a smile on their face.

My lovely and wonderful wife loves chocolate, and I can never go wrong surprising her with this gift. Another beauty of fine, hand-crafted chocolate is that normally it is packaged in an eye-catching way. Boxed chocolatiers are beautifully decorated and filled chocolates are a true art to be admired. This gift keeps giving rewards. When she opens the box the aroma of fine chocolate is salivating. Then, when she takes a bite, it is mood enhancing. My wife is almost always in a good mood but give her a piece of quality chocolate and she is floating on air. "Chocolate Happiness" is a real thing.

More than this, chocolate is a gift that keeps on giving because of its health benefits. In moderation, it will reduce the risks of certain diseases. There is much scientific proof that dark chocolate promotes better heart health. The antioxidants in dark chocolate have been shown to lower blood pressure, reduce the risk of clotting and increase blood circulation to the heart, thus lowering the risks of stroke and death from coronary heart disease. It is also rich in antioxidant flavonoids, which are healthy for your heart. One study suggests that eating chocolate in moderation each week also reduces the risk of dying.

Chocolate has been proven to help with depression symptoms also. Chocolate contains phenylethylamine (PEA), the chemical known to boost one's mood, and the neurotransmitter serotonin as well, which acts as a natural mood stabilizer to enhance mood and lower symptoms of anxiety and depression. Chocolate consumption also causes your brain to release the pleasure chemical, dopamine, which will put anybody in the mood for love. Another interesting and amazing statistic is that the brain, which is only two percent of a person's body weight, consumes twenty per cent of the used calories.

Eat chocolate regularly and your marriage will experience an ever-growing love that will be coupled with a positive mood enhancer. Chocolate is indeed the gift that keeps giving.

跟她姐妹和朋友们炫耀，她也喜欢在房间里摆放鲜花，而且这是给我们俩共同的礼物，我们可以共赏鲜花、共品花香，也可以在床上抱在一起分享甜点。

买一束鲜花或美味甜点回家并不费事，但出于各种原因，人们往往会忘记。我建议要养成习惯，每周至少带一样上述礼物回家，这样会让你的伴侣快乐，你也会因此而快乐。当我们关心的人面露笑容时，我们会更欢喜。

我可爱美丽的太太喜欢巧克力，送她巧克力作为惊喜礼物绝对不会错。精美手工巧克力的美妙之处在于包装异常亮眼，外盒装饰精美，内置巧克力更是值得欣赏的艺术品，这种礼物效果最佳。当她打开盒子时，精致巧克力的香味令人垂涎，尝上一口会立即改善心情。我太太心情一直不错，要是再来一块美味巧克力，她就会飘飘然。“巧克力幸福”是真实存在的。

更重要的是，巧克力作为礼物可以一直赠送，因为它对健康有益。适量食用巧克力，能降低罹患某些疾病的风险。有很多科学证据表明，黑巧克力能促进心脏健康。黑巧克力中的抗氧化剂已被证明可以降低血压、减少凝血的风险、增加心脏的血液循环，从而降低中风和因冠心病而死亡的风险。黑巧克力还富含抗氧化剂类黄酮，对心脏健康有益。一项研究表明，每周适量食用巧克力能将死于中风的风险明显降低。

巧克力也被证实有助于缓解抑郁症状。巧克力中含有苯乙胺（PEA），这种化学物质可以改善人的情绪，还含有神经递质血清素，是一种天然的情绪稳定剂，可以改善情绪，降低焦虑和抑郁的症状。食用巧克力还会让大脑释放令人愉悦的化学物质多巴胺，能让任何人都有恋爱的心情。另一个有趣而惊人的统计数据是，大脑只占自身体重的百分之二，却能消耗百分之二十的总热量。

经常食用巧克力，伴随着积极的情绪增强剂，能让婚姻更美满持久。巧克力作为经典礼物确实适合经常馈赠。

49. LONG WALKS. MEDITATION, OR A TRIP TO THE GYM ARE GREAT WAYS TO OVERCOME CONFUSION AND FIND PEACE

Being able to find inner peace will help you in every aspect of your life, from business to family, and for the purposes of this book, your love life. When you are overwhelmed, you lose that peace. One of the best ways to get your thinking back on a linear peaceful track is to take a long walk or go to the gym. Physical exertion has a way of increasing focus and clearing your mind. It is proven that physical activity will immediately increase the norepinephrine, dopamine, and serotonin levels in your brain. These all directly affect your attention levels and focus. Exercising also helps your nervous system to relax and remove stress. If your mind is spinning or you are feeling overwhelmed, working out or taking a walk can help to quiet your brain and help you discover solutions to problems, thus reducing stress.

If you cannot workout, meditation has similar benefits. Clearing your mind of all distractions allows it to focus on the things that matter, and thus find conclusions you could never reach by overthinking. The key is to find a way to let your mind relax. For some people, this may be best accomplished through strenuous exercise, for others, it may be a nice quiet walk through nature, or yoga, or meditation.

I have a friend who found that he and his wife had a healthier relationship when he was able to go to the gym at least three times a week. He claimed that this helped him get out his aggressions and focus his mind on what really mattered…his family and relationship. He would return home happy, feeling good, and eager to please.

49 放松大脑

保持内心平静，会对生活的各个层面大有助益，包括从事业到家庭等各方面，也对感情生活更有帮助。当人在不知所措时，内心就会失去平静。能平复心态的最好方法之一就是坚持散步或健身。体育锻炼能使人的思想更专注、思维更清晰。事实证明，体育活动会促进大脑分泌去甲肾上腺素、多巴胺和血清素，这些都直接影响人的注意力。锻炼还有助于让神经系统放松，排解压力。当人思维混乱、不知所措时，锻炼或散步有助于大脑放松，便于找到解决方案，从而减轻压力。

如果你不方便锻炼，也可以用冥想代替。清除干扰因素，集中思维，有助于发现之前很难想到的解决方法。关键在于要想办法放松大脑，对某些人来说，通过剧烈运动就能实现，而对另一些人而言，在大自然中安静散步、做瑜伽或者冥想也能实现。

我有一个朋友，当他每周至少健身三次时，他会感觉自己和爱人的关系更和谐了。他说这样有助于摆脱攻击性，把注意力集中在真正重要的事情上——他的家庭和感情生活。他健身之后回家时会很高兴，感觉很棒，并渴望给他人带来欢乐。

50. BEING KIND IS ALWAYS IMPORTANT

It goes without saying that we should continuously be kind to our significant other. That is obvious, but you would be surprised how often the opposite is true. What is less obvious is the importance of being kind to others outside of your home, and how that can directly affect your relationship with your spouse. When we are kind, we typically receive gratitude in return. This affects our self-confidence and how we view ourselves. It doesn't matter if you are giving a few bucks to a man on the street playing the trumpet, or to a charity helping underprivileged children, or even assisting an elderly person load groceries into their car. The act itself will positively change how we see ourselves, thus altering how we interact with everyone else in our lives. When you see yourself as a kind and gregarious person, you are more likely to behave as one at home with your spouse.

Being a kind and giving person will also affect how your significant other sees you. If you are the type of person to never hold a door open, throw away your trash, or display basic manners, your spouse will notice, and it will negatively influence how they view you. Rather than viewing you like the good person you surely are in your heart, they will see you as an unkind, unloving person, which will naturally damage your relationship. How you treat others outside of the house can directly alter how you are viewed inside the house, and hurt or help your relationship.

It is important to always be kind to everyone you meet. You may not see how it relates to your relationship at home, but it does, and it will. Work to keep your heart open. If you see someone who needs a hand, or perhaps a compliment, be the one to give it to them. You will be making their day, and simultaneously strengthening your relationship.

50 善待他人

毋庸置疑，我们应该一直善待自己的伴侣，这是显而易见的事，令人惊讶的是，事实往往相反。我们不太在意善待外人的重要性，而这恰恰会直接影响你与伴侣的关系。当我们善待他人时，就会得到感激的回报，能增加自信和提升自我。不管是送给街上吹小号的人几块钱，还是给帮助贫困儿童的慈善机构募捐，甚至只是帮助老人把日用品装上车，都是善待他人，这种行为本身会积极改善我们对自己的看法，从而改善我们与生活中其他人的交往模式。当你认为自己是善良随和的人时，就能和伴侣同心同德。

做一个温和善良、乐于奉献的人也会影响伴侣对你的看法。如果你是那种从不帮忙开门、不扔垃圾、缺乏基本礼仪的人，你的伴侣会注意到，这不利于伴侣对你的看法，即使你内心是个善良的好人，对方也会认为你不友善、没爱心，自然会破坏你们的感情。你在外面待人接物的方式会直接改变你在家中的形象，也会影响夫妻感情关系。

要善待遇到的每个人，这一点很重要，虽然这看起来和家庭婚姻没什么联系，但其实不然，它们有很大关系。要努力敞开胸怀，看到有人需要帮助，或者需要赞美，我们就去给予，这样就能让别人开心，同时也可以拉近你们的关系。

51. COMPROMISE IS A MUST

"I'm right."

"No, I'm right!"

"NO, I'm right!!"

"NO, I'M RIGHT!!!"

Sound familiar? Too many relationships experience troubles because of basic miscommunications or an inability to find a compromise. It can be hard to let go of your pride, and once you get angry, it can be near impossible to see a situation from a different point of view. This in turn will lead to bigger fights. The solution? Be open to compromise or to being wrong altogether.

I know my wife is almost always right on the rare occasion when we have a minor disagreement, but when we just cannot see eye to eye, we are always able to find a compromise.

They say in a compromise, no one is happy. I disagree with this. I fully believe that you are almost always able to find a compromise where everyone is happy, or if it is an argument over something stupid, why care? Just agree and move on. Why risk the happiness of your relationship over a disagreement about curtains, or how you should stack your cups? Move on and be happy.

I have a friend who got divorced because he could never let anything go. Whenever he and his wife got into an argument, he would never back down or compromise. Even if she proved him to be completely wrong, he would change his premise and persist that he was right all along. This of course made their home life terrible. He eventually saw the error of his ways after losing his marriage and after much soul searching. He told me how much he regrets always having to be right, and never being able to find a middle ground. He admitted that most of the things they fought about were totally irrelevant, and the few issues that weren't could have easily been solved by meeting in the middle. Thankfully he learned his lesson, albeit too late,

If you have a disagreement with your significant other, find a middle ground that makes you both happy, but first ask yourself, is this even a fight worth having?

51 学会妥协

“我是对的。”

“不，我是对的！”

“不，我是对的！！”

“不，我是对的！！！”

听起来是不是很熟悉？有很多人感情关系出现问题，都是因为简单误解或不知妥协。放下自尊很难，一旦生气了，就不太可能从不同的角度看问题，从而导致吵架升级。要怎么解决呢？只要学会妥协或学会认错。

我和爱人很少吵架，偶尔有小分歧的时候，也基本都是她对，但当我们不能统一意见时，也都能做到妥协。

有人说，一旦妥协，双方都会不满意。我不同意这一观点，我确信能找到双方都可以接受的妥协方式，但如果是为了一些愚蠢的事情而争论，为什么要在意呢？只要同意对方观点就完事了，为什么要为了窗帘或杯子如何堆放的小事而拿两人的感情冒险呢？凡事都要向前看，要快乐地生活。

我有个朋友离婚了，因为他总是看不开，每次和爱人发生争执时，从不让步或妥协，即使对方证明他完全错了，他也会改变说法，坚持认为自己一直都对，这当然迫使家庭生活越来越糟。离婚后他自我反省，终于认识到自己的错误，他说特别后悔之前总是坚持自己是对的，从不妥协。他承认引发争吵的基本都是无关紧要的小事，而且这些小事本就可以通过妥协来轻松解决。谢天谢地他终于吸取了教训，只是为时已晚。

如果你和伴侣发生争执，务必找到让双方都满意的妥协方式，但首先要问自己，这事值得争吵吗？

52. EMPOWERMENT

My wife is a major source of my empowerment. She makes me feel like a million dollars! Her loves gives me the confidence to do things I would never attempt without her presence. I know that even if the risks I take do not workout, she will still be at home, waiting for me, loving me.

Couples need to empower one another. Too often, the opposite occurs. Rather than being the source of each other's strength, they become the reason for their insecurities and low self-esteem, sometimes directly contributing to their downfall. Rather than building each other up, they tear one another down, commenting on the other's insecurities or outright insulting each other. This will not only hurt your relationship, but it can tank your professional aspirations. When the person you love most belittles you, it can break your self-confidence and crush your dreams.

It does not have to be this way. You can be the light that shines and the source of power that helps your spouse to gain enough confidence to face each new day with a positive attitude. For all of the negatives that can result from a soured relationship in which a couple does not empower one another, the world is at the fingertips of the couple who does. When your significant other gives you endless support, you will find confidence you never knew you possessed. It will allow you to develop a winning mindset, which in turn will allow you to take chances and seize opportunities. I empower my wife every chance I get. This is not difficult to do because there are so many positive things about her.

When you are married, you should make a point to empower your significant other. Talk them up, compliment them, and let them know that you support and believe in them. Never let them leave the house thinking that you believe they will fail. Be an undrainable well of love and comfort. It will make a difference in how they perform at work and at home. An empowered person, is a confident person, a happy person, and is a pleasure to be around. Your job is to make your spouse become a person who is unstoppable.

52 赋予力量

我太太是我的力量源泉，她让我觉得自己像个百万富翁！她的爱给了我信心，如果没有她在身边，很多事我永远都不敢做。我知道，即使我因冒进而失利，她依然会在家里等我、爱我。

夫妻需要相互给予力量，但现实往往相反，两人不是彼此力量的源泉，而是让对方感到不安和自卑的原因，这有时会直接导致两败俱伤。两人不是互相扶持，而是互相拆台、指责对方，或者直接污蔑对方，这不仅会伤害两人的感情，还会毁掉双方的职业抱负。被最爱的人轻视，会让你失去自信、梦想破灭。

其实完全可以不必如此，你可以成为伴侣引路的明灯和力量的源泉，让伴侣信心满满，以积极的态度面对每一天。如果夫妻不能互相给予力量，就会产生很多负面影响，而相互给予力量的夫妻能让世界尽在掌握之中。当伴侣全力支持你时，你能激发出全部自信，拥有成功的心态，进而抓住机遇。我总是赋予太太力量，这并不难，因为她身上有很多正能量。

结婚后更应该赋予伴侣力量，要表扬、称赞对方，让对方知道你的支持和信任。永远不要让对方怀着被你轻视的心情走出家门。要源源不断地提供关爱与慰藉，让伴侣在工作和生活中信心百倍。被赋予力量的人，是自信而快乐的人，能给身边人带来欢笑。你要做的就是让伴侣成为勇往直前的人。

53. EMPATHY

What is empathy? It is a word that is bandied about quite a bit. The simple definition is that it is the ability to share and understand the emotions and feelings of another human being. To have a successful marriage, you must be able to empathize with your significant other. That means not only intellectually understand their position on a matter, but also how it makes them feel. This will allow you to put yourself in their shoes, and thus fully understand their point of view and better understand them as a person.

Being empathic is a natural state of being for many people. If you are not one of these people, the good news is with awareness you can learn to be empathetic. To develop empathy, one needs to not only listen, they also need to observe others closely, notice their behaviors, subtle indications, non-verbal expressions, body language, and environmental factors. This cannot be emphasized enough: "Listening is not only hearing words." At times, what someone articulates is only a fraction of the full story. By honing your observation skills, you can have a better understanding of someone else's experience.

It is important to learn the skill of being empathetic as it will make you more aware of the world around you. Being in touch and in tune with what's going on around you is a recipe for success. An empathetic person normally has a high emotion quotient, an "EQ." When it comes to success, many people believe that a high EQ is more important than a high IQ.

The ability to empathize gives us insight into one another's world view. When we only look at the world from our perspective, we miss out on a lot. This can cause conflict in our lives, or perhaps simply be the reason we miss a lot of the beauty life has to offer. You should not only empathize when there is a tragedy, you can also do so to better appreciate the world around you.

Watching my wife appreciate a sunrise from our balcony has helped me to better grasp its beauty, and more fully see it myself. Think about it, a sunrise is all about new chances, hope, and a reminder that yesterday is gone. Her love of certain foods has expanded my palette also. I have learned to better, laugh, cry, and be open through

53 学会共情

什么是共情？这是一个经常被提及的词汇，简单来说是指分享和理解另一个人的情绪和感受的能力。要拥有成功的婚姻，就必须学会与伴侣共情，这意味着不仅要从理智上理解对方对某事的看法，还要了解对方的感受，这样才能让你设身处地为对方着想，从而充分理解其观点看法，进一步理解这个人。

对很多人来说，共情是天性，如果你不能共情，也没关系，只要用心就能学会。要想与人共情，不仅需要倾听，还需要仔细观察，注意对方的行为举止、面部表情、肢体语言和环境因素。有一点特别重要："倾听不仅仅是倾听话语。"有时某人所能表达的只是整件事的一小部分，通过磨炼观察的技巧，就能更容易理解别人的感受。

学会共情非常重要，它能让你更了解周围世界，而与外界发生的事情保持联系和实时同步是成功的秘诀。善于共情的人通常情商（EQ）都较高。说到成功，很多人认为高情商比高智商更重要。

学会共情就能洞察他人的世界观。当人们只从自己的角度看世界时，他们有可能会在生活中引发矛盾，或者会错过生活中的许多美好。在不幸的事情发生时要学会共情，好事发生的时候也需要共情，这能让你更好地欣赏周围世界。

看着爱人站在阳台上欣赏日出，我更能领悟日出的美丽，也对事物看得更全面。想想看，日出代表着新的机遇和希望，提醒我们昨天已经过去。她对某些食物的喜爱也让我大饱口福。通过共情，我了解到她的世界观，让我

empathizing with her outlook on the world. This has made me a better and more well-rounded individual.

When you empathize with a person, you are able to connect with them on a higher plane. For a moment, rather than viewing the universe from two possibly conflicting worldviews, you see it as one. At this point, you are able to better understand the other person's opinions and actions. A big problem with the world is the lack of empathy many people have. Many are so certain their outlook is correct, they refuse to view things from any other perspective. By allowing yourself to see the world from your spouse's point of view, you will grow closer together and gain a new respect for the beauty that is always around you. The bottom line is people who practice being empathic will develop a higher EQ as a direct result.

Success and EQ go hand in glove, meaning that such a person normally has more success than other people at all levels (romance, work, school). With a high EQ, your romance and marriage benefit as you will now be more in sync with your spouse by better understanding their needs and point of view at all levels. Learning to be empathic with your spouse can positively change the course of your marriage. It will help in building your romance to higher and higher levels.

By working on being empathic, you will become a much better observer and listener. Remember, being empathic is much more than words, it is all about observation. It is a well-known fact that good listening skills are a part of the formula for success when it comes to relationships.

54. DON'T ALWAYS BE THE BOSS

Forget always being the boss. As far as I am concerned, you never need to be the boss! I feel no desire to be the "boss" in my relationship. I view it as a partnership. In a partnership, no one is the boss. My wife is not my sidekick, she is my equal, thus we make decisions together. When she has a better idea than I have, which is most of the time, we do what she

成为更好的自己，并学会了欢笑、哭泣以及乐观待人，让我成为更优秀、更全面的人。

当你与某人共情时，就能在更高层次上与对方心意相通。有那么一刻，你们不是从两种可能相互冲突的世界观来看待宇宙万物，而是用同一个世界观去看，这能让你更加理解对方的观点和行为。这个世界的一大问题就是太多人缺乏共情的能力。很多人总是认为自己的观点是正确的，拒绝从任何其他角度看问题。允许自己从伴侣的角度看世界，会让两人关系更亲密，能使人更加尊重身边的美好事物。最重要的是，学会共情的人能直接提高自己的情商。

成功和情商密切相关，情商高的人通常在各个层面（感情、工作、学习）都比其他人更成功。拥有高情商也会在感情和婚姻方面受益，因为你能与伴侣更加同步，能更加理解伴侣在各个层面的需求和看法。学会与伴侣共情可以积极改善婚姻状况，有助于两人的感情越来越甜蜜。

通过与他人共情，你会成为更好的观察者和倾听者。记住，共情不仅仅是听对方所说的话，还要仔细观察。众所周知，在感情关系中，良好的倾听技能是成功的一半。

54 别装老板

不要总是装作老板。在我看来，永远都不要当老板！我不想在感情关系中当“老板”，我认为我们是合作关系，在合作关系中，没有人是老板。我太太不是我的跟班，她和我是平等的，所以我们一起做决定。当她的主意更

has proposed. On the rare occasion that I have the better idea, we do whatever I have come up with. We never have a power struggle or fight over who is in charge, because we already know… we both are.

A marriage is meant to be a partnership, not a hero and side-kick dynamic. In a partnership, each partner has their strengths, and each has their weaknesses. In the best partnerships, one partner's strengths complement the other's weaknesses, so together they are unstoppable. This is true in business, and it is equally true in a marriage. My wife is sweet, empathetic, and loving in a way I could never be. Her attention to detail is impeccable, and she has a fantastic memory. These characteristics are a perfect match for my personality.

When you view a marriage from a boss/worker dynamic, you are just asking for trouble. No one likes to be bossed around. Some people will put up with it for a while, but it is not a healthy long-term strategy. It also implies that only one person's ideas matter. Not only is this not true, you are doing yourself and your relationship a disservice by silencing ideas that may change your life for the better!

Always remember that your marriage is a partnership, and you are both working together for its success. The main takeaway with this point is that if you try to be the boss of the relationship, the odds are you will stop listening. We all know the key to all success is to listen. So, stop trying to be the boss of your spouse, and instead make it your goal to be in harmony with each other.

55.UNDERSTAND THAT PEOPLE CHANGE

I am not talking about your spouse; I am speaking about friends and family. We all hopefully grow and evolve as we get older, but that is something you are supposed to do WITH your spouse, not apart from them. The same is not true for the other people in your life. Things happen in everyone's lives that can change them for the better, and sadly, for the worst also. While we all hope that no tragedy befalls anyone, that is not

好时——而且多数情况如此——我们就按照她的建议去做，偶尔我有更好的主意，就照我想的去做。我们从来没有因为谁做主而吵架，因为我们知道，我俩都能做主。

在婚姻中，两人是合作关系，不是主角和跟班的关系。在合作关系中，双方都有自己的长处，也都有各自的弱点。最好的合作关系，就是双方的优势和劣势能够互补，两方合作就能天下无敌，做生意时如此，婚姻也是如此。我太太和蔼可亲、善解人意、充满爱心，这是我永远无法做到的，她对细节的关注更是令人叫绝，而且她的记忆力超强，这些优点和我的个性正好互补。

如果从老板和员工的角度来看待婚姻，那就是自找麻烦。没有人愿意总被别人使唤，有些人会忍受一时，但绝非长久之计，这也意味着只有一方的想法重要，这不仅是错误的，还会扼杀能改善生活的想法，对你自己和你们的感情都是一种伤害！

千万记住，婚姻是合作关系，你们都在为美满的婚姻而共同奋斗。这一条目的主要结论是，如果你想在婚姻关系中当老板，就不会再倾听。我们都知道，成功的关键在于倾听，所以别再装作伴侣的老板，而要将和谐相处作为目标。

55 人都会变

我不是说伴侣，我说的是朋友和家人。我们都希望随着年龄的增长而成长和进步，但这应该是和伴侣共同经历，而不是独自经历。你生命中的其他人就不必如此了。每个人的生活中都会发生一些事情，这些事情会让人变得更好，也可能让人变得更糟。虽然我们都不希望悲剧降临到任何人身上，但

reality.

You should always be there for your friends and family in their time of need. However, sometimes these events cause people to permanently alter their core personalities. When this occurs, you should not hate them or even judge them. That does not mean you should let it negatively affect your marital relationship. If you find yourself in this situation, you should speak with your significant other about the best path forward. This may mean seeing them less, taking a break from them or not seeing them at all. No matter what conclusion you reach, reach it together. Never do anything independently.

On that same note, you should never criticize your spouse's friends. It is so easy to find flaws in your spouse's friends and point them out, but this is always a mistake. The one exception is if they are dangerous or detrimental. At that point, it is your responsibility to bring it up. This will not be an easy conversation, and there is a good chance your husband or wife will immediately take the defensive position. Hopefully you have enough respect for one another to be able to carry out an intelligent and well-reasoned discussion and come to a conclusion that is best for both of you.

It is a tragedy that life can cause people to change for the worse, but it is also a reality and one that must be faced. To ignore it is to put your relationship, and possibly the safety of you and your wife, at risk. Understand, do not hate anyone, but make the decisions that are best for you and your family.

56.NEVER BE A KNOW-IT-ALL WITH YOUR SPOUSE

Know-it-alls are among the most unliked people in the world. Even a master will tell you there is always more to learn. Such a person will not listen, as they believe they already know everything. With your spouse, this is asking for trouble. Even in areas where I'm an expert, I share my thoughts with my wife, and then I ask for her opinion or insight. Subsequently, I have been humbled to discover I was not as much of an expert on a

有时事与愿违。

在朋友和家人需要你的时候，你应该一直陪在他们身边。然而，有时变故会导致人的性情大变，当这种情况发生时，你不应该憎恨他们，甚至不应该评判他们，但并不意味着让这些人对你的婚姻关系产生负面影响。如果你发现自己处于这种情况，应该和伴侣谈谈最佳解决方式，比如尽量少和这些人接触，离开一段时间，或者根本不见他们。无论你们得出什么结论，都要两人一起商量，永远不要自行决断。

同样，你也不应该评论伴侣的朋友。发现对方朋友的缺点并指出来很容易，但这样做不对，除非他们是危险或有害的朋友，这时你就有责任提出来。这不是一场轻松的谈话，而且很有可能你的伴侣会立即维护朋友。我希望夫妻双方能彼此尊重，进行明智而理性的讨论，并找到对两人都有利的解决方案。

生活可以使人变得更糟，这虽然是一个悲剧，更是必须面对的现实。忽视这些，就是把你们的感情——可能还有你和伴侣的安全——置于危险之中。要明白，你不可能憎恨任何人，但要做出对你和家人最好的决定。

56 学无止境

万事通是世界上最不受欢迎的人，即使是大师级人物也会说学无止境。认为自己是万事通的人不会倾听，因为他们认为自己无所不知。这样对待伴侣就属于自讨苦吃。即使在我的专业领域，我也会和爱人分享看法，征求她的想法或见解，她总能令我自愧不如，随后我会发现，在这一领域里，我并非想象中那样专业。

particular subject as I thought.

When you are a know-it-all, you eliminate your opportunities to learn and grow as a person. Instead, you alienate everyone around you. Know-it-alls believe people respect them for their vast well of knowledge. In reality, people resent them. Even if they are the expert, and do know everything about a subject, people do not like to be talked down to. They also do not like to be talked over, and made to feel like their ideas do not matter. As such, it is irrelevant how much a know-it-all knows, as no one is listening.

This is important to keep in mind when you are dealing with your spouse. If behaving like a know-it-all can have such a negative reaction on strangers, who are not invested in you, imagine how someone who loves you will feel when you treat them with such disrespect. It will cause them to resent you and pay less attention to what you are professing. It is not about being right, it is about being kind, and listening.

In almost every interaction I have had with a know-it-all, they have in fact not known it all. Had they shown a little humility, they could have increased their knowledge. Never act like you know everything, there is always more to learn! The moral of this story is that you need to become a better listener because even a master has more to learn.

57. DON'T FORGET TO SMILE

Smiles are difference makers. They are contagious and have a substantial impact on others. They can entirely turn someone's day around. The most important other is your "significant other." To smile often around your spouse is crucial, even if it is a bit forced. After a while you will no longer need to force the smile, as you will notice the mood changing effects of your smile on your husband or wife, and on yourself. A smile can brighten a boring mood and turn around the environment immediately. My wife and I carry this to a higher level, as we are always laughing at absolutely nothing. We find joy in every moment, and happiness in the strangest places.

I learned the power of a smile in business. Most people know that it is important

当你自认为是万事通时，就会失去学习和成长的机会，也会疏远周围的人。万事通认为自己知识丰富，因而会受到尊敬，实际上却令人厌恶，即使他们是专家，并且对某一领域了如指掌，也会因为其高人一等的态度令人生厌。万事通也不喜欢被别人说服，这会显得他们的想法不重要，因此，万事通的知识再多也没用，因为没有人听。

与伴侣相处时，千万记住这一点。如果在毫无关系的陌生人面前充当万事通，会产生如此负面的反应，那么想象一下，对爱你的人如此不尊重时，对方会是什么感受？这会让对方怨恨你，不在意你的教导。其实，关键不在于谁对谁错，而在于是否能善待他人，是否能倾听他人。

每当和这些万事通打交道时，我就发现，他们实际上并不是无所不知。如果他们能谦虚一点，反倒能增长知识。千万别当万事通，学无止境！最重要的是，要成为更好的倾听者，因为即使是大师也有很多东西要学。

57 时常微笑

微笑能改变一切，且具有传染性，能对他人有很大影响，更能改善人的心情。伴侣是你生命中最重要的人，即便强迫自己，也要在伴侣面前时常微笑，这一点非常重要。一段时间后，你就不需要再强迫自己，因为你的笑容已经改善了两人的情绪。一个微笑可以把烦恼的情绪一扫而光，让周围环境熠熠生辉。我和太太更是把这一点做到了极致，因为我俩经常对着毫无意义的事情发笑，我们每时每刻都能找到快乐，在最奇怪的地方也能找到幸福。

我明白微笑在工作中的重要性。很多人都知道，在开会或其他职业场合

to smile and put on a happy face in meetings and other professional scenarios, but then they often do not carry that knowledge over into their home. Rather than smiling at their significant other, they unload all of their stress onto them. While it is important to be able to do this, it is more important to be able to smile. Find joy, and your stress will disappear like it was never there.

Even if you are in a bad mood, go ahead and smile anyway. Actually, if you are in a bad mood, it is more important than ever to smile. When you smile, it not only brightens the day of others, but it also brightens your own day. Smiling has been proven to elevate your mood and the mood of those around you. Keep an upbeat and positive attitude even when times are tough, and it will carry you to the blue skies we all desire.

When I return home after being out all day, seeing my charming wife smile instantly improves my mood. If I was in a good mood before she smiled at me, I am in an ever-better mood afterward. On the times that I have been in a bad mood, her smile is enough to turn my day around. Suddenly I am happy. I smile back, and we have a great evening.

The takeaway is simple, learn to smile and your marriage will be that much happier.

58. DO NOT STRANGLE YOUR RELATIONSHIP BY PUTTING YOUR SPOUSE ON A BUDGET

Mi casa es su casa is a Spanish phrase that means my house is your house. In marriage, this phrase should be carried further if you believe, like I do, that being in harmony is important. My wife and I share all things. To me, the relationship must be in balance, and putting a spouse on a budget accomplishes the opposite. It gives the other person the idea that you do not trust them. It says you are not 100 percent committed to the marriage, and you do not believe that they are either.

In our marriage, both of us are all in, and we share all assets equally. Yes, we live by an overall budget, but we do not have one between us. Neither of us want to exploit our shared budget and thus will not abuse it. We understand that we share everything, and that means

要面带笑容，却不明白这一理论在家也适用。不仅不对伴侣微笑，还把所有的压力都倾泻给对方，虽然想减轻压力很重要，但能够微笑更重要，找到快乐，压力自会消失，就像从未有过一样。

即使你心情不好，也要微笑。实际上，心情不好的时候，更需要微笑。当你微笑时，不仅能让别人愉悦，也能让自己高兴。实践证明，微笑可以改善自己和他人的情绪。即使在困难的时候，我们也要保持乐观向上的态度，去拥抱我们渴望的蓝天。

当我外出一天回到家时，看到爱妻面露笑容，我的心情顿时好转。如果没看到她笑容之前我心情就很好，那么在看到笑容之后，心情就会更好。在我郁闷的时候，她的微笑能让我转变心情，我会立刻高兴起来，也会对她微笑，然后一起度过美好的夜晚。

结论很简单，时常微笑，你的婚姻会更幸福。

58 共同预算

Mi casa es su casa 是一句西班牙语，意思是我家就是你家。在婚姻中，如果你像我一样认为和谐最重要，那么这句话就应该大为推广。我和爱人共享一切。在我看来，感情关系必须处于平衡状态，而给伴侣做预算则会适得其反，会让对方感觉不被信任，也说明你并没有百分之百地投入这段婚姻关系中，而你也不相信对方会全部投入。

在我俩的婚姻中，双方都是全身心投入，我们平等共享所有财产。是的，我们只有一个共同预算，不分摊。我们都不会占用资源，不会乱用共同的预算。我们明白要共享一切，不会贪占。

not taking advantage.

When you put someone on a budget, you are telling them you think they are an irresponsible person, that they are going to go on shopping sprees and waste tons of money. This lack of trust can in turn cause them to do just that. A couple that respects one another will not waste their resources, no matter how vast they may be. I think of my wife before making any purchase and she does the same, not because we cannot afford it, but because I do not wish to be wasteful. Being wasteful is a terrible habit. It is disrespectful to people with less, it is disrespectful to your maker who blessed you with wealth, and it is disrespectful to your spouse.

In a marriage, a couple should share all things at all times. You are in this life together, and to thrive, you must act as one.

59. CONSIDER HAVING A PET

My wife and I do not have a pet, but for some, it is an absolutely wonderful idea! We are focused on having a family at the moment, so it is not currently a priority for us. A pet can help a couple find love as they will both equally care about the animal. It will also give a couple a common goal and purpose. A lot of couples get a cat or a dog to prepare them for having a child. Having a pet makes you completely responsible for the life and wellbeing of another creature. This is a responsibility that cannot be taken lightly. If you go out for dinner and drinks and forget to feed it, it goes hungry. If you don't take it outside to do its business, it will have an accident inside. If you do not properly discipline it, it will misbehave. Being responsible for another life is the best team building exercise I can think of!

In addition to bringing you and your significant other closer together, pets are known to reduce stress. People with a dog are 24% less likely to die from all cause-related mortality issues. Animals also provide companionship, and most importantly, love. They can be the one missing element that turns a house into a home!

Having a pet to love with the one you cherish is a great way for you and your husband's or wife's love for each other to blossom. The pet will open your heart, and not only will it

如果你给某人做预算，则表明你认为对方不负责任，会疯狂购物、浪费钱财，缺乏信任就会导致适得其反。互相敬重的夫妇，不论多富有，也不会浪费自家的资源。我在买任何东西之前都会想到我太太，她亦如此，不是因为我们买不起，而是因为不想浪费。浪费是特别不好的习惯，是对穷苦人的不尊重，是对赐予财富的造物主的不尊重，是对伴侣的不尊重。

在婚姻中，夫妻双方应该共享一切，今生今世要生活在一起，为了长久的幸福，必须团结一致。

59 养只宠物

我和太太没养宠物，但对一些人来说，这绝对是个好主意！我俩现在正专注于组建家庭，所以目前它还不是我们的首要任务。夫妻一起照看宠物，有助于两人更懂爱，让两人能够拥有共同目标。因为要生小孩，很多夫妇会养猫或养狗。养宠物就要对这个小生命的起居和健康完全负责，确实责任重大。如果你出去大吃大喝而忘了喂它，它就会挨饿；如果你不带它到外面遛遛，它就会在家里生事；如果你不好好管教它，它就会不听话。据我所知，对另一个生命负责，是最好的团队建设训练！

养宠物不仅能让你和伴侣更亲密，还能减轻压力。宠物还能提供陪伴，最重要的是，能提供爱。有了宠物，一所房子就能变成一个家！

养只宠物，和你珍惜的人一起去爱护，是让你和伴侣彼此之爱开花结果的最好方法。宠物能打开你的心扉，会走进你和伴侣的内心。当你俩把宠物从小养到大时，你们会变得更加亲密。在这段时间里，你会与伴侣就宠物的

step in, but so will your spouse. You will grow closer together as you raise your pet from infancy to adulthood. During that time, you will learn to communicate with your spouse about decisions for your animal. Do you get it fixed or do you breed it? Is it an inside or outside pet? Is it allowed on the bed? These are all simple questions, but finding the solution with your partner will deepen the love you share.

Pets are a great way to strengthen an already strong relationship. One of my friends turned his marriage around by getting his wife a dog. He travels almost six months each year and his wife was naturally lonely when he was gone. It was causing her to be insecure and question the relationship. She asked him more than once if he had girlfriends in other cities. After he gifted her the cute dog, all this changed. They are now happy and very much in love.

60. IF YOU WANT A ROMANTIC MARRIAGE, STAY IN SHAPE

Life is a lot easier to enjoy when you are in shape. When it is a struggle to get out of bed in the morning, or to hoist yourself off the couch, life begins to get a bit complicated. When you are in shape, the world is available to you. If you want to go for a hike, all you need to do is find a mountain. If you want to ski, same thing. Even your love life will be much more active if you are in good physical condition. Your spouse will find you more desirable and you will find that you have an increased libido to match theirs.

I get up to exercise first thing every morning, and it is for a different reason than you may think. My first priority is to remove stress from my life. Exercise can be similar to meditation. The exercise will boost your feel-good endorphins, causing you to forget about your troubles. So for me, the physical benefits are just a bonus.

Regular exercise will also increase your self-confidence, improve your mood, help you relax, and lower symptoms of depression and anxiety. Exercise can also improve your sleep, which is often disrupted by stress, depression, and anxiety. It can ease your stress levels and give you a sense of command over your body and your life. The result will be a much better

问题进行沟通，是否给宠物绝育？是室内宠物还是室外宠物？可以放在床上吗？这些都是简单的问题，但是和伴侣一起找到解决方案能加深你们之间的爱。

宠物能加强本就牢固的感情关系。我的一个朋友送给他妻子一条狗，因而使他的婚姻有了转机。丈夫每年要出差将近六个月，当他不在的时候，妻子自然会很孤独，因而没有安全感，开始质疑两人的感情。妻子不止一次质问丈夫在其他城市是否有女人。当丈夫把这只可爱的狗狗送给妻子之后，一切都变了。他们现在很幸福，非常相爱。

60 保持体形

身体健康才能享受生活。如果每天早上起床都很困难，或者要费好大力气才能从沙发上起身，生活就不那么美好了。当你拥有好身材时，整个世界都会向你招手。如果想徒步旅行就找一座山去旅行，想要滑雪就去滑雪。身体健康还会给爱情生活增添活力，你的伴侣会更满意，而你也能在各方面满足伴侣的需求。

我每天早上起床的第一件事就是锻炼，个中原因可能和你想的不一样，我主要是想减压，锻炼有时类似于冥想。锻炼身体有助于分泌内啡肽，能让人忘记烦恼，所以对我来说，身体健康只是意外收获。

经常锻炼还能令人增加自信、改善情绪、放松身心，并能缓解抑郁和焦虑的症状。压力、抑郁和焦虑容易造成失眠，健身则能改善睡眠。运动能减轻压力，让人能把握自己的身体，从而把握人生，享受美好的爱情。运动之后会让人感觉很棒，能更轻松、更平静地对待生活。压力小的人婚姻会更

love life also. You will be feeling good all the time and approach life in a more relaxed and calm manner. A person with lower stress levels certainly will have a better marriage.

The main reason you should want to be in shape is for yourself and your own health. If you want to live life to the fullest, you need to be able to remain active. If your wife or husband loves to hike and you want to go with them, you need to keep yourself in good physical shape. You do not want to be huffing and puffing behind them while they blaze up the trail. What fun is that? The second reason you should want to be in shape is to extend your longevity. People who take care of their bodies typically live longer, happier lives. That is more time you get to spend with the love of your life. You do not want to check out early because you could not stop drinking milkshakes and eating hamburgers! The third reason is obvious. Think about all the fun you can have when you and your significant other are in great shape! You are not limited by your physical condition. Plus, as a fringe benefit, you will look amazing doing it! So, you better take some pictures.

Exercising with your spouse is a great bonding activity. It gives you a common goal and purpose you can pursue together. It can also help you to reach goals you never thought were possible. It is amazing what you can do when you have the person you love beside you, supporting you all the way. Stay in shape together, laugh together, love life together!

61. IF YOU WANT TO SHOW YOU CARE, BUY HEALTH INSURANCE

It's easy to assume health will never be an issue for you or your spouse. Let's hope good health is your normal situation forever. However, sometimes things are out of our control and a good health insurance policy can be your spouse's saving grace. Talk about showing you care, buy you and your spouse a good supplemental health insurance policy, and no, I'm not an insurance salesperson. Most people have some sort of health insurance, but it is rarely enough to cover major medical expenses.

I have seen what can happen when tragedy strikes and people are unprepared. It is

美满。

保持体形的主要原因是为了自身健康。要想生活更加充实，就要保持活力。如果你的伴侣喜欢徒步旅行，而你也想参加，就需要保持良好的身体状态。你一定不愿意在伴侣火速前进的时候，自己却气喘吁吁地拖人后腿，这样多没意思！保持体形的第二个原因是能延长寿命。在意身体的人通常活得更长久、更幸福，也会有更多时间陪伴挚爱。你不会想因为无节制地食用奶昔和汉堡而让自己提早退出人生舞台吧！第三个原因很明显，想象一下，当你和伴侣都处于良好状态，不受身体状况的限制时，你们就能拥有所有乐趣！另外，你还能有意外收获，你会看起来很棒！所以要多拍些照片。

和伴侣一起锻炼能更好地增进感情，让你们拥有共同追求的目标，还能助你实现超出预期的梦想。当挚爱在你身边一直支持你的时候，你就能突破自我。一起健身，一起欢笑，一起热爱生活！

61 健康保险

人们很容易相信自己或伴侣永远不会出现健康问题，真希望大家都能永远健康。然而，有时候事情不由我们控制，买份健康保险能成为你和伴侣的救命稻草。要表示关心，就给你和伴侣买一份优质的补充健康保险。当然，我不是推销保险的。大多数人都有各种形式的健康保险，但都不足以支付重大医疗费用。

我看到过悲剧发生而人们毫无准备时的情景。很不幸，重大疾病就医时

unfortunate but true that a major illness requiring medical care can cost millions of dollars. With good health insurance, the policy will cover most of the costs.

You love your significant other and you want to be with them for as long as possible. One of the best ways to insure that this happens is to take steps to make certain they receive the best medical care, if they ever need it. If they never do, and we hope they do not, you have still given them the gift of peace of mind. They know that no matter what occurs, they will be covered, and they will be all right.

Health is one of the most precious things you have. It is paramount that you do everything in your power to make sure you do not lose it. Having a healthy diet, avoiding risks, and exercise are of course the most important part of that, but so is having insurance to cover you in case of catastrophe.

I love my wife. I want her to be with me forever and remain healthy throughout our lives. If there is something I can do to help her stay healthy, you better believe I am going to do it. The same is true for me. Everyone should have a family policy.

Health insurance is expensive, but I look at it as an investment. In fact, it is the only investment that I have ever made where I hope to lose my money. It is my goal to stay healthy and never get sick. I hope that I will never use the insurance policy.

Buying a good health insurance policy may be wasted money if it is never used. However, if a major illness occurs, it will be the best investment you have ever made. Keep yourself healthy, plan for the best, but prepare for the worst. Show your spouse you care by purchasing a supplemental health policy.

62. AT TIMES, YOU MUST GET OUT OF BALANCE TO BE IN BALANCE

The title of this point seems contradictory, but it's true. Relationships are a little like a pendulum. The important thing is to keep it from swinging too far to the left or right. To be equal and in balance all the time is an unrealistic goal. Life ebbs and flows, to expect it

真的需要花费数百万美元。如果买了优质的健康保险，它就能支付大部分费用。

你爱你的伴侣，愿意和对方永远在一起，那就要采取措施确保一旦伴侣需要，就能得到最好的医疗服务。如果对方不需要，那样更好，你也能让对方安心，知道无论发生什么，有保单托底，一切都能解决。

健康是人生最宝贵的事情之一，最重要的是，我们要想尽办法确保自身健康，均衡饮食、避免风险和锻炼身体当然是其中最重要的部分，但拥有保险同样重要，能以防万一。

我爱我太太，我希望她身强体健，永远和我在一起。如果能有什么方法让她永远健康，我一定会去做，我自己也是如此。

每个人都应该有一份家庭保险。健康保险不便宜，但我会视其为一种投资，实际上，这是我唯一希望赔钱的投资。我的目标是保持健康，永不生病。我希望永远都用不上保单。

买一份优质的健康保险，如果从来不用，可能就是浪费钱，然而，一旦发生重大疾病，这将是你所做的最好投资。要保持身体健康，就要做最好的打算，也要做最坏的准备。买份补充健康保险来表达你对伴侣的关心吧。

62 保持平衡

要保持平衡就要先打破平衡，这听起来似乎自我矛盾，但是事实如此。感情关系就像钟摆，关键要控制左右摆动的幅度不能过大，但一直保持摆动均衡不太现实。人生起伏不定，如果期望生活总是完美无缺，则注定要失

to always be picture perfect is to invite failure. You need to learn to appreciate the swings of the pendulum. It may be swinging to the left at the moment, but these tough times will only serve to make you better appreciate things when it swings back to the right. The key is to keep it from ever going too far in one direction.

People find peace in balance. Things can only be great for so long, they will always swing back the other way. A wise man will build a life to account for this motion and limit the violence of the pendulum's variations.

To have a happy relationship, you must not only focus on finding balance externally, you must find it inside of yourself. If you are not personally in balance, you cannot hope to maintain balance elsewhere. The key to finding balance within yourself is to not be led by your emotions. Understand that they are natural and should not be bottled up, but at the same time they should be examined and deciphered before being appropriately displayed. Many times you will find your emotional response to some stimuli was over the top or inappropriate. That is why you must have self-control until you figure out why you had such a response. A wise man will not overreact. Such reactions can hurt your relationship with your spouse also and be difficult to repair.

Keep balance with your partner and in your life, then all will work out right.

63. DON'T FLIRT YOUR WAY INTO TROUBLE

Being nice to everyone you meet is a great approach to life. To be kind and friendly is in my DNA. To give genuine compliments is a must in developing a strong relationship. However, I advise to be especially careful with the compliments that you give to people of the opposite sex. A compliment can easily be perceived as flirting if you are not careful.

First and foremost, it is never a good idea to mislead anyone. The words you say can often be taken in the wrong way. Instead of a compliment as you intended, a comment can be taken as "this person likes me." This can lead to big trouble, as suddenly that person may start chasing you for romance. Later, they may feel jilted if you don't respond to their

败。要学会欣赏钟摆的来回摆动，目前可能向左摆动，但这些艰难的时刻只会让你更加心存感激，并等待它摆回右侧。关键在于摆幅不能过大。

人们在平衡中找到安宁。事情的美好只能持续这么短的时间，之后总是会向相反的方向发展。智者会用人生的起伏来诠释这种摆动，并限制摆幅的剧烈程度。

为了拥有一段幸福的感情，你不仅要注重寻找外在的平衡，还必须找到自己内心的平衡。如果你自己不能保持平衡，就不能指望其他方面平衡。找到自我平衡的关键是不要被情绪所左右。要明白，情绪是天然的，不能隐藏，但同时在表露情绪之前，应该先检查和了解原因所在。很多时候，对一些刺激的情绪反应是过度或不当的，因此必须自我控制，弄清情绪反应的原因。聪明人不会反应过度，这种情绪也会伤害你和伴侣的关系，而且很难修复。

在生活中与伴侣保持平衡，一切都会好起来的。

63 避免调情

善待周围每个人是很好的生活方式，温和友善是我与生俱来的品质，真诚的赞美能让感情更牢固。然而，我要提醒一下，赞美异性时需要谨慎，如果你不加小心，赞美很容易被误认为是调情。

首先，误导别人很不好。人说话时特别容易被误解，当你想赞美别人时，对方可能理解为“这个人喜欢我”。这就会造成大麻烦，因为那个人可能突然开始追求你，之后如果你不回应，即使什么都没发生，对方也会觉得

advances, even though nothing has happened. Worse, the person may actually become vindictive. We have all seen movies where a person who feels misled calls and stalks the spouse.

Second, it makes your spouse look bad if it is perceived that you are flirting with people of the opposite sex. This can develop into a vicious situation where rumors are started and quickly spread. More than once, I have observed gossip become the basis of real trouble. At a minimum, such a situation can cause uneasiness in your relationship, and that is never good.

I am an extremely outgoing person. In my profession, I meet pretty, elegant, educated ladies every day. Because I am kind and considerate, I must be very extra careful that my behavior is not misinterpreted. I am very careful about never sending the wrong signal to someone I am chatting with. Needless to say, my wife is a beautiful lady, and she is also very guarded with men for this same reason.

We cannot control what other people think, but we can do things that manage the situation. If I am talking with a pretty woman, I immediately bring up my wife in the conversation. I might say those earrings you are wearing remind me of a pair that I bought for my wife. Or I might say I love your perfume, please give me the brand name because I would like to buy it for my wife. From the beginning, I set the table that I am a happily married man, and that I am not available.

It is so important to be loyal in a relationship. The issue often comes down to the fact that perception is often as powerful as reality, meaning you should not do anything that makes people think things that are not true. Realize that the way you act and the words you say are important. You want to always avoid creating the wrong impression.

My mindset says: "My marriage is the most important thing in my life. I will behave in ways to make this marriage lasting, loving, empathetic, romantic, and caring." I will do nothing to jeopardize this situation. It's as simple as that. I am loyal to my wife, and I will do nothing to compromise this position.

In summary, flirting never leads to anything good. Be aware that there is a fine line between flirting and giving compliments, and it's easy to cross. I realize that life is challenging enough without creating trouble for no reason. I do love my wife, and I am at all times loyal to her.

被你抛弃，更糟的是，此人很可能怀恨在心。我们都看过这样的电影：某人感到自己受骗，打骚扰电话并跟踪已婚夫妇。

其次，如果伴侣认为你和异性调情，就会很难堪，还会发展成恶性局面，谣言四起并迅速传播。我发现，很多时候，流言蜚语就是真正麻烦的根源，至少会让你们感情不稳，总之绝不是好事。

我是非常外向的人。在我的职业生涯中，每天都会遇到漂亮、优雅、有教养的女士。因为我善良体贴，所以必须格外小心，不能让他人误解。我很注意，从不向交谈之人发错误信号。不用说，我太太特别漂亮，她也同样对其他男人非常谨慎。

我们不能控制他人的想法，但可以做一些事情来控制局面。如果我和一位漂亮女士交谈，我会在谈话中提到我太太，比如说：你戴的耳环和我给太太买的那副很像。或者说：我喜欢你的香水，是什么牌子，我也想给我太太买。从一开始，我就表明自己是幸福的已婚男士，别人没有机会了。

恋爱时保持忠诚非常重要，出现问题时，感觉和事实一样重要，不能做让人误解的事。要时刻注意自己的言行，避免给人留下错误的感觉。

我的心态是：婚姻是我生命中最重要的事。我会注意言行，让我俩拥有持久甜蜜、相互理解、浪漫关怀的婚姻。我不会做任何危害婚姻的事，就是这么简单，我忠于我的妻子，这事没商量。

总之，调情没有任何好处。要知道，在调情和赞美之间有一条微妙的界限，而且很容易逾越。生活本就困难重重，不要再无端制造麻烦。我爱我太太，我对她永远忠诚。

64. LEARN TO TAKE THE BLAME AND APOLOGIZE

Taking the blame is an interesting concept. There are levels to it. You can take all the blame and profusely apologize, you can apologize and take part of the blame, you can apologize and take NONE of the blame (this is known as being passive aggressive), or lastly, you can put all the blame on someone else, be it your spouse, a stranger, a friend, or another family member. The last two should obviously be avoided when applicable. It is a tricky game, because sometimes a situation actually is not your fault, but someone else's entirely. Even then, it is important to be able to apologize for your involvement in it, no matter what that may be, and explain what happened.

For instance, if I take my wife to a restaurant that has good reviews and the food is terrible, I would simply apologize that the dining experience wasn't everything I had hoped. She would, of course, appreciate my apology. It does not matter that it was in no way my fault, and in fact, I was trying to do something nice. The apology is a gesture. I am basically apologizing that we didn't have the night I intended. Luckily, we can have fun anywhere!

For those who cannot apologize under any circumstances, I am sorry to tell you the bad news, but your chances of a happy marriage are very low. Such a person has an unhealthy life outlook that will not serve them well, either professionally or personally. I have met a few people like this, and while they can be cordial enough, once something goes wrong, they always manage to make a bad situation worse by refusing to apologize. If you have noticed these tendencies in yourself, try hard to open up and be more vulnerable. This behavior usually stems from childhood. If a child was punished whenever they were wrong, for example, they sometimes grow up unwilling to accept fault.

As a mature, self-actualized adult, you should be able to apologize when you have made a mistake, and even when it appears in your eyes that you have not made one. We all make mistakes as a normal part of life. In a relationship, you MUST be able to apologize. This does not show weakness, instead it shows strength and caring. It shows your dedication to the

64 学会道歉

承担责任这个概念比较有意思，分为几个层次：真心道歉并承担所有的责任；道歉并承担部分责任；道歉但不承担任何责任（被称为消极抵抗）；把所有的责任都推到别人身上，他可能是你的伴侣、陌生人、朋友或其他家庭成员。最后两种情况在实际运用时显然应该避免。担责是很棘手的问题，因为有时实际上根本不是你的错，而是别人的错，即便如此，别管什么事，也要因参与其中而道歉，并解释清楚。

例如，如果我带爱人去一家评价不错但实际菜品很差的餐厅，我就会道歉，告诉她非常遗憾是这种情况。她当然会感激我能道歉。这绝不是我的错，但没关系，我就是想表现得绅士一点。道歉是一种姿态，我是因未能按预想欢度夜晚而道歉。幸运的是，我们在任何地方都能玩得开心！

对于那些从来都不道歉的人，说来很抱歉，这种人很难拥有幸福的婚姻，他们的人生观很不健康，无论是工作还是生活方面，都不会有好结果。我遇到过这种人，虽然他们很热情，但一旦出了问题，总是拒绝道歉，把情况弄得更糟。如果你发现自己有这一倾向，就要学会以诚意待人，放下身段。这种行为通常源于童年。例如，如果某人小时候因犯错而受到惩罚，长大后就不愿意承认错误。

作为自我实现的成年人，犯错误时，要勇于道歉，即使感觉自己并没做错。我们都会犯错，这是生活常态。在感情关系中，你**必须**学会道歉。这不是软弱的表现，而是实力和关心的表现，表明你对感情的全心投入，以及你

relationship, and your willingness to be open and vulnerable with your partner, even when it ostensibly makes you look bad. Learn to apologize. You will find out that people will respect you more for it, not less.

65. WRITING NOTES CAN ALLEVIATE STRESS

I write notes all day, every day. I write myself reminders so I do not forget about important obligations, I write down ideas that pop into my head when I am working or exercising, I write affirmations to myself to keep a positive outlook, and I write notes to my beautiful wife. Notes help me to keep my life organized and to live up to the model person that I want to be. For instance, if I tell my wife I will pick something up for her at the store, but I do not write it down, there is a chance I may forget. Since I do not want to ever disappoint her, I write a note, and I always remember! It is an easy trick that has been around as long as pen and paper, possibly longer. Many people use note taking apps on their phones as well. Whatever works.

Writing notes is a great way to better communicate as well. Granted, text messages have replaced the physical note in many respects, but if used properly, they can still be a sweet gesture. I like to write her little love notes and leave them around the house for her to find when I am away from the house. She loves to receive them, and I love to write them. I hide them in clever places where she will discover them at some point during the day.

I also take notes to remember those small, off-topic comments she makes. I first learned this skill in business. Whenever I had an important thought, I would just jot it down to later jog my memory. One day I realized why not also do this to help my marriage. It has been a great tool for helping us have a happy loving marriage. If she mentions she wants to go to a certain restaurant, or likes a certain brand of chip, I write it down. This way, I make sure I buy her what she likes, her preferred brand, not what I think is good.

Notes are a helpful tool in every relationship. They give you a sweet way to communicate, and they are a great way to remember all those little things that make your spouse happy!

愿意对伴侣开诚布公、放下身段，即使这样会让你略显难堪。学会道歉，你会发现自己更加受人尊重。

65 写备忘录

我每天都写备忘录。我会写下提醒事项，以免忘记重要事情；我也会写下在工作或锻炼时突然出现的想法；我会写下自我肯定的话，以保持积极的态度；我还会给我美丽的太太写便条。写备忘录能让生活更有条理，让我成为理想中的自己。例如，我告诉太太会去商店给她买东西，如果我没记下来，就有可能忘记。我不愿让她失望，记下来就永远不会忘！这个小窍门，在纸和笔出现时就已存在，甚至可能更早。很多人会在手机上写备忘录，同样有效。

写便条也是很好的交流方式。短信确实在很多方面已经取代了实体便条，但如果使用得当，便条仍然能成为贴心的表达方式。我喜欢给太太写便条，藏在家里某处，当我不在家的时候，让她能找到。她喜欢这些便条，我也愿意给她写。我把便条藏在巧妙的地方，以便她能在某个时候发现。

我还会写下她说的那些不重要的小评论。我第一次学会这个技巧是在工作中，每当我有重要的想法就会记下来，以免忘掉。有一天，我忽然发现这样做也有助于我们的婚姻。写备忘录是很实用的工具，能帮助我们拥有幸福美满的婚姻。如果她提到想去某家餐馆，或者喜欢某个牌子的薯条，我就会写下来，这样我就肯定能买到她喜欢的东西、她中意的品牌，而不是我认为好的。

写备忘录是感情关系中很实用的工具，是贴心的沟通方式，也是记住所有能让伴侣拥有小确幸的好方法！

66. STOP ONLY LOOKING AT YOUR PHONE

There is no quicker way to make someone feel like they do not matter than to spend all of your time with them while on your phone. Notice, I am not proposing that you should never be on your phone in front of your significant other. You live together, after all, and to never look at your phone whenever you are at home would be foolish. My rule of thumb is that I am never on my phone when my wife and I are having a conversation, eating together, or on a date. In those instances, I give her my full attention.

Being on your phone all the time has become so commonplace you hardly even recognize when you are doing it. This is not because you are a bad person, or because you are inconsiderate, it is because that is how society has been evolving. I am not immune to this behavior any more than anybody else, but I am aware of it, and thus able to counterprogram myself.

When you are on your phone with your spouse, you are not giving them the attention they deserve. Yes you are physically present, but mentally you are off in social media land, or still at work. This makes the other person feel unimportant, or at the very least, less important than whatever you are doing on your phone. This will not build a strong relationship, and it will inspire resentment, and possibly even jealousy.

Your significant other deserves your complete attention. They love you and they want to enjoy their time with you. They cannot do that if you are mentally checked out. When you are having a conversation or spending one-on-one time with the person you love, put your phone aside. It is not going anywhere.

66 少玩手机

如果你一直在伴侣面前玩手机，就会让对方觉得自己不重要。注意，我并不是说你在伴侣面前永远都不能看手机。毕竟你们生活在一起，如果在家里的任何时候都不能看手机也不太正常。以我的经验，在和太太聊天、吃饭或约会时，我从不玩手机。在这种情况下，我会专心和她在一起。

手机时刻不离视线已经成为普遍现象，以至于人们感觉不到自己一直在玩手机。玩手机不代表人品差，也不代表不体贴，这是社会发展的产物，我也深受其害，但我意识到了这一点，因此能够想到反制措施。

在伴侣面前玩手机，就不能给予对方应得的关注。没错，你人虽在场，但精神已经离开，忙着刷视频，或忙工作上的事，这会让对方觉得自己不重要，或者至少没有你在手机上做的事情重要，因此两人的感情就不会牢固，而且会激起怨恨，甚至嫉妒。

伴侣值得你全身心的关注。伴侣爱你，希望能和你在一起享受美好时光，如果你忙着玩手机，伴侣就没法和你共度时光。当你和爱人交谈或两人独处的时候，把手机放在一边，它不会跑。

67. BUILD TRADITIONS AND KEEP THEM ALIVE

Traditions are a lot of fun! You can turn anything into one. That is their beauty. They spice up life and give you something to look forward to. My wife and I like to make a lot of silly traditions. Whether we decide to wear the same color shirt on a specific day every week, or we plan to cook each other a meal every Wednesday, these traditions are fun! They give us something to look forward to and to plan together.

Beyond simply having a good time, traditions are important to building a meaningful life with your significant other. They establish a special ceremony that belongs to just you and your spouse. This will strengthen the bond between you and further build your relationship. Traditions can be big and grandiose, or they can be small. The important thing is to establish them, and then stick to them.

There are larger social traditions that we all follow as members of society, be they religious or federal in nature. What I like to do is to make holidays personal. For example, I might like to eat a certain type of food every year on a particular holiday. For example, it is said that if you eat black eyed peas on New Year's Day, you will have good luck all year, and I do exactly that. This personalizes the holiday and makes it that much more fun. Anticipation of traditions is also a great tool when it comes to love and romance.

I have a friend who loves nature and goes to The Grand Canyon with his wife every Labor Day. They look forward to the trip all year around, and plan how they are going to make THIS year different and special. Their shared anticipation and planning bring them together more than the actual trip ever could. On top of that, it is a special tradition that they share. It belongs only to them and is thus incredibly important.

Traditions serve to bring people together for a common purpose. They strengthen bonds by creating special events that belong to just you and your spouse, and are important in any healthy relationship. And do not forget to take lots of photos on such a trip to commemorate these special occasions.

67 形成传统

形成传统是非常有意思的事！任何事情都能变成传统。传统之美在于能为生活增添乐趣，令人期待神往。我和太太喜欢把很多愚蠢的事变成传统，比如我们会在每周特定一天穿同色衬衫，我们还会在每周三给对方做一顿饭，这些小传统都很好玩！让我们能一起规划，共同期待。

除了享受美好时光之外，形成传统还有助于两人一起度过有意义的生活，能形成一种特殊的仪式，它只属于你和伴侣，因而能够加强两人的关系，使两人的感情更牢固。传统可大可小，关键在于能够形成传统，然后坚持下去。

作为社会中的一员，我们都遵循大的社会传统，无论是宗教传统还是联邦传统。我喜欢让节日变得更加个性化，例如，我愿意在每年的特定节日吃某种食物，据说如果在元旦那天吃黑眼豆，一整年都会有好运气，我就是这么做的。这能让节日更加个性化、更有意思。在婚恋方面，对传统的期待也大有益处。

我有一个朋友喜爱大自然，每年劳动节都和爱人去大峡谷，他们全年都期盼着这次旅行，并计划让这一年比往年更特别。他们一起规划、共同期待的过程，会比实际旅行更能让两人团结。此外，这是他们自己的特殊传统，只属于他俩，因此非常重要。

传统能让人们为了共同的目标而走到一起。让只属于你和伴侣的特殊传统来加强两人关系，这对稳固感情很重要。别忘了在旅行中多拍些照片来纪念这一特殊时刻。

68. NEVER QUESTION IF YOU MADE A GOOD DECISION ONCE YOU ARE MARRIED

I have never questioned my decision to marry my wonderful wife, but I have friends and acquaintances who have questioned the wisdom of their own marriages. I personally think this is the most ridiculous thing in the world. You are already married, so do everything you can to make it a win for both of you. To me, a marriage is not just something that you can trash. Once you are married, it is too late. The time for a couple to question their marriage was before they said, "I do." After you have made those vows, it is up to you to make it work. If you quit, you will probably make the same mistake over and over again. Stick with your decision, and with effort, even the most difficult of marriages can turn the corner and be loving, caring, and lasting.

When you question your marriage, you admit at least subconsciously that you may have made a mistake. This kind of negative thinking can only lead to trouble. Rather than asking, "Did I make a mistake?" Remind yourself why you married that person in the first place. Think of their positive qualities and how you are going to work things out. You should be asking, "How can I fix my relationship, not how can I end it?"

Relationships can live or die because of a couple's mindset. If they both honestly work to get along and improve their relationship, odds are they will get along better and their relationship will improve. If instead they bemoan and question the legitimacy of their relationship, things will only get worse. A committed person will never be looking for a sign to break up. Instead, they will only be focused on reasons for staying together. One is a very positive approach that will create a win, while the other is very negative and can only lead to losing. You should believe that to stay married is your only option, and the only true road to happiness. If a happy life is your goal, you will heed my advice.

Be thankful for your spouse and your marriage, even when times get tough. You married each other for a reason. Find a way to make it work and to get along. Love is strong. It sometimes takes a lot of work, but in the end, it will always be worth the effort.

68 不要质疑

我从来没有质疑过是否应该娶我太太，但我的一些朋友和熟人却会质疑自己结婚是否明智。我个人认为这是世界上最荒谬的事，你已经结婚了，所以应该竭尽全力让两人和谐相处。对我来说，婚姻不能随意放弃，一旦结婚，就是既成事实，如要质疑，应该是在说“我愿意”之前，而在婚礼宣誓之后，就要靠自己的努力让婚姻和谐美满。如果你放弃这段婚姻，很可能之后会重蹈覆辙。要坚持自己的决定，通过努力，即使是最难磨合的婚姻也会有转机，能变成充满爱意、互相关怀和持久的婚姻。

当你质疑自己的婚姻时，至少在潜意识里认为自己可能犯了错误，这种消极的想法只会带来麻烦。别问自己“我是不是错了”，而应该想想当初为什么要和对方结婚，想想对方的优秀品质，以及如何解决问题。你应该想怎样修复两人关系，而不是怎样结束关系。

夫妻关系的好坏取决于双方的心态，如果双方都有诚意一起努力并改善关系，就能相处得更好，感情也会更牢固。相反，如果总是抱怨并质疑两人关系是否合理，事情就会变得更糟。一个全心投入婚姻的人永远不会寻找分手的信号，而只会关注两人在一起的原因。一种是非常积极的方法，能够带来成功，而另一种是非常消极的方法，只会导致失败。你应该相信，稳固婚姻是唯一的选择，也是通往幸福唯一正确的道路。如果你的目标是幸福生活，就会听从我的建议。

即使在艰难的时候，也要感谢你的伴侣和你们的婚姻。你们当初结婚肯定出于某种原因，要想办法让那个原因发挥作用，好好相处。爱很强大，虽然有时需要经过很多努力，但最终都会值得。

69. TOUGH TALKS ARE BEST WHEN WELL THOUGHT OUT

No one likes to have tough talks, no matter what they happen to be about. They are awkward, uncomfortable, and usually quite daunting. The key to navigating any such conversation with your spouse, or anyone else for that matter, is to completely think everything out beforehand. Of course, "everything" is an exaggeration, as it is impossible to know some of the details beforehand. The key is to prepare to the best of your ability.

When you confront your spouse, try to empathize with them and understand their point of view. Their opinion on the matter will almost certainly differ from your own. I am guessing you have differing outlooks, otherwise it wouldn't be a tough talk. Find a non-confrontational way to broach the subject, and enter it with an open mind. Do not charge in and insist that your way of thinking is correct. Listen to your spouse and hear what they have to say. Once you know exactly where they stand, you can better address their concerns, or if they make a good point, perhaps you can change your opinion about the issue. I go into such conversations open to being wrong.

No one likes to have hard talks, but in a relationship, they are occasionally necessary. If you avoid these conversations, animosity can grow over time. If you truly love your partner, you will be willing to discuss any issue, even those that are uncomfortable. If you think through the conversation in advance, empathize with your partner, and carefully listen to what they say, you and your significant other will grow closer together. The hardest iron is forged in the hottest fire, and these difficult conversations can serve as that flame.

Trust your partner to treat you with the same respect as you treat them. My wife and I have no trouble talking about anything because we both greatly respect one another's opinions. It is that respect that makes any conversation simple. We each know that the other person is looking out for our best interests, and on that basis, we can find a solution to anything!

69 艰难对话

没有人喜欢艰难的对话，无论什么内容，都会令人难堪、不适，且心生畏惧。与伴侣或其他任何人进行此类谈话时，一定要事先通盘考虑一切细节。当然，“一切”有点夸张，因为事先不可能知道所有细节，关键是要做好充分准备。

如果和伴侣对话，要尽量体恤对方，理解对方的观点。伴侣对这件事的看法肯定会与你相左。我估计你们观点各不相同，否则就不会是艰难对话。用平和的语气引出话题，并以虚心的姿态进入话题，不要自以为是并坚持自己的看法正确，要倾听伴侣的说法。明确对方的立场更有利于解决问题，或者如果对方提出很好的观点，你也许会改变看法。我在这样的对话中就很容易是错方。

没有人喜欢艰难对话，但在感情关系中，有时却很有必要。假如避免这些对话，憎恶之心会随着时间而增长。如果你真的爱你的伴侣，就会愿意讨论任何问题，即使是那些令人不适的话题。如果你事先想清楚对话的内容，能够同情伴侣，仔细倾听对方的话语，你和伴侣就会更加亲密。最坚硬的铁器是在最炽热的火焰中锻造出来的，而这些艰难对话正如火焰。

要相信伴侣能够尊重你，就像你能尊重伴侣一样。我和爱人可以谈论任何话题，因为我们都非常尊重对方的意见。正是这种尊重使任何谈话都变得简单。我们都知道对方在为两人的最大利益着想，以此为基础，我们可以找到任何问题的解决方案！

70. ARE HOROSCOPES ACCURATE PREDICTORS OF FUTURE MARRIAGE HAPPINESS?

Many people believe in the power and accuracy of horoscopes. However, scientific testing has found no evidence to support the purported accuracy of astrology. There are many naysayers who believe that astrology is just a waste of time. I have heard it said more than once that people who believe in astrology are fools.

On the other side of the coin, there are many people who live by astrology. These people are amused at the so-called scientific evidence. Personally, in the past I have always been skeptical of systems like astrology. I do not want to know about bad events that might happen. However, before my pending marriage, I took a leap of faith and hired a well-known astrologer to give me answers about our compatibility and our future as a married couple. At first, I must admit I was more than a little nervous. I had been warned that this person has a reputation of being blunt and telling it like it is. Luckily, she told me that we are the perfect match and will have a happy marriage forever. She said, of course there will be challenges, but you will make it through each one being more in love and committed after each such episode.

Many people might think I am a fool, and maybe they are right, but I always go “all in” on everything I do, so I decided to tempt fate. A happy marriage is absolute, according to these experts. We are perfect for each other and will have a happy marriage forever.

I am sure that our stars are aligned. That is an extraordinarily good thing. What would I have done if the opposite results were predicted by the astrologer? The answer is simple. I would still have married my wife. I love her that much. Nothing could have stopped me from marrying her, but these people did give me comfort in my decision to marry this lovely lady.

As you can tell from this book, we are very happy together. We have many ways to communicate beyond merely the spoken word that help our marriage grow and remain strong. We are unique, and I believe this has helped us. In summary, are horoscopes accurate or not? I do not know, but often “where there's smoke there's fire.”

70 星座占卜

很多人相信星座占卜的预测能力和准确性。然而，科学实验没有证据表明占星术所谓的准确性。有很多反对者认为占星术只是浪费时间。我不止一次听人说，相信星座占卜的人都是傻子。

另一方面，有很多人依靠星座占卜而生活，这些人对所谓的科学证据感到好笑。就我个人而言，过去我一直对占卜持怀疑态度，我不想知道会有什么坏事发生。然而，在即将结婚之际，我做了一次大胆的尝试，请教了一位著名的占星师，询问我俩是否般配以及婚后情形，我承认一开始非常紧张，因为有人提醒过我，这个占星师以直言不讳和实话实说而闻名。幸运的是，他告诉我，我俩是天造地设的一对，会永远幸福地生活在一起。他还说，当然会有挑战，但我们会渡过每一个难关，在这些插曲之后，会更加相爱并彼此忠诚。

有些人可能认为我傻，也许我是傻，但我做任何事都会“全力以赴”，所以我决定挑战命运。根据这些说法，我和太太肯定会有幸福的婚姻，我俩特别般配，我们的婚姻将永远幸福美满。

我确信我俩星座吻合，真是太好了。但是如果占星师预测的结果正好相反，我会怎么办？答案很简单，我还是会娶我太太，我就是爱她，没有什么能阻止我娶她，而这些大师确实在我决定娶这位可爱女士时，给予我安慰。

正如你从本书中所了解的，我们在一起很快乐。除了言语交流，还有很多方式能让我们的婚姻更加幸福稳固。我们与众不同，相信这一点很有帮助。总而言之，星座到底准不准确？我不知道，但“空穴来风，未必无因”。

71. WINE, DINE, AND HAVE A HAPPY MARRIAGE

It has long been said that the way to a man's heart is through his stomach. I read an article in which scientists at the University of California-San Diego School of Medicine have proven that women also respond to romantic cues better on fuller stomachs. The study seems to prove that there is a correlation between food and sex. But to me, food is just one piece in a more complicated puzzle.

In the study, scientists evaluated the theory by viewing brain activity in response to romantic stimulation in women who had fasted versus women with full stomachs. They concluded that women demonstrated greater brain activation in reward-related neural regions after eating, meaning they are more sexual shortly after a satisfying meal.

The fact is meals play a huge role in romance. They are significant part of the way we court. For me, it has never been just the satisfaction of eating a meal that enhances romantic moods, but everything about the dining experience together. If you want more love dust in your romance and another arrow in your romantic quiver, meals can be important. Like a previous point on packaging, you can make what would be a bland meal something special with a few extras. Candlelight dinners are nice. Breakfast at sunrise on the beach or on a terrace is super romantic. Creating the appropriate ambiance with meals is always a win when it comes to romance. In summary, dining can be an intimate experience. Combine delicious food with a romantic atmosphere and choice elements such as a glass of good wine, pretty tablecloths, nice music, and you will be dancing with love in the air. Your marriage will be alive and well.

It is not necessary to wait to go out to a restaurant. Do these things in your own home and do them several times each week. The rewards of a more romantic and loving marriage will be worth the effort. A good dining experience will do more than create great memories, it will also act as a catalyst for immediate feelings of love between the couple.

71 美酒佳肴

一直以来，人们都说要抓住男人的心，先抓住男人的胃。我读过一篇文章，文中称加州大学圣地亚哥分校医学院的科学家证明，女性在饱腹时对情感暗示更有感觉，这项研究证明了食物和情欲之间的关系。但对我来说，食物只是复杂拼图中的一片而已。

在这项研究中，科学家通过观察禁食女性和饱腹女性在情爱刺激下大脑的活动对比来评估这一理论。结论是女性在进食后大脑中与奖励机制相关的神经区域表现得更活跃，这表明女性在一顿美餐之后会有更强的欲望。

实际上，饮食在恋爱中扮演了重要角色，这也是主要的求爱方式之一。对我来说，不仅是美餐，整个就餐感受都能提升浪漫情怀。如果你想在恋爱中获得更多浪漫氛围，那么就请在爱情箭筒中再添一箭，注重饮食非常重要。就像前面提到的包装一样，你可以花点心思把一顿平淡无奇的饭食变得与众不同。烛光晚餐很不错，日出时分在海滩或露台上吃早餐也超级浪漫。说到浪漫，在用餐时营造适宜的氛围会事半功倍。总之，用餐是亲密的体验，将美味的食物与浪漫的氛围结合起来，外加一杯美酒、漂亮的桌布、好听的音乐等点缀其间，你与爱人翩翩起舞，你们的婚姻会更美满。

没必要去餐馆吃饭，在自己家里做饭也一样，每周做几次，会让婚姻更加浪漫和甜蜜，一切都很值得。美好的就餐氛围不仅能留下特别的回忆，还能让两人即刻产生爱意。

72. ROUTINES ARE THE OPPOSITE OF BORING—THEY WILL ADD SPICE TO YOUR LOVE LIFE

Developing healthy habits and routines is important to sustaining a healthy marriage. My wife and I practice "HRR,"which stands for the creation of healthy habits, rituals, and routines. In many places throughout this book, I emphasize the importance of spontaneity in a healthy relationship, and that message applies here. Of course, routines should not govern all aspects of your life. For example, we both enjoy perfect health and want to keep it this way. We love looking marvelous for each other, so going to the gym daily is a must. Slack time with nothing to do is also important, but let's get back to gym time. I found out long ago that to be consistent with attending the gym requires going at the same time every day. For us it is 6:00am. That routine begins each day with a sense of positive achievement and assures there are no conflicts with other activities.

In any relationship, a set routine can help provide a sense of stability and security for each partner. Regardless of how you are feeling about the relationship, starting a new routine is an excellent way to show each other love in a consistent manner.

With routines, there should always be room also to allow for spontaneity. Life just happens, and some evenings we do not have time to connect the way we'd like, but our goal is to strive for that connection. Focusing on our routines helps in protecting the quality time we spend together. Routines allow us to say "no" to others. Routines help in keeping our priorities in order. Open communication stems from spending quality time together. A sense of trust and closeness is built between us because we know we will be together during the scheduled activities at certain times in each twenty-four-hour period. Believe it or not, routines will protect your marriage as they do ours. Time together is a must for love to grow.

Most late evenings are reserved just for us. We look at late evenings and early mornings as sacred space for connecting. During this time, we resolve conflicts, share ideas, engage in small talk, pray, communicate often at deep levels, and of course we become intimate with

72 日常习惯

养成健康的生活习惯对维持幸福婚姻很重要。我和太太实行“HRR”，意思是养成健康的习惯、仪式和常规。我在书中多次强调过在良好的感情关系中自发行为的重要性，在这里也适用。当然，不能让习惯控制生活的所有方面。就我们而言，我俩都希望自己能够一直健康，都愿意看起来精神饱满，所以每天都要去健身房。无事可做的闲暇时间也很重要，但让我们先回到健身时间这一话题。我很久以前就发现，要想坚持去健身房，就必须每天在同一时间去，对我们来说是早上 6 点。因为每天都坚持这个习惯，我就会带着积极的成就感开始健身，而且也不会与其他活动发生冲突。

在所有感情关系中，固定的习惯都能让双方感到稳定和安全。不管你如何看待这段感情，养成新的日常习惯，就是用始终如一的方式向对方表达爱意。

要养成日常习惯，也要给自发行为留有余地。生活就是这样，有些夜晚，我们没有时间按喜欢的方式联系，但我们的目标是为这种联系而努力。按照习惯行事能保护两人在一起的美好时光。习惯能让你对他人说“不”，也有利于保持做事的优先顺序。共度美好时光能让两人坦诚交流，彼此就会更加信任、更加亲密，因为我们知道，在每天的特定时间里，我们都会一起按时活动。信不信由你，日常习惯能保护你们的婚姻，就像我们一样。只有经常在一起，爱情之树才能常青。

有无数个夜晚留给我们共度，我们把深夜和清晨视为神圣的交流时间。在这期间，我们会化解矛盾、分享看法、一起闲聊、共同祈祷，经常进行深

each other. Our routines have become part of who we are. Small talk is super important because it keeps the relationship loose and alive. To always be serious is just not a good idea.

We perform our routines without thinking about them because they have become natural and take precedence over other activities. If anyone or anything tries to disrupt that time together, we stick to the routine anyway, with a few exceptions. At times when we are asked to go out for business meals or to social activities with friends, we already have our own date planned, so it is easy to respond with a gracious no and schedule such events for a later date. Our time together is sacred, and we love bonding during those times of real commitment and love.

73. SPOKEN WORDS MEAN LITTLE— ACTIONS MEAN EVERYTHING

Actions speak louder than words. We have all heard this saying before, but nowhere is this truer than with your significant other. You can tell them you love them and promise them the world, but if you never SHOW them you love them, the rhetoric will grow stale. I tell My wife I love her every day, and I believe that regularly saying those words is crucial to a happy marriage, but more importantly, I show her it is not an empty platitude. I give her flowers and surprise her with dinner. I rub her shoulders and am always available. I am fully engaged in our conversations when we are together or speaking on the phone. In other words, I am present.

I have a friend who could not understand why his wife felt like he did not love her anymore. In fact, he was quite angry with her for feeling this way. He just did not understand it at all. Once we began speaking about their relationship, I realized that he did truly love his wife. He even told her each day of his love for her. However, he did not show it. He was a businessman and always in the office trying to make money for his family. He believed this was showing his love, and for him it was, but he was never home. When he did go home, he fell asleep immediately. He never took her anywhere. It was only empty words to her with

层次的交流，当然，我们因此更加亲密。日常习惯已经成为我们生活的一部分，闲聊很重要，能让两人的关系轻松而活跃，不能总是那么严肃。

我们会不假思索地按习惯行事，因为习惯成自然，而且比其他活动更重要。如果有人或事会扰乱我们在一起的惯例，我们也依然坚持，只有少数例外。比如有人邀请我们出席商务餐会或与朋友参加社交活动，而我们已经有安排好的惯例，就可以礼貌地拒绝，并将活动延后。我俩在一起的时间很神圣，我们愿意在这个承诺和关爱的时间里稳固两人的关系。

73 实际行动

行动胜于言语，我们以前都听过这句话，说得没错，尤其是和伴侣在一起的时候。你每天都说很爱伴侣，并向伴侣承诺给她整个世界，但如果你从来没有爱的行动，这些花言巧语就会让人厌倦。我每天都告诉太太我爱她，我相信经常说这些话对幸福婚姻很重要，但更重要的是，我会用实际行动表明所说不虚。我会送她鲜花，给她惊喜晚餐，替她按摩肩膀，随时陪伴左右。当我们一起聊天或打电话时，我会全心投入，换句话说，我一直陪伴在她身边。

我有一个朋友，他爱人总感觉得不到他的爱，实际上他对爱人的这种想法很生气，只是他一点也不明白为什么。当我们说起他俩的关系时，我发现他确实很爱妻子，他甚至每天都用言语表达爱意，但并没有任何实际行动。他是个商人，总是努力工作、为家赚钱，他觉得这样就是在表达爱意，对他来说确实如此，但他总是不回家，即便回家，也是马上睡去。他从没带爱

no action she could identify. To him, it was the opposite, as he believed by making more and more money, she could tell he was showing his love. "Wrong"? Yes, wrong as his wife wanted him present and she wanted at least a little personal attention. She wanted him to cuddle, to dine with him, just to spend a little personal one on one time with him. In his mind he was killing himself at work to make his wife happy, but all she wanted was to spend the evening with him once in a while.

I explained that you need to give love for it to be felt. He didn't understand the concept at first but agreed that it was worth a try. Sure enough, his relationship began to improve. Instead of staying late at the office five days a week, he cut it down to three. The other two were for his wife. Like magic, their relationship has improved, and they have never looked back.

This book contains several points about the importance of words, but words are worth nothing alone. You also need to show your love every day. Give your spouse a kiss in the morning and another one when you get home. If their back hurts, rub their shoulders. If they are sad, talk to them. It is the little things that make a marriage, and a good marriage leads to a successful life.

74. FOMO – THE FEAR OF MISSING OUT

The fear of missing out, or FOMO, is exactly what it sounds like. You are afraid of missing a party, an experience, or an opportunity. This typically leads to a lack of commitment to the moment because you are focused on preparing up until the last second. This type of behavior can be poison in a relationship. Let's say you will not commit to dinner with your spouse because you think something better or more important may come up. This will, of course, make them feel undervalued. They do not want to be your last choice, they want to be your first. There is nothing wrong with wanting to plan the best events, but there is a lot wrong with not honoring your commitments to your relationship.

人去过任何地方，只有空话，没有任何让对方认同的行动，但是他却相信，通过赚更多的钱，爱人就能明白他的爱。“错了？”是的，错了，因为他妻子需要陪伴，至少需要关注，想得到拥抱，两人能一起吃饭，能单独相处。在他看来，他拼命工作就是想让爱人高兴，但对方却只想两人能偶尔共度良宵。

我告诉他，要付出让对方能感受到的爱。他一开始并不理解这个概念，但认为值得一试。果然，他俩的关系开始好转。他不再一周五天都晚归，而是减至三天，另外两天留给爱人。就像施了魔法，两人的关系改善了，现在一切都已步入正轨。

本书有几个条目都涉及言语的重要性，但光说不练毫无意义。每天都要用实际行动表达爱意，早上给爱人一个吻，回家后再来一个吻。如果伴侣背部疼痛，就帮忙按摩；如果伴侣伤心难过，就耐心开导。正是这些小事成就了婚姻，而拥有美满的婚姻才能拥有成功的人生。

74 活在当下

害怕错过，或称错失恐惧症（FOMO），正如字面上的意思。人们害怕错过某个聚会、某个经历或某个机会，这会导致不能专注眼前的事，因为你会时刻准备着做某些事，直到最后一秒才考虑当下。这种行为对于感情关系而言就是毒药。比方说，你不想和伴侣共进晚餐，因为你认为可能会有更好或更重要的事情而不想错过。当然，这会让伴侣觉得受到轻视，伴侣不想成为你的备选，而想成为首选。想要参加最好的活动并没有错，但不履行对感情的承诺就是大错特错。

Some people are so paranoid about missing out on something that they actually miss out on everything. Such people are like butterflies, never landing long enough to enjoy anything. To jump from one thing to another due to a fear of missing out (FOMO) can only lead to frustrations and disappointments. Paranoid behavior always creates the opposite effect. When you are somewhere enjoying whatever it is you're doing, never be in a hurry. Instead, follow the philosophy of *carpe diem* and seize the moment. Life is made of special moments. Special moments must be enjoyed when they happen since it is impossible to repeat them. If you want to enjoy life, be in the moment.

Be grateful for what you have, and work to maintain it. Everything in life requires maintenance, from your home, to your body, to your marriage or your significant other. If you are always waiting for a better event, you will miss out on what you already have waiting for you at home. You will never find peace. What appears to be a better situation can never compete with the love you and your significant other share. There will always be another party, but you only get one life to spend with the person you love.

It is common to have a fear of missing out. We all want to optimize our time and experiences, but nothing can compete with the love you have with your spouse. It needs to be tended. The only thing you should be scared of missing out on is time with them.

It is always best to value now as the most important time of your life. Living in the now creates success, from business to a happy marriage. I advise you to forget the past and give little thought to the unpredictable future. Stay in the moment.

75. UNDERSTAND YOUR PARTNER'S SPIRITUAL NEEDS

It is easy to understand our partner's basic physical needs. They need food, water, sleep, and affection. Understanding their spiritual needs is not quite as easy. This takes a deep awareness of who they are as a person, their hopes, their dreams, their fears, and their faith. Such knowledge can only be gained by prolonged intimate contact. In other words, you must

有些人太过偏执，不愿错过某些事情，而实际上会错过更多。这样的人就像蝴蝶一样，从来不会在某处多作停留。由于害怕错过（FOMO）而从一件事跳到另一件事，这样只会导致挫折和失望，偏执的行为总是产生相反的效果。当你在某处享受当下的时候，千万不要着急，而应该遵循及时行乐的哲学，活在当下。生活是由许多特别的时刻组成的，在这些特别的时刻就应该享受其中，因为美好时光不可复制。如果你要享受生活，就要活在当下。

要感激你所拥有的一切，并努力呵护这一切。生活中的很多方面，包括家庭、身体、婚姻、伴侣，都需要精心呵护。如果你总是等待更好的事情，就会错过在家中等你的人，你的内心得不到安宁，你所认为的更好事情永远无法与你们的爱相比。人生总会有另一场派对，但你只有一次生命能和挚爱一起度过。

害怕错过是普遍现象，我们都想优化自己的时间和经历，但没有什么能与你们的爱相比。爱情需要呵护，你唯一应该害怕错过的是和伴侣在一起的时光。

最好把眼下视为生命中最重要的时刻，活在当下才能成功，从生意场到幸福的婚姻都是如此。我奉劝你要忘记过去，也不要忧虑未来，要活在当下。

75 精神需求

我们很容易了解伴侣的基本生理需求，比如吃饭、喝水、睡眠和情感，而要了解伴侣的精神需求就没那么简单了，需要深入了解伴侣，知悉对方的愿望、梦想、恐惧和信念，这些信息只能通过长期亲密接触才能获得，换句话说，你必须向伴侣敞开心扉，说出自己的恐惧，倾听对方的恐惧，了解对

truly open yourself up to your partner. Share your fears and listen to theirs. Find out what they care about, not what they tell the world they care about, but what truly drives them. What is their purpose for getting out of bed every morning? Once you can answer these questions, you are on your way to understanding your partner's spiritual needs.

It takes time and effort to fully get to know someone, and sometimes it is impossible. Many people are closed off and will never share what is truly in their hearts. That is why it is your job to make your spouse feel comfortable enough to open up. This takes love, time, and trust. You do this by being vulnerable yourself, by sharing your own spiritual needs. You cannot expect someone else to bare their soul when yours is locked away in a vault. If this does not come easy, start small. Share little things until you are comfortable enough to share the bigger secrets of your heart.

Once you understand your partners spiritual needs, your relationship can evolve to the next level. You will grow closer and become stronger partners. You will find peace and strength in one another and truly understand what makes the other person tick. This understanding will allow you to help each other reach those dreams of the heart you may have been too scared to mention. It will also give you the opportunity to support each other in overcoming the past traumas that still keep you up at night. It is hard work, but it is worth the effort. Understand your partner's spiritual needs, and your relationship will blossom.

76. START SMALL ON NEW VENTURES

Many people tell you that you should dive headfirst into any new venture. In other words, you should commit yourself 100% immediately. While this strategy works with certain activities, it is not a universal truth. With many things, it is wise to start small and grow step by step. By committing yourself 100% from the get-go, you deny yourself the chance to acclimate. Think of it as stepping into a hot tub. It may be too hot to fully immerse yourself immediately, so you put your feet in, then enter to your knees, your waist, your chest, and finally you are in the water, enjoying the heat and relaxing. The same is true when

方的关心所在，不是那些对外宣称的，而是真正在意的事。一旦你能回答这些问题，就开始了解伴侣的精神需求了。

完全了解某个人需要时间和精力，而有的人根本无法了解。很多人都封闭自我，永远不会说出内心的真实想法。所以，要营造舒适的氛围让伴侣能够敞开心扉，这就需要关爱、时间和信任。要做到这一点，你自己先要放下身段，说出自己的精神需求。当你自我封闭时，就不能指望别人打开心锁，如果不容易做到，那就从小事说起，先向对方吐露不重要的小事，水到渠成时再分享内心更大的秘密。

一旦能够了解伴侣的精神需求，你们的关系就会升华到更高层次，两人会更加亲密，感情也会更加牢固。你们能相互给予力量和内心的平静，并真正了解对方的动力，能够帮助彼此实现心中因胆怯而不敢提及的梦想，也能让你们互相支持，抚平过往那些让人夜不能寐的心灵创伤。这是一项艰苦的工作，但值得努力。了解伴侣的精神需求，你们的感情才会开花结果。

76 谨慎投入

很多人都会说，做新的项目时应该直接投入，换句话说，应该立即全部投入。虽然这一策略适用于某些情况，但并不是普遍真理，对于多数情况，明智的做法是先谨慎投入，然后逐渐增加。如果从一开始就全部投入，就会剥夺自己适应新环境的机会。可以想象成泡澡时人们进入浴缸时的情境，如果水温太高，就不能直接全身浸泡，要先把脚放进去，然后膝盖、腰部、胸

starting a new activity or venture. It may seem overwhelming to jump all the way in right away, but by slowly entering the water, you will acclimate, and by the time you are fully submerged, you will be comfortable.

Starting small gives you the chance to find out if you like what you are trying without committing yourself. Once you commit yourself, you feel an obligation to keep going, or else you feel like a failure. For example, my wife and I wanted to learn salsa dancing, so we first took a sample class. We still have not decided if we will enroll for the entire class, but this was a good start. If you do not like what you are doing, this will lead to strife, and simply put, a bad time. If you start slowly, you can pull the rip cord and back out without any damage to your self-esteem or relationship. However, if you do like it, you can slowly get further into the activity with your significant other and grow closer all the while.

My wife and I love to try new things, from food to new interests. We have learned that we have the best time and the most success when we try them out before fully committing. This allows us to determine what we like and how to best use our time. We can have a good time anywhere, and we often do, but why not use the time for the things you really enjoy doing? Start slowly, then ramp up as you learn and become comfortable. We are now thinking of taking an art class together and planning the first step in that new adventure.

77. AT TIMES IT IS IMPORTANT TO GIVE A FIRM NO, BUT NOT OFTEN

Compromise and teamwork are the backbone of any partnership. When you are married, it is important to work with your significant other to make decisions. You should also do everything in your power to adhere to their wishes; however, sometimes the request may be outside of your comfort zone. In these rare scenarios, it is okay to respond with a firm, but always respectful "No." Most of the time, you should work with your spouse to find

部，最后全身进入水里，享受热水浴，让身心放松。在开始一个新的活动或项目时也应如此，直接入水会让人难以承受，但是慢慢入水就能适应，当你完全进入水中时，会感到很舒服。

谨慎投入，能让你在全部投入之前，有机会发现自己是否喜欢这件事。一旦全部投入，就有责任坚持下去，否则就会觉得自己很失败。例如，我和太太想学萨尔萨舞，所以我们先报了一个试学课程，并没有决定是否要报整个课程，但这是很好的开始。如果你不喜欢正在做的事情，就会很麻烦，简单来说，很糟。如果你谨慎投入，可以随时结束，然后全身而退，这样不会对你的自尊或两人感情造成任何伤害。当然，如果你真的喜欢这件事，就可以慢慢和伴侣深入活动中，两人关系也会更加亲密。

我和太太喜欢尝试新鲜事物，比如美食和一些新的爱好。我们发现，在完全投入之前先尝试一下，就能让我们拥有美好时光，且更容易获得成功，这样可以让我俩能够决定喜欢做什么事，及如何更好支配时间。我们在任何地方都能玩得开心，也经常这样做，那为什么不把时间用在自己真正喜欢做的事情上呢？慢慢开始，然后随着熟悉和适应而逐渐增加。我们现在正在考虑一起上美术课，计划尝试新的爱好。

77 偶尔拒绝

妥协让步和同心协力是任何合作关系的支柱。当你结婚以后，要和伴侣一起做决定，要竭尽全力遵从伴侣的意愿，然而，有时这一要求可能会令你感到不适，在这些仅有的情况下，你可以坚定而礼貌地说“不”。大多时候，你应该和伴侣一起找到折中方式，但有时不太容易。

some middle ground, but this will not always be possible.

Being able to say no on important issues and have that response accepted shows respect, but constantly saying no is not good. Only say no on rare occasions, and when you do, make sure you have a good reason, although that reason could simply be that you are uncomfortable. That infrequent "no" should be respected by your spouse, and that respect should be appreciated and reciprocated. If your significant other cares enough about you to respect your no, you must respect theirs.

"Yes" is what I always want to say and hear. But there are times when "no" is the appropriate response. Sometimes a firm but gentle no is the only choice. I advise exploring the no in a manner that provides alternatives. I cannot agree with this and must say "no," but maybe we can find another solution. It may be an entirely different solution, but one where we are both happy. If you say "no" too often, it will lose its power. If used sparingly, it is the ultimate sign of respect.

78. HELP ME UNDERSTAND

Most fights are a result of miscommunication. A lot of the time, both parties are in agreement, but they verbalize their position in such a way that they are misunderstood. Think about how much smoother interactions would be if we always knew exactly what the other person was saying. That would be magnificent! That is why it is important to take the time to understand your partner's thoughts and opinions and to explain your own. It is a two way street, and you both must be going the same direction.

I had a friend who would constantly fight with his wife. Whenever we would talk, he would complain about her. I couldn't understand where he was coming from, because I was friends with her as well. She was very nice, and I told him as much. One day, they got into an argument in front of me, and I quickly realized they were both saying the same thing, but in different ways. I pointed this out, and they were both embarrassed to admit that I was right. This is not uncommon.

能够在重要问题上说“不”，并得到伴侣的认可，是伴侣对你的尊重，但不能总是说“不”，只能在极少的情况下拒绝伴侣。当你拒绝的时候，要有适当的理由，哪怕是令你不适的理由。这种偶尔的“不”应该得到伴侣的尊重，而伴侣的尊重应该得到赞赏和回报。如果你的伴侣足够关心你，尊重你的拒绝，你也应该尊重伴侣的拒绝。

“是”是我最想说和最想听的回应，但有时“不”才是恰当的回应。有时候，坚定而温柔的拒绝是唯一的选择。我建议探索一下替代说“不”的方式，但是实在找不出替代方案时，必须说“不”。也许我们能够找到另一个解决方案，一个完全不同的折中方法，能让两人都高兴的方法。如果你经常说“不”，拒绝就会失去力量；如果使用得当，则能更受尊重。

78 深入理解

多数争吵都是源于沟通不畅，很多时候两人想法本就一致，但因表达方式不同而引起误解。想象一下，如果两人都能真正理解对方的意图，沟通就会特别顺畅，这种感觉简直太棒了！所以，一定要花时间深入理解伴侣的想法和观点，并解释自己的想法和观点，这很重要。沟通是一条双向的路，而两人必须朝同一个方向走。

我有一个朋友经常和爱人吵架，每次闲聊时，他总是抱怨妻子。我不明白他的抱怨从何而来，因为我和他爱人也是朋友。他妻子人很好，我也总跟他这么说。有一天，他俩在我面前吵了起来，我很快发现两人说的是一回事，只是表达方式不同。我指出这一关键所在，两人都很不好意思，承认我

Communication is about conveying an idea to another individual, but the problem is, we do not all speak or think the same way. What is in our heads, is not always what comes out of our mouths. This can spell disaster in a relationship if it is not addressed. Worse, it can sometimes come out right, but the other person still misunderstands what you said. The only way to combat such a situation is with patience and understanding. Before you get angry about something your partner said or did, try to understand why it happened. A lot of the time we make assumptions about their intentions, and our assumptions are wrong. Had we taken the time to actually discover the reasoning behind what they said or did, there would be an entirely different outcome.

"Help me understand" is a great opening line to resolve disagreements before they get out of hand.

79. LEARN BODY LANGUAGE (HOW TO READ AND HOW TO USE IT)

Body language can tell you a lot about what is going on in the confines of someone's head. It can tell you if they are happy, aroused, angry, scared, nervous, etc. The ability to read it can help better facilitate communication between you and your significant other, while misinterpreting it can spell disaster.

I have made a point of reading books and watching videos on this point. I am almost a master at reading someone's energy and body language. This has helped particularly in my marriage because my wife's first language is not English.

In a relationship, cues such as eye contact, touch, proximity, and an open stance between partners can signal attraction, happiness, comfort, and affection. On the other hand, a closed stance, physical distance, and avoiding eye contact can indicate nervousness, anger, or fear. It is important to be able to recognize these signs in your partner, as they may not always be comfortable saying exactly what is on their mind. If you can read their body language, you can react to help them through whatever it is they are feeling.

是对的。这种情况很常见。

沟通是将自己的想法传达给他人，但问题是，我们说话或思考的方式并不相同，我们口中所说并非都是心中所想，如果不解决这一问题，就会影响两人的感情。更糟的是，有时候你说出了自己的想法，但对方仍会误解你的意思。避免这种情况的唯一方法就是要拥有耐心并体谅对方。在因伴侣所作所为而生气之前，先要深入理解为什么会这样。很多时候，我们会猜想对方的意图，而这些想象可能都是错误的。如果我们花时间去真正了解对方所作所为的背后原因，就会有完全不同的结果。

“给我讲讲”是一个很好的开场白，可以在失控之前解决分歧。

79 肢体语言

学会肢体语言能了解他人心中所想，能知道对方是否快乐、激动、生气、害怕、紧张，等等。理解肢体语言有助于你和伴侣更好地去沟通，而误解肢体语言则会造成麻烦。

在这方面，我很重视通过看书和视频进行学习。我很擅长理解肢体语言，这对我的婚姻很有帮助，因为我太太的母语不是英语。

两人在一起时，伴侣之间的眼神交流、身体接触、亲密无间和接纳的姿态等暗示可以发出喜欢、幸福、舒适和爱慕的信号。另一方面，拒绝的姿态、肢体疏离、避开眼神等可能表明紧张、愤怒或恐惧。能够辨别伴侣这些暗示很重要，因为对方可能不便直说自己的想法，如果你能了解肢体语言，就能想办法帮助对方应对这些感受。

理解肢体语言有助于夫妻更好地沟通。非语言交流配合语言交流，让你

Being able to read body language can help couples better communicate. Nonverbal communication, in concert with the spoken word, makes it easier to understand and empathize with your partner. You can decipher what your significant other is saying based on their words and their body language, which helps you to better appreciate their emotional state. If they are telling you something and are displaying signs of nervousness, you must be patient and understanding. While if their body language says they are happy, it invites you to get excited.

Beyond being able to read body language, you need to be open with your own. Show your significant other you love them in how you carry yourself and embrace them. It is a love language not to be neglected, and can forge a stronger bond because it lets them know they have you body, mind, and spirit.

80. KEEP A POWER NOTE OF 25 REASONS WHY YOU LOVE YOUR SPOUSE

The hardest thing about writing twenty-five reasons I love my wife was stopping at 25! I could easily have written an entire book on the subject, and the one you are reading is testimony to that. On that same topic, we are in the process of making a Hollywood movie, titled "THE TRUE ZOOM TO ZOOM STORY OF LOVE, ROMANCE, AND MARRIAGE," which will illustrate many more reasons. Meanwhile, I will not bore you with the items on my own personal list, but I will explain why every married couple should make one.

The list is fun to write. When you write a list of the twenty-five reasons you love your spouse, you get to relive all of the moments that created it. I instantly flashed back to meeting the love of my life at Zoom and everything in between. We have had crazy, fun days and romantic nights ever since, and every one of those has a special place in my heart. Recalling them is heartwarming but keeping my list to just 25 points was as difficult as choosing my favorite song. I have so many favorites I can never choose just one.

更容易理解和同情伴侣。根据其所说话语并结合肢体语言，你就能更加懂得伴侣，更能理解对方的情绪状态。如果伴侣和你说什么事，并表现得很紧张，你一定要拥有耐心并体谅对方。而如果对方的肢体语言表明她很高兴，就是想和你分享快乐。

除了能够理解肢体语言，也要学会运用肢体语言，用行动去拥抱伴侣来表达你的爱。一定要重视这种爱的语言，它能让两人的感情更牢固，让对方知道能够拥有你的身体、思想和心灵。

80 写出理由

要写出“爱伴侣的 25 个理由”对我来说最难的是只能写 25 个！我可以轻轻松松写出一整本书，你正在读的这本书就是证据。我们正在筹拍以我俩为主题的好莱坞电影，片名为《从 Zoom 到 Zoom 的奇缘——关于爱情、浪漫和婚姻的真实故事》。此刻，我不会拿我写的 25 个理由来烦人，但我会解释为什么每个已婚夫妇都应该写出理由。

写出理由很有意思，当你写下爱伴侣的 25 个理由时，就会重温所有过往的美好时光。我立刻回想起在 Zoom 便利店遇到一生挚爱，以及其间发生的一切。我们有过狂热、有趣的日子，也有过浪漫的夜晚，每一时刻都在我心中占有特殊位置。回忆令人感动，但让我把理由控制在 25 条以内，就像选择最喜欢的歌曲一样难，我喜欢的太多了，真是难以抉择。

列出你爱伴侣的 25 个理由，每天看看，会让你想起以前的美好时光。

Having a list of 25 reasons why you love your partner and looking at it daily will remind you of the good times. Be dynamic and update the list once per month. People can get busy, and life can throw you curveballs. It is in these instances that our minds wander, and we may forget exactly why and what it is we love about our significant others. If you have a prewritten list, it will not only remind you of how blessed you are to have your spouse, but it can turn a bad day into a great one. Sometimes a small shift of momentum is all that you need!

When you make your list, do not be afraid to be specific. Go into detail as to why you love your partner. Feel free to include memories of occasions together and how they made you feel. These are all important to the process. The more specific you are, the better your list will be. Then once you are done, share it with your spouse. Not only will it remind you of all the reasons why you love them, but it will let them know how much they are loved.

If you want to carry this a step further, a "love journal" in which you write only good things every day is a powerful reminder of how lucky you are to be married to the person you are with. Most people do not keep journals because they assume it will take too much time. This is not necessarily true. If you take just five or ten minutes every day and write only the headlines, that is all it takes to memorialize each wonderful day in your marriage.

On some days, nothing significant may happen at all, but you can always find something to jot down. For example, you could write something like, "When I looked in my beautiful wife's eyes today, I saw my forever love." Or, "My love for her is stronger and more powerful than ever today. I don't know why, but it has given me more energy than I have ever known." Or maybe even, "Today when we kissed and hugged the world seemed to stop." Later, when you read these journal headlines, they can help you to relive that wonderful day or experience. If you make a habit of writing in the journal every day, it will become a joyful habit. Since you are only writing good things and not secrets, your spouse can also look at it when you want to boost their mood. It will keep the romantic fire burning forever.

你也可以随时变动它们，每月更新一次理由清单。人们越来越忙碌，生活也会麻烦不断，在这种情况下，人的思想就会游离，会忘记当初为什么爱伴侣，爱的又是哪方面。事先写好清单，不仅能提醒你拥有伴侣多么幸福，而且还能改变当前的心情。有时候，你所需要的只是一个小小的转变！

列清单时，别嫌繁琐，要详述爱对方的理由，写下在一起时的回忆和感受，这些对整个进程都很重要，清单越具体越好。写完之后让伴侣看，不仅能让你想起爱对方的原因，还会让伴侣获悉你的爱。

如果想进一步发挥，可以写一本《爱情日记》，每天只写那些美好的事，这样就能不断提醒你，能和爱人结婚是多么幸运。大多数人不写日记，因为太费时间，这也不完全正确，每天花五到十分钟，哪怕只写标题，也可以让我们记住婚姻中每一个美好的日子。

在那些平淡无奇的日子里，你也能记录一些事。例如，你可以这样写："今天，当我看着漂亮太太的双眸时，看到了我永恒之爱。"或者："我对她的爱比往昔更加浓烈，不知为何，我拥有了前所未有的力量。"还可以是："今天，当我们亲吻拥抱时，世界都为之静止。"之后，当你看到日记标题时，就能助你重温那些美好情景。要养成每天写日记的习惯，这绝对是一个快乐的习惯，既然你记下的都是好事而不是秘密，当你想让伴侣开心时，就能拿给伴侣看。这本日记能让爱情之火永远燃烧。

81. WHEN IT COMES TO MAKING LOVE, ALWAYS THINK OF YOUR SPOUSE'S NEEDS FIRST

Years ago, I was sitting at an outside restaurant in Chicago with a friend, a beautiful and elegant lady, but not my lover. A guy walked by with a shirt that read, in big letters, "I do not need Viagra." She looked at the guy and laughed. I asked her what was so funny. She said that guy just does not get it. She then told me that she would prefer to be with a lover who is willing to take Viagra than a person like that. "I want a guy that cares about me."

A guy like that obviously only cares about himself. She wanted to find a guy who cared about her as his first priority, one who would take every step possible to be a better lover. Why should she settle for a man whose only own objective is his own pleasure and not hers? The winning choice for a woman is a guy who puts her needs above his own, and that goes way past having sex.

I let this way of thinking bleed over into all areas of my marriage. This experience impacted me from that day forward and has made me a better man. I am more considerate and caring than ever, and I credit this story to that behavior. The greatest gift a man can get is when a woman gives herself to him.

This goes beyond caring and putting the needs of your lover above your own. I do everything I can to show my wife that I put her desires above my own in every category. By caring first about her instead of myself I create an atmosphere of love and trust between the two of us.

There are so many little things you can do outside of the bedroom that demonstrate this principle, sending her messages throughout the day, for example. If only takes seconds and is a powerful way to show that you care more about your spouse than yourself and that they are on your mind all the time.

Another way of achieving this goal is through the appropriate mindset, showing your spouse that nothing is an inconvenience in your relationship with them. Maybe it is turning

81 伴侣优先

多年前，我和朋友坐在芝加哥一家露天餐厅里，这个朋友是一位美丽优雅的女士，但不是我的爱人。当时有一个男士走过，衬衫上印着大字："我不需要'伟哥'。"朋友看着那个人笑了起来，我问她有什么好笑的，她说那家伙不明事理，然后告诉我，她宁可和愿意服用"伟哥"的情人在一起："我想要一个在乎我的男人。"

那种男人显然只关心自己。她想找一个把她放在第一位的男人，能竭尽一切成为更好情人的男人。女人为什么要嫁给只图自己快乐而不顾及女方快乐的男人呢？对女人来说，最佳的选择是把女方的需求放在首位的男人，而这远远比做爱重要。

我将这种思维方式渗透到婚姻中。从那天起，这件事就一直影响着我，让我成为更好的自己。我比以往任何时候都更体贴、更有爱心，都源于此事。男人能得到最好的礼物就是女人把自己交给男人。

不仅关心伴侣并将对方的需求放在首位，我还竭尽全力向太太表明，在任何方面，我都把她的意愿放在我的意愿之上。通过先关心她而不是自己，我在我俩之间营造出了关爱和信任的氛围。

在卧室以外的世界，有很多小事能证明这一原则，例如，随时给对方发信息，只需几秒钟，就能有效证明你更在意伴侣，整天想着伴侣。

其他一些方式也能实现这一目标，要向伴侣表明，你俩之间不会有任何不便之处。当伴侣做重要事情时，你要把手机调成静音；当伴侣看书时，尽量不要打扰；当你起床时，不要吵醒熟睡中的伴侣；在伴侣没说的情况下就

your phone to silent when they are doing something important or being quiet if they are reading a book. Maybe it is not waking your spouse up from a deep sleep when you get up. Running to the store to grab something for your spouse without even being asked is powerful. Trust creates feelings of safety, security, and caring, and that should be your goal. A smile goes miles in showing you are in love. Every little thing you do to show your spouse that they come first in your life is a win for her and for you.

I always want to know my wife's thoughts because I value her opinion. Knowing her thoughts on a subject helps keep our lives in alignment. It is also a sign of respect to ask her opinion. It shows her that I value what she says. It illustrates that I am working hard on coordinating her thoughts with mine so that we both win. I may sound weak, but honestly, if she feels strongly about something, I just go with her opinion and forget my own. I am always more than willing to adjust my schedule to accommodate hers. I will reschedule other commitments when needed because she always comes first with me.

As a last point, my wife's ongoing safety is priority number one with me. With her I am extremely safety conscience. I avoid all unsafe situations. I want My wife to feel safe and secure at all times. She knows how seriously I take this job, and it is one of the ultimate ways of putting her needs above mine.

82. BE LOYAL AND AVOID ALL TEMPTATION

Temptations are everywhere, and it is natural for someone in a relationship to be tempted to stray. However, it is disastrous to even entertain the thought of disloyalty to your spouse. It is one thing to notice an attractive person—after all, you are not dead—but it is another to ogle them or imagine scenarios where you end up meeting, and perhaps go further. Even thinking about such possibilities is being disloyal and is unhealthy for you and your relationship.

We become what we think about. If you think about other men or women, you will inevitably lust after them. I am not saying it is wrong to appreciate another person's beauty, I

跑到商店给对方买东西效果更好。信任能造就安全和关爱的氛围，这才是目标。微笑能表达爱意，你所做的每一件小事都向伴侣表明，一切都以对方为首，这才是成功的婚姻。

我很想知道我太太的想法，因为我重视她的观点。了解她对某件事的想法有助于我俩在生活中保持一致。询问她的看法也是尊重的表现，表明我重视她所说的话，且努力协调两人的观点，以便实现双赢。我可能看起来很软弱，但老实说，如果她对某件事很坚决，我就会听从她的意见，而忽略我的。我还非常乐意调整自己的日程来配合她，如果需要，我会重新安排其他任务，因为她永远排在第一位。

最后一点，保证爱人的安全是我的头等大事，和她在一起时，我会特别关注安全问题，避开一切危险情况。我希望太太在任何时候都能有安全感，她知道我特别在意这件事，这也是把她的需求置于我之上的终极方式之一。

82 避免诱惑

诱惑无处不在，有伴侣的人被诱惑出轨也常见。然而，即使是对伴侣有不忠的想法都非常可怕。被有魅力的人吸引不算什么，毕竟你是性情中人；但向对方抛媚眼或想象和对方幽会的场景，甚至想更进一步，那就另当别论了，即使只是在心里琢磨也属于不忠，会危及你和伴侣的感情。

人很容易被自己的想法支配，如果你总想着其他异性，就会产生欲望。我并不是说不能欣赏别人的美，我是说，一旦超出简单的欣赏时，就会出问

am saying there is a problem when it goes beyond simple appreciation. Thoughts should be directed back home towards your significant other.

Infidelity is one of the biggest breaches of trust imaginable in a relationship. Its repercussions can be life altering. Not only can you lose your relationship, but you will crush your partner's heart and soul. It is very possible they will never be the same after such a betrayal. It leads to headache, heartbreak, and quite frankly, a recipe for disaster!

Appreciate what you have at home. Instead of wasting your energy lusting after people outside of your relationship, use those resources and that energy to improve what you already have. Maybe you feel like the romance is gone from your relationship, thus it is justified for you to step out. This is misguided thinking. Instead, use that effort to improve your current relationship and restore the romance. You and your significant other are forever. Do not throw it away over a pretty face.

Always cherish what you have. If you have given up on romance in your current relationship, you will probably give up on it in your next. Keep what you already have alive and love your partner with everything you have. That is the best and the only choice for me.

83. UNDERSTAND THE GOALS OF THE ONE YOU LOVE AND HELP THEM ACHIEVE THEM

In a relationship, one of your primary goals should be to help your significant other achieve and realize their dreams. You and your partner should prioritize being healthy and happy. People are happiest when they have a purpose. Chasing and achieving one's dreams provides such a purpose. For this reason, it is crucial for a couple to work together to help each other's ambitions come to fruition.

Talk to your spouse and discover what they hope to achieve in life. This can be a very enlightening conversation and can bring you both closer together. I would hope you already have some idea of what makes them tick, but dig deep. Draw out the details. The truth is,

题。你应该把心思放在伴侣身上。

在亲密关系中，不忠是信任的最大敌人，且影响深远。你不仅会失去感情，还会让你的伴侣心力交瘁。经历这种背叛之后，你的伴侣再也不会回到从前，从此身心俱疲，简直后患无穷！

要珍惜现有的一切，与其浪费精力去追求外人，不如利用这些资源和精力来改善现有的感情。或许你感到两人的关系已经情淡爱弛，因此你有理由离开。这是错误的想法。你应该努力改善现有的感情，重拾浪漫。你和伴侣要永远在一起，不能因为外来诱惑而放弃。

要永远珍惜你所拥有的一切。如果你放弃现在的感情，将来很可能重蹈覆辙。要让现在拥有的感情越来越好，尽你所有去爱伴侣。这对我来说是最好也是唯一的选择。

83 实现梦想

在亲密关系中，你的主要目标之一应该是帮助伴侣实现梦想。你和伴侣应该首先考虑健康和快乐，有目标的人最快乐，而追逐和实现梦想正是人生目标，因此，夫妻双方要共同努力，帮助彼此实现梦想，这一点至关重要。

和伴侣谈谈心，了解对方的人生目标，这会很有启发，能拉近两人的关系。我想你已经知道对方的一些梦想了，要深入了解，问出细节。就我而言，太太说的很多事我并不了解，她总会有新奇而令人兴奋的梦想。如果你认为已经了解了伴侣的所有梦想，那么相信我，你并没有。如果你和伴

I do not know all the things I want, and there are always new and exciting dreams. If you think you already know all your spouse's dreams, trust me, you do not. If you explore those dreams with your spouse, you may discover new and exciting goals you can achieve together. Find out how they hope to accomplish their goals. Put together a timetable and discuss steps on how you can make it happen together. It may take a little sacrifice from both sides, but it will be worth it in the end, and your relationship will come out stronger.

My wife and I discuss our goals regularly. We have a great time planning how we will achieve them. It is fun to imagine, and it is even more fun to put into action. When you see your significant other's goals coming to life, it warms your heart to know you helped make that happen.

Working together to achieve your partners goals can be laborious at times, depending on what their goals may be, but it is great fun once you begin to make progress. It will strengthen your relationship and connect you in ways you never imagined. It will also make for a happy and productive home life. It is always good to have direction and purpose. Working to achieve your significant others goals provides that.

84. EVERY DAY IS VALENTINE'S DAY

Valentine's Day is just an excuse for people to do what they should already be doing. You shouldn't need a holiday devoted to love to show the one you love how much you care. That should be an everyday occurrence. Every time you wake up, you should be thinking about how you can make today special for your spouse. Give them flowers or little gifts randomly throughout the week and show them why they are special. Call them in the middle of the day just to tell them you love and appreciate them. Valentine's Day is fun, but to me, gestures mean less on a holiday where you are obligated to behave a certain way. It means much more to do it on your own reconnaissance.

To me, every day is Valentine's Day. I don't need the calendar to tell me to treat my wife special. I make sure she knows it every hour of every day. I tell her I love her. I treat her

侣一起探索这些梦想，就会发现新奇而令人兴奋的目标，你们可以一起实现。要了解伴侣希望如何实现目标，然后制定计划，并讨论如何共同实现这一目标。可能双方都要做出一点牺牲，但最终都会值得，你们的感情也会更牢固。

我和爱人会定期讨论我们的目标，规划如何实现梦想。一起畅想未来很有意思，而付诸行动则更有趣。当伴侣在你的助力下实现目标时，你就会很欣慰。

一起努力实现伴侣的目标可能会很辛苦，这取决于目标是什么，而一旦取得进展，就会很有趣，能加强你们的感情，更能让两人前所未有地团结，还能让家庭生活幸福美满。一定要有目标和方向，要努力帮助伴侣实现梦想。

84 天天过节

情人节不过是个借口，好让人们去做本该做的事。其实没必要非要等一个专门的节日来向爱人示爱，示爱应该是日常习惯。早上醒来时，想想今天要怎样表现才能让伴侣感到特别；每天都送鲜花或小礼物，让伴侣心情愉悦；随时打电话，向伴侣表达爱意。情人节很好，但对我来说，在必须按规定行事的节日里，再怎么表现都意义不大，而你平日里诚心实意的行为更有意义。

对我来说，天天过节。我不需要日历来提醒我要好好对待太太，我要让她每时每刻都明白我爱她，她是我的唯一，事实如此。我绝不让她感到被忽

like she is the only person for me, because she is. I never want her to feel like she is being neglected, and I make a conscious effort to see that happen.

Couples are often happiest on Valentine's Day because they are actually showing one another how much they love each other. Why wait? Wouldn't life be better if every day was like that? Yes, you will not be making a grand gesture and dining at a fine establishment every evening, but that doesn't mean you can't make a meal at home romantic. My wife and I like to set up candles and eat on our balcony, overlooking the city. It is just as romantic as any restaurant, and we get to enjoy the privacy of our own home.

Find ways to make every day special for your significant other. When every day is Valentine's Day, your life will be a holiday and your love will be in full bloom!

85. STAYCATIONS WORK, SO MIX IT UP

Who says you have to visit exotic locations or fly halfway around the world to have a great vacation. Why not do it near your home? A staycation is exactly that. It is a when you go on vacation near where you live and treat your hometown as if you were a tourist. This is a lot of fun. It allows you to see and experience parts of the city you never would as a resident. Typically, when we live somewhere, we do not spend our time visiting the tourist traps. As a result, you can live in a city for years, and never see or experience the sights that made it famous. Get together with your significant other and decide where you want to stay. Perhaps rent a room for the night in your downtown area, or maybe in a nearby city you have never explored.

The key to a successful staycation is to treat it like you are on the other side of the planet. Disconnect from everything. Be fully present and get excited. Do not think about work or inviting others to join your party even though they may be right down the block. As far as you and your spouse are concerned, they are a million miles away.

See your city with new eyes. Spending a staycation where you live, or in a nearby city, can help you and your partner see your city in a new light. Rather than looking at where you

视，我会竭尽所能保护她。

情侣在情人节时最幸福，因为每个人都会在此时向对方表达爱意。为什么非要等那一天呢？如果天天过节，生活不是更美好吗？是的，你不可能每天晚上都在高档餐厅吃豪华大餐，但可以在家里做一顿浪漫的晚餐。我和太太喜欢在阳台上点上蜡烛共进晚餐，一起俯瞰城市，浪漫情调堪比任何一家餐厅，还能在自己家中享受二人世界。

要想办法让伴侣感觉每天都很特别。如果每天都是情人节，就能每天都生活在假期中，你的爱情之花就会盛开！

85 周边度假

谁说一定要去异国他乡或飞越半个地球才能享受美好假期？为什么不能就近度假？所谓周边度假，就是在家乡附近度假，把自己当作游客，这样很有意思，能让你体验作为居民永远发现不了的城市面貌。通常，当我们居住在某地时，不会花时间去本地的旅游景点，因此，即便在这个城市生活多年，也从未去过当地的著名景地。和伴侣一起规划行程，比如在市中心租一间房过夜，或者去之前没去过的附近小城。

周边度假成功的关键是要把自己当作异乡客，要断绝一切联系，全心投入，尽享欢乐。别再想着工作，也不用邀请其他人一起玩，即使他们可能就住在街区对面，对于你和伴侣来说，他们离你有十万八千里。

要用全新的眼光观看你居住的这座城市。在你所住城市或附近小城度过假期，有助于你和伴侣重新看待这座城市。不要把你的家看作只是居住地而

live as a means to an end, you can get excited about everything it has to offer. Life is about challenging perceptions, and you will do just that.

In my experience, when I return home from a staycation, I still feel like I am on vacation. I can roll those romantic feelings and that excitement seamlessly into the next week.

86. TAKE TIME TO RECHARGE FROM A HARD WEEK, MONTH OR YEAR. SLOW DOWN AND ENJOY YOUR LOVE NEST WITH YOUR PHONES TURNED OFF

You cannot go, go, go, go, and never rest. Eventually, you will run out of gas. Sometimes even a vacation can be overwhelming if you are overworked and overstressed. Instead, plan some time with your spouse to stay home and totally disconnect from the world. Shut off your phones, and let everyone who needs to know that you will be incommunicado for a few hours or days. Spend that time being present with your husband or wife. Enjoy each other's company and let the rest of the world wait.

My wife and I love to shut ourselves up in our room and cuddle in bed. We pretend we are the only people on the planet. I find that during this time, all of my stress and exhaustion melt away. Sometimes we will do this for a few hours. I always hope it can be for a few days, but I am so busy. Even a few hours are mood changing, however. Whenever we rejoin the world, we feel happy, refreshed, and motivated to take it on!

Take comfort in your spouse and find peace. When things outside feel like they are getting to be too much, remember that you have the love of your life at home. Your home is your fortress, and the love you and your partner share is the guard. Take solace in one another and enjoy each other. Spend some time pretending the rest of the world doesn't exist and just be together.

The only problem with retreating into your love nest is reemerging. It is so nice and

已，要对周围的一切感兴趣。生活就是挑战观念，你肯定能做到。

根据我的经验，在周边度假之后，我依然会觉得自己还在度假。我可以把那些浪漫的感觉和兴奋的时刻延续到下一周。

86 二人世界

你不能一直前进、从不休息，这样最终会耗尽体力。如果工作过度，压力过大，就算外出度假也会让你不堪重负，那不如就和伴侣待在家里，完全脱离外界，关掉手机，通知相关人士你将在几小时或在几天内不愿被打扰，和自己的伴侣一起度过这段时间，享受彼此的陪伴，忘掉其他一切。

我和我太太喜欢把自己关在房间里，依偎在床上，假装地球上只有我们二人。我发现，在这种时候，所有的压力和疲惫都会消失。有时，我们会这样待几个小时。我一直希望可以这样休息几天，但是我实在太忙了。然而，即使是几个小时，我的情绪也能好转。每当我们重新回到现实世界时，都会感到心情愉悦、精神焕发，并能积极面对生活！

你可以从伴侣那里得到安慰、寻求平静。当你感到外面的世界难以承受之时，要记住家里有你生命中的挚爱。家是你的堡垒，你们的爱则是守卫。彼此安慰，彼此欣赏，假装整个世界都不存在，只有你们的二人世界。

回归家庭、享受二人世界之后的唯一问题是要重新回到现实世界。和爱人独处是如此美好和舒适，我永远都不想离开，所以，我需要极大的毅力才

comfortable being alone with My wife, I never want to leave. It takes all of my willpower to rejoin the real world, but when I finally do, I feel better than ever. Take time to cut off the world, bask in your significant other's love, and shower yours upon them. The world will wait.

87. GENTLEMEN, DO YOU WANT MORE ROMANCE AND SEX IN YOUR MARRIAGE? SIMPLY CLEAN THE BATHROOM

Every woman in the world with, no expectations, including my wife, cherishes a clean bathroom. The biggest complaint married women have about their husband is not caring about the hygiene of the bathroom. Sorry guys, they are right! Sure, not all men are guilty but many of you are. If you are one of them, it is time to develop a new mindset.

A clean bathroom will have more impact on your relationship than a dozen roses every day. Cleaning the toilet cannot beat a new diamond, but even here it is a close second. It's simply good common sense if you think about it. For real love, the kind that lasts for forever, it is not just the grand gestures that give the relationship ongoing romance, it is cleaning the bathroom!

Women do not want to be with a man who doesn't take care of himself. That starts with being clean. I try not to think about all the nasty things that go on in the bathroom. It is a catchall for all things filthy. It is a virtual cesspool of disease. Bad germs and viruses are just the start of what a dirty bathroom represents.

From the perspective of your wife, simply cleaning the bathroom is monumental in their minds. We are only talking basic hygiene, which you should also want, but many men do not understand the importance of a clean bathroom, and the impact on their relationship. It is a meaningful commitment to your wife and yourself, and that's the foundation of any healthy relationship.

Hygiene experts recommend cleaning the bathroom once a week. Personally, I clean

能重新回到现实世界，回来以后，我会感觉更好。要留出时间切断与外界的联系，沐浴在伴侣的爱情中，也把你的爱全部奉献给伴侣，暂时忘记外面的一切。

87 清洁浴室

世界上所有女人，包括我太太在内，都喜欢干净的浴室。已婚女子对丈夫抱怨最多的就是不注意浴室卫生。对不起，伙计们，确实如此！当然，不是所有男人都有问题，但多数男人都不注意卫生。如果你也是其中一员，那就要赶紧改变观念。

清洁浴室要比每天送一打玫瑰对感情的影响更大。干净的卫生间虽比不上一颗新钻石，但也仅次于它。请你仔细想想，这是最普通的常识，对于真正的爱，那种能持久的爱，不是那些高大上的举动才能让感情持续浪漫，而是清洁浴室这种小事！

女人不愿意和不修边幅的男人在一起，人首先要爱干净。我尽量不去想浴室里的各种卫生问题，包括所有污秽的东西，它们实际上就是疾病的温床，有害细菌和病毒只是肮脏的初步问题。

对于妻子来说，清洁浴室是其心中执念。我们指的是最基本的卫生，这也是丈夫需要的，但是很多男人并不理解干净浴室的重要性及其对夫妻关系的影响，这是对两人感情的全心投入，是美满婚姻的基础。

卫生专家建议每周清洁一次浴室。就我个人而言，我每天都打扫，因为只需要几分钟。实际上，我在每个卫生间里都放了清洁用品，这样打扫起来

it daily, as it only takes a few minutes. I actually keep the cleaning supplies in each of the bathrooms to make it easy. You do not need to be like me, but trust me, cleaning the bathroom once per week will create a mood of love.

A central theme in this book has been the preaching of consistency and the importance of the little things. Cleaning the bathroom is the ultimate in a meaningful little thing. For most people, it is not fun to clean the bathroom. I have made it a routine, habit, and ritual, and I now I just do it on autopilot. It is actually weirdly romantic if you think about it. At times we both drop what we're doing, grab some paper towels and cleaning solution, and then tackle the bathroom cleaning duties together. Sometimes we even make love after such a job. Of course, a shower comes before the love making. Clean is our theme with this point.

Keeping your bathroom clean should not only be done because you love your spouse, but also because you respect yourself. Just because you do it initially for selfish reasons, like the fact it will improve your love life, doesn't take away from the fact you did it.

88. WORK ON ALWAYS BEING A BETTER PERSON. IT SHOWS YOU CARE

Working on yourself is one of the most selfless and caring things you can do for your significant other. It may not seem like it when you say it out loud, but if you take a second to think about all it implies, the reason will be clear. I certainly wouldn't write "I'm working on myself" in a Birthday card, and give it as a present, but that is exactly what it is. It's a gift that keeps on giving, and not just to you or your spouse, but everyone who comes into contact with you.

Life is about growing, and while we cannot help getting older, we can continually work on our physical, mental and spiritual health. When these three things are in balance, the world is a totally different place. Things that were once obstacles are now easily overcome. You will have a brighter worldview, and subsequently enjoy life at a higher level. This will

更方便。你没必要和我一样，但是相信我，每周清洁一次浴室能产生爱的氛围。

这本书的中心思想是主张一致性和提示小事情的重要性。打扫卫生间就是一件极有意义的小事。对大多数人来说，清洁浴室很没意思。我已经将之形成日常习惯，现在每天都会打扫。你仔细想想，这其实是一种奇怪的浪漫。有时，我们会放下手头的工作，拿一些纸巾和清洁液，然后一起清洁浴室，甚至打扫完毕后会做爱。当然，做爱前要先洗澡，毕竟卫生是第一位的。

清洁浴室不仅是因为你爱伴侣，也是因为你尊重自己。如果一开始清洁浴室是出于自私的原因，比如这样就能改善爱情生活，那么，你也做到了。

88 提升自我

努力提升自我，是你能为伴侣所做的最无私、最体贴的事情之一。说起来可能没那么重要，但如果仔细想想其中深意，你就会明白。我当然不会在生日贺卡上写出“我正在努力提升自我”，然后作为礼物送给太太，但这确实是礼物，是能一直馈赠的礼物，不仅能送给自己或伴侣，更能送给每一个相处之人。

人生意味着不断成长，虽然我们无法避免衰老，但可以通过不断努力来保持身体、心理和精神的健康，当这三者达到平衡之时，世界都将焕然一新，能让我们更容易克服困难，并拥有更积极的世界观，享受更高层次的生

lead to increased success and a happier home.

Conscious effort to keep improving who you are is a must. Your physical, mental, and spiritual health must be maintained. Work hard on being in balance to be able to enjoy life to its fullest.

Spend time each day working on all of these. Do not neglect any of them, as they are all equally important and tied together. Go for a walk, hit the gym, meditate. Each will help you with enjoying good mental and physical health. Say a prayer or read your bible for your spiritual wellbeing. There are countless ways to improve yourself. Find what works best and put together a routine. This can be a fun activity to do with your spouse. There is no rule that says you have to improve yourself alone. A lot of the time, these exercises are more effective when done with someone you love and trust.

Working on yourself is a wonderful gift to give your spouse. Everyone can always be a better version of their current self. Everyone has room to improve. Becoming a better you should be your goal. Being a better you is a golden key for a stronger and healthier marriage.

89. KNOW WHAT WILL CALM BOTH YOU AND YOUR SPOUSE DOWN THE FASTEST, AND LEARN A TECHNIQUE TO MAKE THAT HAPPEN

I hope you know what works best to calm yourself when you get angry or upset. In a relationship, you must be able to control your emotions. You do not want to be at the mercy of your most primal urges. This will not be healthy for your spouse, your relationship, or you. Similarly, you must learn what your significant other needs to get back to baseline when they are agitated, and learn to put it into practice when you see them entering that emotional state.

Too often, couples have the urge to poke the wound. When someone sees their partner is angry or upset, particularly if they are involved, they oddly feel a need to make the

活，也让我们的人生更成功、家庭更幸福。

要不断努力提升自我，保持身体、心理和精神健康，努力保持平衡，才能真正享受生活。

每天都要努力保持平衡，不能忽视任何一方面，因为各方面相互交织且同样重要。散步、健身、冥想都有助于身心健康，做祈祷或读《圣经》有利于精神健康。有无数方法可以提升自我，找出最有效的方法，并养成习惯。和伴侣一起做这种活动会很有意思。没人规定要一个人独自提升自我，很多时候，和相爱且信任的人一起做会更有效。

努力提升自我是送给伴侣最好的礼物。每个人都可以成为更好的自己，也都有上升空间，应该以此为目标。做一个更好的自己是通往更牢固、更健康婚姻的金钥匙。

89 快速冷静

在生气或心烦的时候，但愿你能知道让自己快速冷静下来的方法。在感情关系中，你必须控制好自己的情绪，你肯定不愿被最原始的冲动所摆布，这对你的伴侣、你们的感情或你自己都很不健康。同样，你必须知道，当伴侣焦虑不安时，要怎样才能让对方快速冷静，当你看到伴侣进入那种情绪状态时，就要付诸实践。

很多时候，夫妻都会有戳人伤疤的冲动，当某人看到伴侣生气或心烦，尤其是自己也卷入其中时，就奇怪地想让情况变得更糟，这多半是出于冲动，而不是有意为之，就像你忍不住用舌头去舔已经咬破的嘴唇一样，人们

situation worse. Usually it is an impulse more than a conscious thought. Just like you can't help but prod your bit lip with your tongue, they are compelled to stick the knife in a little further. It goes without saying, this is an unhealthy behavior. It is why small disagreements balloon into apocalyptic throw downs. Instead of going with your natural instinct, learn to do the opposite.

Discover what works best to calm you and your partner down. Perhaps it is going on a walk around the block to clear your head. If that is the case, tell your partner what you are doing, so they do not believe you abandoned them, then take a stroll and try to relax. With any luck, a little distance and time will allow both parties to calm down and revisit the situation a bit more rationally. Or if it was unimportant, you can drop it entirely.

If your spouse is upset, and they are the type of person who needs space, give it to them. If they like a peace offering, bring them a donut or something, even if you think they are wrong. Do what is necessary to de-escalate the situation. It is not always easy in the moment, but through determination, you can learn to keep things on an even keel. This will result in a much happier and less tumultuous relationship.

90. ASK YOUR SPOUSE IF THERE ARE THINGS THAT YOU DO THAT ARE ANNOYING, THEN MODIFY YOUR BEHAVIOR

We all have tendencies that we are unaware of which can be grating to another human being. Perhaps you never throw you dirty socks in the clothes hamper, or maybe you always put the dishes back in the wrong place. These are little things, but over time, they have the propensity to become the straw that broke the camel's back. If your spouse is already upset about something, and they go to get a plate but cannot find it because you put it back in the wrong place, despite being asked to be more careful a hundred times, the tipping point may be reached. We can all agree, this is best avoided, so why not take the time to ask them if there is anything else you do that bothers them before the explosion occurs. After all, it is not that

会忍不住把刀插得更深。毋庸置疑，这种行为很不好，正因如此，小小分歧会演变成世界末日般巨大的争吵，所以千万不能一时冲动，要反其道而行之。

找出能让你和伴侣快速冷静的最有效的方法，或许是绕着街区散步，让头脑清醒。如果这样有效，要告诉伴侣你散步的原因，以免对方误解，然后出去走一走，试着放松一下。离开一段时间会让双方冷静下来，然后再重新思考问题，如果是不重要的小事，就算了吧。

如果你的伴侣生气了，而对方又是需要空间的人，就要给予对方空间。如果伴侣想要和解的礼物，那就送一个甜甜圈之类的礼物，即使你认为对方错了。要想方设法缓和局势，这种时候确实不容易，但要坚定信念，慢慢让事情平稳过渡，你们的感情就会更幸福、更和谐。

90 做出改变

我们都有自己意识不到的癖好，而有些会令他人感到不快，比如总是忘记把脏袜子扔进洗衣篮里，或者总是把盘子放错位置。这些都是小事，但长此以往，就有可能成为压垮骆驼的最后一根稻草。如果你的伴侣已经为某事生气了，这时去拿盘子却找不到，因为你把盘子放错了地方，尽管以前跟你说过一百次别再放错，但这次就会达到引爆点。我们都不愿发生这样的事情，所以为什么不在伴侣爆发之前问一下，你是否有哪些恼人行为困扰着对方？毕竟把盘子放回正确的位置并不难，所以我建议第一次就放对位置。

hard to put your plates back in the right place, so my advice is to do it right the first time.

Communication and action are key. Taking a few minutes to adhere to such small requests is so easy and will most likely make all the difference to your significant other, bringing love and romance to higher and higher levels. However, if you do not take the time to talk with them and find out what these things are, they could become a big problem down the line.

Have a conversation with your spouse about the things you each do that may annoy the other. This is not about taking shots, or insulting the other person. Tell them clearly that you will not take offence during the talk. Instead of taking it personally, you will listen and enthusiastically do as they ask. This exercise is to strengthen your relationship. If done in the right way, it will never lead to a fight. If it is you that is asking them to change, start with a well thought out list and convey it lovingly. Simultaneously, be open and accepting of all the critiques they may have to make about you. These kinds of conversations are easy if done from the point of love and respect. Take it seriously, and be willing to make the effort these changes require.

91. PUBLICLY PRAISE YOUR SPOUSE. MAKE THEM NOT ONLY LOOK GOOD, BUT AMAZING!

I publicly and privately praise my wife every chance I get. I love to talk about her. In fact, I think I may talk about her a little too much. My friends are probably sick of hearing how great she is, but I don't care, I am going to keep telling them.

Do not just show your love at home or when your significant other is around. Share your feelings with the world. Do not be shy about praising your spouse on all occasions. I will tell everyone how lucky I am, from a checkout clerk at the ZOOM store, to my business partners. I do not do it to brag, I do it because I feel so blessed and want to share the joy. Think about it, you are reading this book and it's all about how much I love my wife.

沟通和行动是关键，只需几分钟就能很容易遵守伴侣的小小要求，而且会让对方万分高兴，你们会更相爱。然而，如果不和伴侣沟通，不了解哪些行为令对方烦恼，就会将其彻底变成大问题。

和伴侣聊聊各自有哪些恼人行为，不能相互攻击或侮辱人格，告诉伴侣谈论这些时你不会生气，你会倾听并真心按照对方的要求去做，而不会介意。这样做能让你们的感情更牢固，如果处理得当，根本不会争吵。如果是你在要求对方做出改变，要事先想好，并充满爱意地表达出来，同时，对伴侣可能提出的所有批评都要敞开心胸并虚心接受。如果从关爱和尊重的角度出发，这类对话会很顺利，要认真对待，并能够心甘情愿地做出改变。

91 当众赞扬

我一有机会就当众或私下称赞我太太。我很喜欢提起她，实际上，我觉得提到她的次数太多了，总是说她有多棒，估计我的朋友们已经听烦了，但我不在乎，我要继续跟他们说。

不要只在家里或伴侣在场的时候示爱，要和全世界分享你的感受，在任何场合都不要羞于赞美你的伴侣。从 Zoom 便利店的收银员，到我的商业伙伴，我会告诉所有人自己多么幸运。我这样做不是为了炫耀，是因为我感到很幸福，想要分享快乐。想想看，你正在读的这本书，字里行间满满都是我对太太的爱。

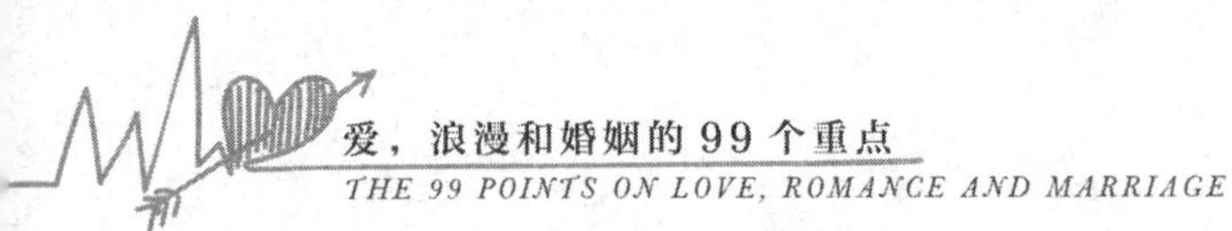

Don't hide your love or your enthusiasm for your partner. Let everyone know how you feel. This will certainly affect how they view you, but in the best way possible. They will see you as a loving and caring partner. Who does not respect that?

It is important to talk about your partner and praise them publicly. It shows them that you care about them and are not afraid to show it. Your love is not secret or shameful, it is joyous and wonderful. Your love for each other is something that should be celebrated daily.

Make a point to let the world know how happy you are with your spouse. Don't be nervous about getting specific with the details or sharing pictures. Tell people how attractive you find them and how intelligent and motivated they are. Let the world know how much you support them, and that support will be felt back home.

92. NEVER TELL OUTSIDERS YOUR PRIVATE MATTERS. INSTEAD TELL YOUR SPOUSE. OPEN COMMUNICATION IS A MUST

Secrets are secrets for a reason. Do not air your grievances with your significant other in public. Only a fool would go around sharing their darkest secrets with the world. People are social animals, and we like to chat. We particularly like to share juicy gossip. In an age of social media, people are less and less sensitive to sharing private information in a public forum. This, of course, is unacceptable when you are married. You should never be sharing you or your spouse's personal information with anyone, whether with a friend or on a social media site.

This sort of behavior undermines trust in a relationship. How are you supposed to connect with someone on a deep level if they cannot trust you? If you have abused your partner's trust, it will take time to gain back, and in that time, you will drift apart. You want your home to be a sanctuary where you both feel safe to be your true selves. You do not want to have to worry about people outside of your home judging you for something you privately

不要隐藏你对伴侣的爱恋和热情，要让所有人都知道你的感受。这当然会影响别人对你的看法，而且是以最好的方式，他们会知道你是充满爱心和善解人意的伴侣，谁会不尊重这样的人？

当众提及并赞扬伴侣很重要，这表明你关心对方，而且愿意当众展示，你们的爱不是秘密，也不丢脸，而是欢乐、美好的感情，每天都应该庆祝你们对彼此的爱。

让全世界都知道你和伴侣在一起有多幸福，不要因提及细节或分享照片而紧张，告诉别人你认为伴侣有多迷人、多聪明、多上进，让全世界都知道你有多支持自己的伴侣，而你的支持也会被对方感受到。

92 保护隐私

秘密之所以被称为秘密，一定有其原因，不要在公共场合抱怨你的伴侣，只有傻子才会到处宣扬自己家的隐私。人是群居动物，乐于交往，更喜欢闲聊八卦。在网络时代，人们越来越不在意上网分享私人信息，当然，已婚人士绝对不能这样，无论和朋友提及还是在网上发帖，都不行，不应该向任何人透露自己或伴侣的私人信息。

向外人透露隐私会让伴侣对你失去信任，没有信任两人就不会有更深的感情。如果你辜负了伴侣的信任，要想重获信任就需要时间，而这期间两人就会渐行渐远。你希望自己的家是安全的港湾，在家里你们都能做真实的自己。你和伴侣私下谈论的事，绝不愿传给外人去品头论足，那样你会非常烦心，一旦如此，就不愿再跟伴侣吐露心声了，你们的感情也不可能亲密。

told your significant other. If you do, you probably will start sharing with them less and less, and the intimacy of your relationship will of course be affected.

The trust you have in your marriage is a sacred thing, and should not be treated haphazardly. I don't care how mad you are with your spouse, do not betray their trust. When you share that sort of information, it can affect how people view your partner and your relationship, which in turn can have long term negative effects on your marriage.

Cherish your relationship and marvel that your partner trusts you as much as they do. Never take it for granted or betray that confidence. I love my wife and I show it every way I can, which includes keeping what is private exactly that way...private. The funny thing is there are no negatives with her, but if there were, I would keep them to myself.

93. SAY THANK YOU EVERY SINGLE DAY, BOTH IN PRAYER AND TO YOUR SPOUSE. SHOW GRATITUDE

You are blessed. Every day when you wake up, take a moment to realize and remember just how lucky you are. Many people go through life without ever finding the wonderful love that you are fortunate enough to sleep beside every night. Do not take it for granted, and instead give thanks. Know how lucky you are. It is in gratitude that we find happiness. Psychological research has proven that gratitude is strongly and consistently related to increased happiness. It helps people to feel more positive emotions, improve their mental health, and strengthen their relationships.

Show your spouse your gratitude. Let them know how thankful you are to have them. You can do this in words, or you can show them through your actions. Why not do both? I let my wife know that she is appreciated daily and can never be replaced by another. She knows that she is the only person for me, that I realize this, and count my blessings.

I tell her daily how much she means to me, and how grateful I am to have her in my life. I am so grateful to have this wonderful lady as my wife. I thank God for bringing us

婚姻中彼此之间的信任很神圣，不应该被随意对待，不管你对伴侣有多气愤，都不要辜负对方的信任。当你向外人透露隐私时，会影响他人看待你的伴侣及你俩关系的态度，也会对你们的婚姻产生长期的负面影响。

要珍惜你们的感情，感谢伴侣能够如此信任你，永远不要认为这是理所当然的，更不要辜负对方的信任。我爱我太太，并尽我所能表达我的爱，包括保护隐私。有意思的是，她身上没有负面的东西，即便有，我也不会说。

93 感恩之心

你是有福之人，每天醒来时，要想想自己多么幸运。很多人终其一生都找不到真爱，而你却有幸每晚都有爱人睡在身边，不要认为这是理所当然的，要有感恩之心，明白自己有多幸运。只有学会感恩，才能得到幸福。心理学研究已经证明，感恩与增加幸福感密切相关，感恩能让人更加积极向上，并能改善人的心理健康，还能让感情更加牢固。

要感谢你的伴侣，让对方知道你的感激之情。你可以通过语言或行动表达感谢，或两者兼顾。我要让我太太知道，我会每天感恩，她是我的唯一，没有人能取代，我明白这一切，并惜福感恩。

我每天都会说，她对我有多重要，能拥有她我是多么感激，能娶这么优秀的女士做太太，我由衷欣慰。感谢上帝让我们走到一起，正是由于上天的恩典，我们才会相遇，我们的感情才能开花结果，并最终走向幸福的婚姻。

together. It was only through his grace that we were able to meet as we did, and for our relationship to have flowered and eventually result in marriage.

Being appreciative is so important when it comes to maintaining good health and love. I make it a point in prayer to thank God for the wonderful blessings that have been brought into my life. Treat every day like a gift and be thankful for every moment you have together. Show your thanks in how you live your life. Be an honorable and upright person. Be there for others. Show the world through your actions just how grateful you are!

94. GAME NIGHT

Plan a game night with your spouse. You can include other couples, or the two of you can keep the party private. During your evening of friendly competition, choose what game you want to play. If you can't agree, flip a coin. Or perhaps take turns. I personally like to play poker or shoot baskets, but you can play any number of board or video games. If you are feeling really ambitious, or happen to have the equipment at home, you can go bowling, play pool, or whatever tickles your fancy. Test your mettle against your husband or wife. This sort of friendly competition is a ton of fun, and a great activity to bring you two together. I recently bought both a karaoke machine and a PlayStation to make such nights even more fun.

A little friendly competition can help you and your significant other stay engaged, motivated, and most importantly, build a deeper connection. The key is to keep it friendly and not become contentious. The first piece of advice is whether you win or lose, do so gracefully. No one likes a winner who rubs in their victory, or a loser who sulks. Let you competition be an opportunity to improve your skills and enjoy each other's company. Silly games allow you to just let go. They are stress releasers.

By engaging in friendly games, you and your spouse can speak openly and freely without worrying that you will be criticized. This freedom encourages honest conversation, as you can share your thoughts without fear of retribution. Competition also helps develop a trusting relationship.

要想身体健康、爱情幸福，就要学会感恩。我在祈祷时特别感谢上帝，给予我生命中最美好的祝福。要把每一天都当作上苍赐予的礼物，感谢和伴侣在一起的每一刻。在生活中用行动表达感谢，要做一个正直诚实的人，并乐于助人，用行动告诉整个世界你的感恩之心！

94 游戏之夜

和伴侣一起策划游戏之夜，可以邀请其他情侣参加，或者只有你们俩，让比赛更私密。在游戏之夜，先选择想玩的游戏，如果意见不一，可以抛硬币决定，或者依次轮换。我个人比较喜欢打扑克或投篮，但你可以玩各种桌游或电子游戏。如果你真的有兴趣，或者正好家里条件允许，还可以打保龄球、打台球，或者进行任何你喜欢的运动，和伴侣比试一番。这种友谊赛非常有意思，也能让两人关系更亲密。我最近买了一台卡拉 ok 机和一台 PS 游戏机，它们能让游戏之夜更加有趣。

小小的友谊赛能使你和伴侣全心投入、积极向上，最重要的是，让两人的关系更紧密。这种比赛关键在于要保持友好，不能争执。我的建议是，无论输赢，都要态度从容。没有人喜欢胜利者沾沾自喜，或者失败者郁闷生气。把比赛当成提高游戏技能的机会，并享受彼此的陪伴。无聊的游戏也能让你释放自我，起到减压的作用。

一起参加友谊赛，你和伴侣就能开诚布公地交谈，不用担心受到批评，这种自由的状态能让两人真诚地沟通，可以分享自己的想法而不用担心报复，比赛也有助于彼此建立信任。

A healthy game night can encourage your relationship to grow and develop. It helps to inspire creativity, increase motivation, and bring a sense of accomplishment. It teaches you and your spouse how the other fares under pressure, and how they react when put into a corner. You can also get a better insight into the way their mind works.

Most importantly though, the point of game night is to have FUN!

95. EXPLORE YOUR NEIGHBORHOOD

I love to explore my neighborhood. Whenever I move somewhere new, I will typically walk all around the area and see what it has to offer. This is a great way to meet wonderful people, find exquisite restaurants you would have otherwise never seen, and discover useful shops. Many people live in an area for years and are unfamiliar with what is down the street. While there is nothing wrong with this, you could be missing out on something great.

My wife and I enjoy walking around and exploring our neighborhood together. It is great for several reasons. First, we are out walking. I like to walk to clear my mind, and for the limited light cardiovascular exercise it provides. Second, I am with my beautiful wife. Even if we were walking around the world's most boring track, I would enjoy her company and conversation. Third, we get to enjoy the sights and sounds of our city. Fourth, if we find someplace that looks cool, we can explore it together!

Take your spouse and tour your neighborhood. It is a lot of fun to find a hidden gem together. Many times, some of the best restaurants are understated or relatively unknown. The only way to find them is to look for them. You and your spouse can make an evening out of it. Instead of making dinner plans, walk around your neighborhood and investigate the options. The shared purpose is a great bonding activity. So is the sense of accomplishment when you find a winner. If you accidentally choose a place that has terrible food, it is still okay. You will have a funny story you can laugh and tell friends about.

Instead of ordering food in, or going to your usual spot, grab your spouse and go discover someplace new. It is so much fun to explore and discover new places.

有益身心的游戏之夜能让你们的感情更牢固、更长久，并有助于激发创造力、增加积极性，并带来成就感，能让你和伴侣知道对方在压力下的表现以及在陷入困境时的反应，也能更好地了解对方的思维方式。

最重要的是，游戏之夜的意义在于能一起度过美好时光！

95 周围环境

我喜欢探索周围环境，每当搬到新的地方，我都会在周围四处走走，看看有什么新鲜好玩的去处。这个办法特别棒，能遇到热情好客的人，能发现巷子深处的精致餐馆，也能找到实用的商店。有些人在某地居住多年，却连街道周围都不熟悉，虽然这样没有什么错，但可能会错过一些很棒的东西。

我和太太喜欢一起四处走走，探索周围环境，这样做会有很多益处：第一，我喜欢通过散步来整理思绪，散步也能保护心血管。第二，我能和爱妻在一起，即使在世界上最无聊的街道上行走，只要能和她聊天做伴，去哪都行。第三，我们可以欣赏城市的风貌。第四，如果能发现感觉不错的地方，就可以一起去探索！

带着伴侣去附近转转、一起寻宝很有意思。很多时候，那些最好的餐馆都很低调朴素或鲜为人知，只有四处探索才能被发现。你和伴侣可以晚上出去侦查一番，与其预定晚餐，不如在周围走走，看看有什么新的发现。拥有共同的目标能让两个人更团结，就像成功的人能拥有成就感一样。如果不小心选了不好吃的餐馆，那也没关系，就当个笑话，回去告诉朋友就好了。

不用在家里点外卖，也不用去常去的餐馆，带上你的伴侣，去发现新大陆，探索和发现新奇的周围环境会非常有趣。

96. DO SOMETHING THAT FRIGHTENS YOU

We all have something that we are afraid of, so face your fears with your partner. When I say face your fears, I do not mean for you to something that includes an element of danger; for example, parachute jumping, bungee jumping, driving at high speeds, riding motorcycles, or anything that could result in injury or death. Those must be left on the avoid list. People will argue these are not dangerous if you're careful, and most of the time this is true. It is the exception that is the problem. My wife and I stay away from them as a hard and fast rule.

For all those other fears, if you cannot face them together, you will never face them at all. Talk with your spouse and find out what they are afraid of, and then help them to conquer that fear. Once you are able to rely on your partner to understand what frightens you, and then trust them enough to overcome that fear, your relationship will be unstoppable.

This story may seem silly, but I have always found it romantic. I had a friend who was terrified of heights. He could be in a tall building, but would never get near the windows. If there was a balcony, he wouldn't even approach it. Oddly enough, he didn't want anyone to know. When he was forced to be in a skyscraper, he would always position himself as far from the windows as possible and face the interior. He told me that one day he decided to share this crippling phobia with his wife. Rather than thinking less of him, or laughing at him as he had feared, she slowly helped him to overcome it. They started slow, going to the window on the third floor, then the fourth, fifth and so on, until they were going out onto my balcony on the 69th floor with no fear. He says he would have never been able to do it without her, and they have subsequently been closer than ever.

The goal in a relationship is to better one another. The ability to open up the world to your partner in a way that they could never experience otherwise is a wonderful way to improve your lives. My friend could not enjoy a majestic mountaintop view before his wife helped him get over his fear. Now they live in a skyscraper. Never underestimate the power of love.

96 克服恐惧

人们都有惧怕之事，所以要和伴侣一起面对恐惧。当我说面对恐惧时，并非指有危险的事，例如跳伞、蹦极、高速驾驶、骑摩托车及任何可能导致伤害或死亡的运动，这些都要避免。有人会说，如果小心一些的话，这些运动并不危险，多数情况下的确如此，但是不怕一万，就怕万一。我和爱人都会远离这些运动，这是我们的硬性规定。

对于类似危险以外其他方面的恐惧，如果两人不能一起面对，就会永远无法面对。先和伴侣谈谈，问出对方所怕之事，然后帮助对方克服恐惧。一旦能够信赖伴侣并让对方理解你的恐惧，相信对方能够帮助你克服恐惧，你们的感情就会牢不可破。

这个故事说出来可能有点傻，但我一直觉得很浪漫。我的一个朋友患有恐高症，他能进入高层建筑，但绝不会靠近窗户，如果有阳台，他也绝不会靠近。奇怪的是，他不想让任何人知道。当他被迫待在摩天大楼里时，总是尽量远离窗户，面朝屋内。有一天，他决定把自己恐高的事告诉妻子。他爱人并没有像他担心的那样看不起他、嘲笑他，而是慢慢帮助他克服了恐高症。他们一点一点慢慢来，先靠近三层的窗户，然后再去四层，五层……直到他们毫无畏惧地来到我家位于六十九层的阳台上。他说如果没有爱人，他永远都无法克服恐惧，后来他们的感情更加亲密了。

两人相爱的目标是让彼此更好，要用伴侣永远无法体验的方式帮对方打开新世界，这一能力可以改善两人的生活。我的朋友在爱人帮助他克服恐惧之前，无法欣赏壮丽的山顶景色，而现在他们住在摩天大楼里。永远不要低估爱的力量。

97. DOUBLE DATE

As much as I value my alone time with My wife, it is sometimes fun to go on a double date, triple date, quadruple date, or heck, just invite the whole population of Dubai! A double date with another couple can mix up the conversation and add a new element to the evening. It is a great way to get exposed to new things, and if you are in a rut, to break it. Couples have a habit of forming routines, and while this is important, it can lead to things getting a little dull. By going out with other people, you get to try something new. They have their routines, and you have yours. When you join forces, you will end up doing something original and maybe unexpected. No matter what it will be exciting!

It is particularly fun to do a game night with another couple. You and your spouse can team up and work together. This is great to build trust, and it is a whole lot of fun to boot. It is also a good way to meet your partner's friends, and to form a relationship with them. It is important that you know your spouse's friends, and going out with them and their significant others is a great was to accomplish that. The closer you all become, the more involved you and your partner will become in each other's lives, and the stronger your bond will grow.

It is always nice to meet new people and have new experiences, by inviting other people to join you and your wife for an evening, you open up the possibility of making new friends and learning something new. You all get to benefit from the group's knowledge and enjoy each other's company.

Go on a double date with your spouse and their friends. You will be surprised by how much fun you can have!

97 四人约会

虽然我很珍惜和爱人独处的时光，但有时，四人约会、六人约会、八人约会也很有趣，或者干脆邀请全迪拜的人一起玩！与另一对情侣进行四人约会能拥有更多话题，并为约会之夜增添新意，这也是接触新鲜事物的好方法。如果你每天都一成不变，现在正好改变一下。情侣们容易养成特定的习惯，虽然很重要，但也容易变得无趣。如果和其他人一起玩，就能尝试一些新鲜事物。他们有他们的习惯，你们也有你们的常规，当两方结合起来时，就会做出一些新奇且意想不到的事情，不管怎样都会很刺激！

和另一对情侣一起进行游戏之夜会特别有趣。你和你的伴侣可以组成一队，有助于彼此信任，而且会带来很多乐趣，这也是结识另一对情侣的好方法，并能和他们成为好友。了解伴侣的朋友很重要，和他们一起玩有助于相互了解，和他们越亲近，你和伴侣在生活中就会越亲密，你们的关系也会越牢固。

能认识新朋友、体验新乐趣，多么美好。邀请其他人一起玩，就有机会结交新朋友和学习新事物。大家都能从群体知识中受益，并享受彼此的陪伴。

和伴侣的朋友来一次四人约会吧，它能给你带来无穷的欢乐！

98. MOOD SWINGS

Mood swings are a normal part of life. They can be caused by just about anything. Occasionally mood swings are caused by emotions, and at other times, it is just circumstances. The majority of the time mood swings will have little to do with you. Understanding and not overreacting are at the core of any healthy marriage. To ensure that you have a happy, loving, giving, empathetic, and romantic relationship it is always best, so slow down and never overreact.

The best cure for mood swings is a nice hug and to listen. It is possible your spouse might need a few hours of alone time to put things in perspective and return to their normal personality. At times, everybody experiences mood swings. With some people their mood swings are dramatic and pronounced, while with other people, they are noticeable but not severe.

Regardless of the cause of a mood swing, it is your job to be there with support for your spouse. You are the solution, so please do not exacerbate it by overreacting. Remember you are your spouse's best friend and a built-in support group when needed. It is in these times that you must be there to listen, love, hug, care, and understand.

I have often observed situations where the man or woman only thinks about themselves instead of the spouse who is the one suffering from the mood swing. They start asking what they did wrong. Quit making assumptions and listen before becoming defensive. Mood swings in your spouse are not always about you. In fact, such mood things are nature's way of pulling a person back in balance. A mild mood swing is actually healthy, as it helps in letting go of what is bothering the person. It is unhealthy to bottle up emotions. By being supportive, you can help your spouse by letting go of whatever it is that is upsetting them.

While mood swings may seem horrible and disruptive, in most cases they are temporary and will pass quickly with no damage. I compare mood swings to the rainbow after the storm. There is nothing wrong with the occasional mood swing. It does not need a medical term tagged onto it, like bi-polar disorder. Please relax and realize that your

98 情绪波动

情绪波动是人之常态，凡事皆可引起。有时，情绪波动是由心情引起的，有时则是环境使然。在多数情况下，伴侣的情绪波动与你无关，善解人意且不过度反应是良好婚姻的核心，这样才能拥有幸福、关爱、宽容和浪漫的感情，所以要慢慢来，不要反应过度。

治疗情绪波动最好的方法就是拥抱对方并倾听对方，你的伴侣可能需要独处几小时来看清问题、恢复常态。每个人都会经历情绪波动，有些人情绪波动起来剧烈且明显，而另一些人虽能被人察觉到，但并不严重。

不管因为什么引起了伴侣情绪波动，你都应该陪护在伴侣身边并给予支持，你就是解决问题的良药。所以，千万不要因过度反应而使问题恶化，要记住，你是伴侣最好的朋友，需要时，你就是内置的支持小组。正是在这些时候，你必须陪在他身边，倾听、关爱、拥抱、照顾和理解伴侣。

我发现，人都是只考虑自己，而不顾及遭受情绪波动的伴侣。你首先要问自己做错了什么，不要自行揣测，在为自己辩解之前先倾听对方，伴侣出现情绪波动并不都是因你而起。实际上，这种情绪变化正是让人能回归平衡的自然法则。轻微的情绪波动实际上有益健康，能让人释放烦忧，压抑情绪则会影响健康。要给予伴侣支持，助其放下所有的烦心事。

虽然情绪波动看起来很可怕，且具有破坏性，但一般都是暂时性的，很快就会过去，也不会造成任何伤害。我把情绪波动比作暴风雨后的彩虹。偶尔的情绪波动并没有什么问题，也不需要贴上医学术语的标签，比如双相情感障碍。请放心，伴侣和你一样，都是正常人，需要的不是看病，而是关

spouse, like you, is human, and diagnosis is normally not required. Instead, it is caring, understanding, and hearing (to listen is important, but you must also hear in order to understand).

Try a little tenderness and being understanding. That is the best medicine to help a person overcome a change in mood. With a little time and patience, your spouse will quickly recover and be back to normal after most mood swing episodes.

99. MIND READING NEVER WORKS

If you want a healthy, loving, romantic relationship, do not count on being able to read your partner's mind. I have often heard the story where one person says to their spouse, "You should have known what I wanted without asking." The problem is, we can all fall into this trap. When you are with a person all the time it is natural to think that you can read their mind. The truth is, when you are talking clarity of thoughts, I rarely even know what I am thinking. How could I possibly read the mind of another person?

It is easy to think that you have gotten to know someone so well that that you know what they want before they do. Sometimes this is true. The problem is that more often than not, it is not true, and this is when the trouble begins.

Believing that an attentive spouse knows your needs is a huge mistake. This is an easy mistake to make. You believe that as you and your spouse grow closer, and your relationship solidifies, you know everything about them. To some degree it is true that your spouse knows you inside and out, possibly even better than you know yourself. But to equate this with reading their mind and knowing what they want is a path to disaster. If you think you can read the mind of your spouse, think again. Nothing could be further from the truth.

All of us are constantly changing. Life experiences, maturity, and the accumulation of wisdom alter who we are and how we think. There is no way your spouse can know exactly where you are emotionally and intellectually. Sure, they can probably guess pretty accurately,

心、理解和用心聆听（倾听很重要，但为了理解，你必须用心聆听）。

要尽量温柔体贴，这才是克服情绪变化的良药，给你的伴侣一些时间和耐心，相信对方很快就会恢复常态。

99 避免猜测

如果你想拥有健康、互爱、浪漫的感情，千万不能依靠猜测伴侣的心思来实现。经常发生这种情况，某人对伴侣说：“你不用问就应该知道我想要什么。”问题是我们都被骗了，当你一直和某人生活在一起时，自然会认为能读懂对方的心思。而实际上，有时候我甚至不知道自己在想什么，怎么可能读懂别人的心思呢？

人很容易认为，如果自己非常了解某人，会在对方没说的情况下就知道对方想要什么。确实有这种可能，问题是一般情况下不太可能，这就是麻烦的开始。

认为体贴的伴侣能够了解你的需求是非常错误的想法，这是特别容易犯的错误。你可能认为，随着和伴侣越来越亲密，感情越来越牢固，你就能了解对方的一切。在某种程度上，你的伴侣确实对你了如指掌，甚至可能比你自己还要了解。但是，如果将之等同于能读懂对方的思想，知道对方想要什么，那后果会不堪设想。如果你认为能读懂伴侣的心思，那就再想想吧，事实并非如此。

所有人都在不断变化，生活的经历、年龄的增长和智慧的积累都能改变

but it is not a catch all. Stop assuming you know what your spouse is thinking. Instead, take the responsibility and ask. Never get upset with your spouse if they did not do something you wanted if you failed to tell or ask them. You must articulate what you need each and every time.

Your partner might be reading your signals wrong. Your partner might be reading into what you said incorrectly. When you make a point, you must check to see if it was heard the way you intended it to be. Not only is mind reading a dangerous practice, not drilling down when you do talk is also a mistake. Don't assume your partner knows what you meant because it was so clear in your own mind. They have their own minds. Your spouse is no better at reading your mind than you are at reading theirs.

Even if you could read someone's mind, like some sort of superhero, you could probably not see through all of the clutter. That is the stuff of comic books. For example, if your spouse is thinking "I want a new, sexy dress," you read her mind and act. You take that information and run with it. The problem is that there is not enough information to actually get what she wants. You do not care about the missing information and only focus on buying a sexy dress. You know her size and you decide to buy her the gift as a surprise, then, you cannot believe it when she does not like the dress. The reason is simple. You acted on too little information. I doubt that your spouse even knows the exact dress she wanted, as it was an incomplete thought. Until she went shopping and saw what she was looking for, it would be hard to know which sexy dress was the right one. Is it a pink dress? What style would the dress be? Just knowing what someone is thinking is normally not enough to keep your spouse happy.

Tying to anticipate you partners needs is a good practice, but it is best to stop there and forget mind reading. Do not expect your spouse to read your mind. Never say to your spouse, "You should have known."

Have you ever been mad at your spouse because you believed they should have known or done something, then they failed to live up to your expectations? Now, you're angry at your spouse, and you're both unhappy. This needs to change, and it is not hard to alter this unhealthy behavior pattern.

All you need to do is to change your mindset and stop assuming things. Start with being more straightforward and ask.

我们，也改变了我们的思维方式。你的伴侣不可能在情感上和心智上对你完全了解。当然，对方可能会猜得相当准确，但并不能完全掌握。不要认为你知道伴侣在想什么，而应该承担责任并直接提出要求。如果你想做某事却没有告诉或要求伴侣去做，而伴侣也确实没做，请不要因此生气，你必须每次都清楚地表达自己的需求。

伴侣可能会误解你的暗示或误会你说的话，当你表达观点时，一定要确保对方能听明白。读心术这种方法很不靠谱，说话时不加思考也会引起误会。不要因为自己心里很清楚就以为伴侣也知道你的意思，对方也有自己的想法。你的伴侣并不能读懂你的想法，你也读不懂对方的想法。

即使你像超级英雄一样，能读懂别人的思想，也不可能看清一切，再说那都是漫画书里的故事。举个例子，如果你的伴侣心里想“我想要一件性感的新衣服”，你读懂这一想法并采取行动。你会依照这个信息去做，可是信息太少，你不可能让对方满意。你不去思考自己知道得太少，只关注要买一件性感的衣服。你知道伴侣的衣服尺码，决定将其作为礼物给对方一个惊喜，结果你的伴侣居然不喜欢这件衣服，这简直让你不敢相信。其实原因很简单，你掌握的信息太少了。我觉得你的伴侣可能自己都不知道想要哪种衣服，当时很可能只是一个不成熟的想法，除非亲自购物并看到想要的衣服，否则她自己也很难知道喜欢哪种性感的衣服，是一件粉红色的连衣裙吗？是什么样式的？仅仅知道对方在想什么，并不足以让对方开心。

试图猜测伴侣的需求没问题，但最好到此为止，千万别用读心术。不要指望你的伴侣能读懂你的心思，永远不要对伴侣说：“你早就该知道。”

你是否因为相信伴侣应该知道或应该做些什么但对方没有达到要求而恼火？结果你很生气，你们俩都不开心。你要改变现状，而改变这种不健康的行为模式并不难。

需要做的就是改变心态，避免猜测，首先要做到直接提出自己的要求。

You are lucky as I have added one bonus point to end the book. Thank you for reading and I hope it helps you in having an enduring and happy marriage, full of love and passion.

"YES, I DO"

"Yes, I do" are the three most important words that have ever been said to me. These three words changed my life for the better and forever the day I married my wife. When she said, "Yes, I do," I was reborn as a new person.

"Yes, I do," meant she was now my wife. It was a dream come true to find the perfect person and one whom I love so much. I even have these words as the screen saver on my phone. Seeing these words is a constant reminder of just how lucky I am to have her as my wife.

By seeing "Yes, I do" every day, it reminds me of the vows I have made and the promises I must keep to my lovely wife. That I should never give up when we disagree. To be there through sickness and health. It is more than just the vows, it is the commitment that we are together forever that matters most. That we believe in the love we have found and must cherish it for all time. That we must respect each other, be best friends, and love each other forever.

This last point is the fundamental core of this book. It is to constantly remind yourself of how blessed you are to have this person as your spouse. Love and romance are easy when you go back and remember what got you there. What got me here was these three little words, "Yes I do."

When you constantly remind yourself of just how lucky you are to be married to the love of your life, your love will stay fresh in perpetuity. You will automatically do many of the things that are suggested in this book naturally. Your marriage will flow with peace, love, and tranquility by following the advice of this small book. Just always remember these three little words, "Yes, I do," and your love will stay in full bloom forever.

"Yes, I do" – I love you – "Yes, I do."

你很幸运，因为我在书的结尾要再赠送你一条重要信息。感谢你阅读本书，我希望它能助你拥有一个持久和幸福的婚姻，让你的生活充满爱恋和激情。

“是的，我愿意。”

“我愿意”是我听过的最重要的三个字。从我结婚那天起，这三个字就永远改变了我的生活。当她说“是的，我愿意”时，我便获得了新生。

“是的，我愿意”意味着她现在是我的妻子了。能找到如此完美、如此挚爱之人，我绝对是梦想成真。我甚至把这句话作为手机屏保，每当看到这句话，它就会不断提醒我，娶她为妻，我是多么幸运。

每天看到“是的，我愿意”，我就会想起所说的誓言，以及必须对爱妻信守的诺言。当我们意见不一时也绝不轻言放弃，无论疾病还是健康都要同甘共苦，这不仅仅是誓言，更是我们要永远在一起的承诺。我们相信彼此之爱，会永远珍惜。我们彼此尊重，互为好友，永远相爱。

最后这条是本书的基本核心，就是要不断提醒自己，能拥有此人做自己的伴侣是多么幸福。当你回忆两人为何走到一起时，会很容易想到爱情和浪漫。我之所以是现在的我，就因为这三个字：“我愿意。”

当你不断提醒自己是多么幸运时，便能与生命中的挚爱结合在一起，你们的爱情之火就会永生不灭。按照书中的建议去做，遵循本书的思想，你的婚姻将充满和平、关爱和安宁。只要记住“我愿意”这三个字，你的爱情之花就会永远盛开。

“是的，我愿意。”

我爱你。

“是的，我愿意。”

图书在版编目（CIP）数据

爱，浪漫和婚姻的 99 个重点：英、汉 /（美）江柏德著 . -- 北京：华夏出版社有限公司，2024.3

ISBN 978-7-5222-0612-7

Ⅰ . ①爱… Ⅱ . ①江… Ⅲ . ①爱情－通俗读物－英、汉②婚姻－通俗读物－英、汉 Ⅳ . ① C913.1-49

中国国家版本馆 CIP 数据核字（2024）第 009930 号

爱，浪漫和婚姻的 99 个重点

作　　者　[美] 江柏德
译　　者　王　梅
责任编辑　赵　楠

出版发行　华夏出版社有限公司
经　　销　新华书店
印　　装　三河市万龙印装有限公司
版　　次　2024 年 3 月北京第 1 版　2024 年 3 月北京第 1 次印刷
开　　本　710×1000　1/16
印　　张　16
字　　数　208 千字
定　　价　68.00 元

华夏出版社有限公司　地址：北京市东直门外香河园北里 4 号　邮编：100028
网址：www.hxph.com.cn　电话：（010）64663331（转）

若发现本版图书有印装质量问题，请与我社营销中心联系调换。